Spelling

and

Handwriting

A Guide for Teachers and Parents

Published by Brendan Culligan

ISBN 978-0-9531664-1-1

Printed by CRM Design and Print
Unit 6, Bridgecourt Office Park,
Walkinstown Avenue,
Dublin 12.

Contents

Appendices

Acknowledgements

I wish to express my sincere thanks to the many children, parents and teachers who have helped me to complete this work. I am especially indebted to Gene Mehigan (Coláiste Mhuire, Marino) and Dr. Martin Gleeson (Mary Immaculate College, Limerick), who boldly read their way through a very early draft! I thank them both for their invaluable insight, suggestions and encouragement. Finally, a very special thanks to my wife, Joan, for her encouragement and patience while I worked through the various drafts of this work.

Introduction

We have experienced many changes in education and teaching since my publication of 'Improving Children's Spelling' in 1997. Technology in particular, has seen astonishing growth. However, despite all this progress, the need for teaching children to write has not diminished. Handwriting will always remain a vital skill that children need to master. Within writing, there are two roads children must travel, namely, creativity and penmanship. There is ongoing debate in research literature as to which road must first be travelled in a child's life. This work argues that both deserve simultaneous direction. Young children need to be encouraged and directed to use their language to 'write' their stories even before they have mastered letter formation. For many children, very early in their journey, spelling will become a barrier. Spelling is a sub skill of writing, but nevertheless it often gets too much attention to the detriment of the child's language and thoughts. This is where the role of the teacher is crucial. If spelling is the cause of the writing break-down, the teacher needs to be in a position to look under the 'spelling bonnet,' (Chapter Five) notice how spelling is developing and adapt accordingly.

Although it is the subsidiary skill, spelling occupies the first part of this book. The first couple of chapters give a historical perspective on the subject. The importance of spelling is dealt with at length (Chapter Three) and its relationship with other curricular areas is examined in Chapter Four. Another obvious change in education since 1997 was the introduction of the Revised Curriculum in 1999. Chapter Six analyses its content in relation to spelling, while Chapter Fourteen examines its treatment of handwriting. Assessment of spelling is very much to the fore with both parents and teachers. Chapter Seven argues that the manner in which progress in spelling is measured needs to be reviewed. It is regrettable that ten years on from the introduction of the Revised Curriculum, many traditional practices in both spelling and handwriting are still the norm in many schools. Chief amongst these is the Friday Test. Chapter Eight deals specifically with this practice and argues for its abolition.

As with handwriting, spelling is a very individual skill and Chapter Nine demonstrates how an individual spelling programme may be managed in a whole class situation. Case studies are included in Chapter Thirteen to illustrate how even the weakest of spellers can benefit from such an individual approach. The teaching of handwriting and spelling should not be left up to a few enthusiasts but rather should be a whole school affair. Developing a whole school policy is detailed in Chapter Twelve. Very often in the debate on the teaching of spelling, the views of parents and children are not included. Their attitudes to spelling are contained in Chapters Ten and Eleven.

The final three chapters return to the question of handwriting; its importance in a technology driven world; how it should be taught and what style of handwriting children should use. Fundamental to the acquisition of free flowing penmanship is the whole question of fine motor skills, and these are dealt with in Chapter Sixteen. Fine motor skills are too important to be left to chance and Appendix One contains ten pages of activities to develop these skills.

Also to be found in the appendices are name and word webs; picture mnemonics; and an examination of letter strings/words in children's names. Finally, in response to many, many requests from teachers, I present Corewords Three and Four along with two sets of dictation sentences for each, culminating in various revision exercises.

Brendan Culligan
2009

For
Joan,
John, David, Brian and Jane

In memory of my parents
Michael & Rita,
who valued education so highly.

History of Spelling

T his first chapter will examine the development of spelling from its origins right through to the end of the twentieth century. It will study the historical perspectives on the approaches to the teaching of spelling here at home and in both Britain and United States of America. How these trends impacted on the teaching of spelling in Ireland will also be discussed.

Early Development

McGuinness (1997) informs us that written English had its infancy in the seventh century. It was then that the Venerable Bede (to whom the first history of England is attributed) wrote that Bishop Aidan from Ireland assisted King Oswald from Northumbria to translate Irish into English. Vallins (1965), Scragg (1975), Mudd (1994), Montgomery (1997) have also given detailed accounts of the development the English language from its origins right through to Modern English. Their accounts outline the major outside influences on the evolution of the language as we know it today. Of these, the Anglo – Saxons, the Romans, the Greeks, the French and the Normans were dominant forces of change. In its infancy, English was merely a spoken language while Latin and French were the two written languages of England. The importance of the former was seen both in copying the Gospels and also in spreading the word of Christianity. The role of generations of scribes cannot be understated, as Vallins (1965) concludes that the "printers' spelling derives from the manuscript of the scribe."

After the Battle of Hastings in 1066, French became the language of the royal court. Mudd (1994) discloses that at the beginning of the 13th century, the French language began to be learned and read widely, especially among the upper and/or educated classes. This remained the same until the reign of Henry IV, who became the first king after the Norman Conquest to have English as a first language. The development and use of English was further enhanced as it now became the spoken language of parliament, although proceedings were still recorded in Latin.

Middle – Ages Development

Both Geoffrey Chaucer and William Caxton greatly influenced the development of English in the late fourteenth and early fifteenth centuries. A huge change occurred when Chaucer, although fluent in French and Latin, chose to write his works in English. Caxton's importance lies in the standardisation of the language through the medium of printing. Prior to Caxton's printing press, it could be argued that everyone would have been a proficient speller as there was no uniformity. As Bragg (2003) states 'this magnificent fertility of English spelling was everywhere; the variety was profligate.' He suggests that there were over five hundred ways of spelling the word 'through' and over sixty of the pronoun 'she'. Although scribes in monasteries strove for uniformity, spellings differed widely according to the various dialects. For example, the word *merry* as we know it was written as *myry, miri, meri, myri, merey,* or *merie* (English Express, B.B.C. 1994).

The Renaissance of the sixteenth century further influenced the development of the English language with the introduction of more Latin and Greek words. Many of these were reshaped and blended, for example 'dette' became 'debt'. Mudd (1994) also comments that it is

> 'both interesting and very relevant (especially with respect to the teaching of spelling) to note that though many spellings were thus changed, their pronunciations remained the same (hence the misspellings of those who spell mainly according to sound).'

Although Caxton receives much credit for developing the written language, Scragg (1975) asserts that

> 'between 1550 and 1650, there was tremendous growth of universal acceptance by printers of the stable spelling system, which with very few modifications is in use today.'

The established spelling conventions of seventeenth century printers led to Samuel Johnson's (1755) publication of the *Dictionary of English Language*. Consequently, there was only one *accurate* way to spell a word. Bragg (2003) argues that 'the printing press reinforced the importance of a common written language.' As Vallins (1965) states

> 'from then almost up to our own day, the ability to spell according to the fixed pattern has been looked upon as the outward sign of a literate man.'

Johnson's legacy is not a perfect system of spelling. Again, Bragg (2003) argues that 'just because the spelling was being regularised did not always mean that it was being simplified or made to follow rules of common sense.' McGuinness (1997) describes a perfect spelling system as having 'no alternatives for the same sound… and no overlap in the code where one spelling pattern stands for different sounds.' For example the sound of 'e' may be written as in *me, see, sea, chief, receive, mammy,* and *key.* The overlap in code may also be seen with *ough* in such words as *bough, cough, fought, rough, through, thorough,* etc. Not only did Johnson standardise spelling but also McGuinness (1997) informs us that he 'emphasised word derivation as a major source for spelling and provided etymological roots (in five languages) for many words.' Bragg (2003) argues that the importance of a common written language had been now established and that this 'brought great power to writing.'

In United States of America however, many of the 'uniform' spellings of English were not acceptable to Noah Webster (1758 – 1843) as he found some of them illogical. The purpose of Webster's *Spelling Book* published in

1783, was to liberate the language of these inconsistencies. As a result of his efforts we now find differences in American spelling, such as, *or* in place of *our* in *color*, and *er* in place of *re* in *center*. This *Blue Backed Speller*, as it was also called, became a best seller for nearly one hundred years.

There were other attempts at spelling reform down through the centuries. Early in the twentieth century George Bernard Shaw was to the forefront in advocating change. His proposal for a new alphabet to embrace each of the sounds of the language was unsuccessful, and presently we are in the situation that 'spelling is the only fixed element in language', (Vallins, 1965).

Spelling Instruction – Pre Twentieth Century
Research literature is very definite on how spelling instruction was catered for down the centuries both in relation to specific time allocation and what exactly the children were expected to do in the classroom. An account of the spelling process in earlier centuries is given by Montgomery (1997) in which she relates that the traditional method of teaching both reading and spelling was by an alphabetic method in which the children had to master the names of the alphabet and then their sounds. The children then had to master names and sound of syllables, forwards and backwards (ab, eb, ib, ob, ub. / ba, be, bi, bo, bu. / ac, ec, ic, oc, uc, etc.) until 'each meaningless syllable was fully memorised' (Montgomery, 1997). Such rote memorisation activities stultified the initiative of the favoured children and those who failed were usually punished.

Although this reliance on memorisation was not appropriate to the learning needs of many children, this methodology remained largely unchanged from medieval times to the middle of the eighteenth century. A crucial turning point at this stage was the introduction of children's stories and fables to help them learn the alphabet. There was now an increasing awareness of the importance of the sounds of letters. The fundamental feature of the phonics approach was that the sounds of single letters and blends became the ultimate goal for children's learning. The main argument for the use of such an approach was that when the child had mastered the sounds of letters these could now be used in a simple way to decipher text. Sentences such as '*The fat rat sat on the mat*,' became popular as teaching tools. This gave rise to the development of stilted sentences, for example, '*The dog on the log got lost in the fog*.' As a consequence, able children soon got bored with such repetitive practice, whereas those who did not grasp it usually had to repeat a year in the same standard.

By working through all their *sounds*, the children were expected to use this information in deciphering other words. Their awareness of rhyme was very important because it showed that they were able to categorise words on the basis of their sounds and therefore make analogies. This connection between analogy and phonological awareness has been the subject of much recent research. Goswami (1991) has investigated how children make use of analogies, both *onset* (initial consonant sounds) and *rime* (endings of syllables) to help them in the beginning stages of reading. Her findings demonstrate that many young children could use the spelling pattern of one word to help them decipher other words. Goswami's work indicates that children, who receive training in analogy show significant gains in reading ability from those, who were not trained to use analogies. Such findings support the work of White and Cunningham (1990), who argued that reading by analogy is very appropriate for children who are slow in beginning to read.

Marsh et al. (1980) produced evidence that older children (10 years and upwards) can make analogies in spelling. However, if a six-year-old child could emulate this procedure, spelling ability could be greatly enhanced. Goswami (1988b, as cited in Sturges & Sterling, 1994) indicated that children had the ability to make analogies in spelling as well as reading, and that these analogies were a natural and important part of children's reading and spelling. Goswami concluded that six and seven year olds were able to spell test words by analogy to known words and that they could do this from their stored spelling knowledge. Sturges & Sterling's (1994) study supports Goswami's (1988) finding that young children can make analogies in spelling. However, when speaking about children making analogies or associations, many teachers relate this work as being tied to sound, as it is viewed primarily as an activity to prepare children for reading. It is very important that, from as early as possible, children are encouraged to put words together according to how they look, in order to prepare them for spelling. The best way to initiate this work is by having children examine the letters in their own names. (This will be developed further in Chapter Nine). In Ireland, there is little evidence to suggest that training in both visual awareness and visual association occurs as early as it should in the child's schooling.

During the early 1900s most of attention was focused on spelling vocabulary, as teachers were concerned with what words children ought to be learning. By tackling both the *how* and *what* questions, the *Futility of the Spelling Grind* (Rice, 1897), helped raise educational awareness of children's spelling ability. In 1980, Venezky argued that thinking on spelling was only minutely advanced beyond what Rice promoted in the 1890s. More than one century later, it does hold true that some of Rice's suggestions for improvement of spelling ability are still very relevant; for example, he advocated the use of spelling strategies; he argued that precedence ought to be given to common words; and he stressed the importance of the teacher's role in bringing about such an improvement.

Spelling Instruction in the Twentieth Century
Since the close of the nineteenth century, theorists and practitioners have been debating the importance of spelling ability in the acquisition of literacy. Explanations offered for children's spelling difficulties were varied, sometimes consolidated by studies and research, but more often just a matter of opinion. Initially, the arguments focused on how spelling competence could be attained, and then during the first two decades of the twentieth century, the

debate switched and centred on what words children should spell. Various lists, derived from different sources became the focus of attention. These two divergent focal points dominate the principal literature of the time, and I shall refer to them as the *how* and *what* debate.

Studies of children's spelling during the early half of the twentieth century are scarce as research into reading dominated. Fresch (2002) argues that

> 'reading and writing instruction have changed down the years; as research improved, so did thinking and practice. Spelling instruction, however, has remained largely unchanged since the 19th century.'

The phonic approach to teaching spelling was to remain the basic methodology until the 1920s, when the Look and Say method was introduced in the United States of America. Fernald (1943) provided a whole word multi – sensory technique for helping children to learn how to spell. In her work she argued that the spelling process should involve activity and suggested a kinaesthetic strategy very close to the Look - Cover - Write - Check technique, which is widely used today in schools in many countries.

Fernald believed that the strategy ought to involve a motor cue (kinaesthetic training) and she believed that finger tracing the word was the best way to accomplish this. She proposed that the teacher would say and write the word on a flashcard using cursive writing; the child would then trace the word on the tabletop or in the air while saying it several times. The next step involved the child writing the word from memory, sub-vocalising each syllable. This sub-vocalisation was to be natural, with no distorted sounding out of letters or syllables. As the child progresses s/he is weaned off the tracing element and learns by looking, saying and writing.

When Look and Say was introduced into Britain in the 1950s, systematic phonics teaching was almost eliminated. The use of the simple print script for children (introduced in 1912) coupled with the Look and Say approach, meant that spelling 'took the back seat' and was only picked up incidentally during reading and copying exercises. Very little progress was evident until after the 1960s when there was a gradual introduction of various methodologies. These strategies advocated moving away from phonics to developing an interest in words, their patterns, meanings and structure.

The considerable research of the last three decades forcibly argues that for many children, spelling cannot be caught incidentally

This changed rather dramatically from the 1960s onwards. Research on *how* children acquired spelling ability once again occupied centre stage. Debates about the relationship between reading and spelling and how one impacts on the other, began to flourish. The considerable research of the last three decades forcibly argues that for many children, spelling cannot be *caught* incidentally through reading and writing activities alone. Various researchers and practitioners have presented models of spelling competence. Some of these models were based on an auditory approach while others proposed a visual approach. The theory that children pass through different observable stages of spelling development further stimulated the debate. Spelling was finally accepted as being a vital part of children's schooling and necessitating a place in the school curriculum.

Those to the forefront in advocating change in Britain were Cripps (1978), Peters (1967), and Torbe (1977). The investigations of Adams (1990), Gentry (1981), Lerner (1985), Read (1980), Henderson and Templeton (1986) in the United States, and Arvidson (1977) in New Zealand ensured that spelling had emerged from the shadows of reading research. Each of these researchers produced very rational and powerful investigations, but more importantly, each suggested strategies and learning techniques. This had a dramatic effect on the thinking on spelling. The body of research evidence now showed that spelling *had to be taught* and that the child's spelling requirements could not be picked up incidentally.

The *taught* or *caught* debate is encapsulated in Peters' work (1985). She argued that spelling is caught by certain favoured children and less favoured children need to be taught rationally and systematically. Peters indicated that attention should be drawn to details of word structure, similarities of letter sequence and the varying probabilities of such sequences. She argued that an incidental learning approach to spelling is hazardous for all children, but particularly for those with learning difficulties. She was one of the first researchers to give reasons why children might be failing at spelling and she proposed strategies to overcome these difficulties.

The last decades of the twentieth century saw an enormous development in research into spelling ability, both in Britain and in the United States of America. Brown and Ellis (1994) declared that

> 'spelling research is a growth area... it has received increasing attention as a research topic both in its own right and as a process now clearly seen to be related in important ways to reading development.'

Progress in theoretical understanding of spelling has resulted in better methodologies and these in turn have benefited those with spelling difficulties.

Early Word Lists
Children's spelling vocabulary has 'been a major preoccupation with research workers in spelling' (Peters, 1985). To examine this issue more closely, I will firstly look at the development of lists up to 1945, and then more recent developments. Of the two divergent schools of thought mentioned at the outset (the *how* and *what* debate), the *what* issue, or lists of words children

ought to learn, has been more dominant. A fundamental principle to any spelling list is its relevance to the child's requirements. Lists of words need to be compiled thoughtfully if they are to be beneficial as teaching devices. Some lists were compiled with this in mind, with Cook and O'Shea (1914) perhaps being the first to accumulate a list derived from children's writing. However, most of the earliest lists were gleaned from adult reading material rather than pertaining to children's own needs, or indeed, to the basis of frequency in which they occurred in their written output.

In creating another list, frequency of word occurrences was used by Eldridge (1911), who amassed the 6,000 most common English words from newspapers. This process was developed in 1926, when Horn formatted the *Basic Writing Vocabulary*, which consisted of 10,000 words most likely to be written by adults. Among these words, he registers ten that he felt accounted for 25% of the most prevalent words in English writing of adults. These words were: *I, the, and, to, a, you, of, in, we,* and *for.* These initial attempts at providing a spelling list for schools relied heavily on adults' perceptions of what spelling vocabulary children required. Although Cook and O'Shea (1914) recognised the necessity to base such lists on children's own writing, this concept was only embraced again by Schonell (1932). His *Essential Spelling List,* which comprised 3,200 everyday words, was extensively used in Britain. It was also used extensively in Irish schools. Although it is still in use in some schools it has practically been replaced by spelling books published by Irish publishing companies. Thorndike and Lorge (1944) completed the *Teachers' Word Book*, which comprised 30,000 words. This enormous list did not receive the same attention as Schonell's and was not used extensively.

More Recent List Studies
In England, McNally and Murray (1968) devised a new reading programme for schools, which was accompanied by a list of key words (*Key Words to Literacy*). This list was intended as a minimum sight vocabulary for the teaching of reading and not primarily for use as a spelling list. It was however, widely used as a spelling programme. The concept of a short list of essential words for writing appealed to teachers and was further promoted by Edwards and Summers (1974), who argued that their list of 100 *Most Frequent Words* accounted for 50% of the 250,000 words used in their study. The sourcing of these lists comprised both children's own writing vocabulary and frequency of use. This is in stark contrast to the earliest attempts at list building, which were 'often remote from children's writing needs', (Peters, 1985).

Endeavouring to adhere to his principle that the child ought to be taught the word when he wants to write it, Schonell (1957), was adamant that

> 'the first essential is that children should be taught words which they use frequently in their written work and they should not waste time learning words which they seldom use.'

This concept continues to dominate the teaching of spelling. Culligan (1997) contends that teachers in class 'continually encounter some children who misspell words that they expect them to know, and others who are always requesting to spell words that they have not yet learned'. Geedy (1975), summarised the various opinions concerning criteria for inclusion of words to be studied,

> 'there appears to be the greatest agreement in making selections based on the children's present needs in writing and frequency of need at a given grade level.'

Fernald (1943), who introduced the multi – sensory spelling methodology, argued that the child supplies the most satisfactory spelling vocabulary. In her work, Fernald was extremely critical of spelling books and lists for denying the particular word a writer requires at a specific moment. Despite Fernald's objections to list learning, there was no radical shift away from this practice. Indeed, Peters (1970) discovered that higher achieving children (those on, or above the 75th percentile), all learned lists of some kind. Peters established that if words are derived from the children's own requirements there is significantly greater progress than if printed lists or no lists at all are used.

Studies by Johnson and Majer (1976) disclosed that some words of our language are used over and over again. They stated that over one half of our writing consists of a repetition of one hundred words. Included in this high frequency list would be words such as: - *again, coming, friend, knew, their, too,* and *where.*

The common characteristic of these early lists was that, although high frequency words were stressed, none clarified how to precisely set about learning the words. Arvidson (1963) was one of the earliest to alter this trend. His *Alphabetical Spelling List,* based on frequency of words, didn't have children spending their time learning words they did not require. In 1957 the New Zealand Council for Educational Research established a committee to examine the desirability of creating a basic spelling list for schools. Arvidson's list arose from the recommendations of this working committee. They proposed the preparation of an entirely new kind of list consisting of the most commonly used words, arranged in alphabetical order, with a reference to their relative frequency of use. Target levels were set for the children and when proficient in one, they moved on to the next.

Spelling in Ireland

Investigations such as those mentioned above, were not mirrored in Ireland and evidence of studies into this subject is scarce. Sheahan (1998), who undertook a study of the teaching of spelling in a selected number of primary schools in the Republic of Ireland, argues that 'there is very little quantitative data available on the teaching of spelling in the primary school.' Apart from spelling lists and the occasional research thesis, no major literature on spelling was published (Culligan 1997). From the mid nineteen eighties onwards, the main Irish educational publishing companies did produce books on spelling. These were just lists of words however, and did not offer any methodologies. These publications were organised upon the principle of getting children to learn daily or weekly groups of words of similar sound, with usually the week's words tested on Friday.

The introduction and implementation of the then 'New (Child Centred) Curriculum' (1971) did not generate similar studies into spelling ability. The curriculum itself did not embrace the research findings of the time but it did caution against 'cultivating skills in isolation from their purpose' (Curriculum, Part 1). Although it added that 'a planned approach to spelling has much to recommend it' (Curriculum, Part 1), it did not suggest how this would be done.

Word Lists in Ireland – Pre Revised Curriculum 1999

It is reasonable to assume that Arvidson's, Fernald's, Peters' or Schonell's arguments had little impact on the Irish education system. These research studies and findings did not influence the approach to spelling. The traditional approach to spelling (phonetic list learning) continued as before. Change only occurred in the switch from one list source to another. The advent of the New Curriculum (1971) altered little, and it would take another many years to see Schonell's Essential Spelling List being replaced by Irish produced spelling books. These are the *Fallons Spelling Book* (1985), Sounds *O.K* (Folens, 1990), and *Spelling Workshop* (Educational Company, 1993).

> *These research studies and findings did not influence the approach to spelling. The traditional approach to spelling (phonetic list learning) continued as before.*

The *Fallons Spelling Book* (introduction) affirms that 'a strong phonic element is evident in the early sections of the book...and similar phonic structures recur throughout.' Using 'words of lesser utility' to 'consolidate the particular phonic structure being treated' (Fallons Spelling Book: introduction), runs contrary to the research findings of Arvidson, Fernald, Peters and Schonell. The child with spelling problems was still expected to spend time on learning words, which may rarely be used.

The Folens' publication (*Sounds O.K.*) also presented words that are phonetically based. Many of the words, which are assigned, are selected primarily to correspond to the letter-string in question rather than on frequency, or on the child's own experience and needs. For example, in Box 4 (*Sounds O.K.*) in order to practise '*sc*' the child is asked to learn *scum, scut, scurry* and *scuff*. Questions could also be raised regarding the relevance of time spent learning such words as: – *rasp, scalpel, scroll, midge,* or *girder,* with eight and nine year old children in Third Class. Sipe (2003) is of the same opinion when she states that 'it is an unfortunate reality that published spelling lists, in an effort to teach a particular rule or phonetic pattern, often include words that are unfamiliar and are unlikely to be used in order to have enough words to fill a list.'

The frequent use of phonic rules and tips throughout the edition does not take into consideration that weak spellers do not have the capacity to comprehend so many rules not to mention all the exceptions. Neither is it clarified how the use of tongue twisters and silly words may be beneficial to the imperfect speller. Gillet & Gentry (1993) argue that 'assignments that are boring and time consuming turn spelling into drudgery.' The third publication, *Spelling Workshop* (Educational Company, 1993) also followed a similar procedure. The welcome inclusion of two lists of common words appears to be the only difference.

These publications seem to have overlooked the findings of spelling research available to them at the time of publication. What they offer is similar to what was available in Britain in the 1920s, namely, lists of words phonetically grouped together and no suggested strategy for teaching. Exercises to promote visual recall and activities, which encourage children to look intently at whole words with the purpose of learning and writing them from memory were excluded. Despite much evidence that phonetically based list learning is of doubtful benefit to the learner it is difficult to comprehend why these books are used in so many of our schools. Sheahan (1998) found that 'almost seventy per cent of the teachers surveyed claimed to use a phonically based spelling book.'

Word Lists in Ireland – Post Revised Curriculum 1999

The *Magic Spell* series of spelling books (Educational Company, 2000 and 2001) were published in response to the 1999 Revised Curriculum. The use of Look, Cover, Write and Check strategy is advocated throughout and a special wrap-around flap is a feature of the series. This set of books has worthwhile exercises, but unfortunately there is little variety throughout the series. The focus on high frequency words is laudable, but the activities to 'make the most of these words' are totally sound based, which is at variance with the Look, Cover, Write and Check strategy. It must be emphasised again that the first step in this strategy is <u>Look</u> not *Sound*. Looking for short words in long words, writing new words by deleting letters from longer words, configuration and reference to word origins are worthwhile spelling activities that contribute to children having to look at words with intent. On the negative side however, although configuration is a useful visual activity it is used only once in Book 1 and does not reappear until Book 4. The inclusion of words to suit a particular sound based pattern is a questionable practice as it only fulfils the auditory aspect of spelling knowledge.

In 2001, Primed Publications published a revised *My Spelling Workbook*. Activities such as jumbled words, word searches, fill in the blanks, crosswords, etc. are very similar throughout the entire set of books. However, the Teacher's Guides (also very alike) do offer a metacognitive approach with key questions for children. Another positive feature is that words not yet mastered by the child are carried forward. The 2007 programmes from Folens and Fallons, (both called *Spellbound*) offer similar activities to those mentioned above. It is difficult to see how these three publications, which overemphasise a phonic approach, will broaden children's knowledge of the spelling process. The majority of the exercises involve copying and do not have the children writing from memory. Folens do

> *It is difficult to see how these three publications, which overemphasise a phonic approach, will broaden children's knowledge of the spelling process.*

recognise the importance of configuration, but just like *Magic Spell,* such exercises are not present from the beginning of the series. Working one's way through any of these programmes does not automatically mean that these word lists will be transferred to one's creative writing. These books do little to assist the child in the exploration of word structure.

'Corewords'

Having questioned the value of some spelling lists and identified their limitations, I have suggested the use of a list that avoids these shortcomings and keeps the child's needs to the forefront (Culligan, 1997). In common with other writers, this list evolved from examination of children's errors/miscues over a period of fifteen years as a learning support teacher. What ensued from this examination is a list of high frequency words (*Corewords 1, 2, 3,* and *4*) that cause difficulties for the weak speller. The ten words listed by Horn above, appear in this list only in relation to other words of similar letter-pattern, for example, *you* as in *you*r; *to* as in *to*day; *the* as in *the*y, etc.

Although there is extensive evidence to suggest that alphabetical spelling lists are of limited value such a layout was chosen specifically to assist each child with rapid access and reference to these commonly used words. This is vital if the child's writing flow is to be maintained and safeguarded and if the child is to use the 'Check' element of his/her strategy. Three publications currently available that use a similar lay-out, are; A *500 Word Book* (Learning Materials Ltd., 1990), Arvidson's *Alphabetical Spelling Lists 1- 7, and Target Levels* (Wheaton, 1977), and *My Desktop Dictionary* (Prim-Ed, 1992).

2

Historical Approaches to Teaching Spelling

Many different approaches to teaching spelling have been suggested and developed since the end of the nineteenth century to the present day. Each one had its own advantages and disadvantages. The inherent disadvantage of the earlier approaches was that spelling was not taught to those in need. If the child was good at rote memorisation, then the child succeeded at spelling. Conversely, the specific needs of the child with deficient memory skills were not catered for. This remained the case until the findings of Fernald's (1943) research greatly influenced opinions on the teaching of spelling both in the United States of America and Britain. From then on strategies were developed to assist children who were experiencing problems as spellers. These strategies had their disadvantages also, but the body of evidence suggested that not only spelling had to be taught, but children ought to begin with high frequency everyday words.

Research referred to earlier (Schonell, 1932: Peters, 1967) has indicated that automatic spelling vocabulary should comprise every day words. Once this has been accepted, the next question is how this may actually be accomplished. In the past, children broke up the words into their constituent parts, vocalised these syllables and learned them by rote. Presently, spelling does form part of the curriculum, but this usually means that children learn isolated lists of words (Sheahan, 1998) without having been taught how to learn. Such an approach to spelling is successful only for those who have the ability to cope, but it leaves many children with a sense of failure. Many of these may drop out of the educational system at a young age.

In the United States of America, Fernald (1943) was one of the first to advocate a multisensory approach to assist all children who were failing at spelling. Her methodology involved look, say and do, and there was no evident role for phonics. The child was encouraged to select a word s/he wished to learn and then observed specific steps in the learning process. Fernald reported that it was particularly beneficial for the child to finger trace the word. This was to emphasise the visual aspect and avoid using sound.

Fitzgerald (1955) further developed this theory when he advocated a five stage multisensory procedure in which the meaning of the word was prominent. The child not only had to be capable of reading the word to be learned, but s/he also had to use it in a sentence to demonstrate its meaning. Should the child be unable to verify the meaning of the word in this way, Fitzgerald believed the child was not ready to learn to spell it. For example, if the child could not use the word correctly in context, then s/he ought not to be learning how to spell it. If the child did show an understanding of the word, s/he next got a picture of the word, sub – vocalised each syllable and traced the letters in the air. The child then spelled the word orally and finally wrote it from memory.

Both these approaches were very significant. For the first time children were being directed away from sound based rote memorisation to cognitive strategies, which advocated a visual approach. Subsequently, the *how* question travelled distinct avenues of approach, i.e. a phonic or visual approach. This fundamental disagreement in methodology occupies the theorists in Britain from the mid-1960s to the present day. Criticism of a multisensory approach to spelling was made by Brown (1990). He argued that when the brain has a visual image of a word, then the hand takes over. This concept may be explained by writing one's name and address with one's eyes closed. This is what Brown (1990), calls the *unisensory principle*, which he offers as an alternative to the common multisensory approach with children with reading, spelling and writing difficulties. This methodology involved the blindfolding of the child and the guidance of the hand in tracing the word. Brown (1990) suggests

For the first time children were being directed away from sound based rote memorisation to cognitive strategies, which advocated a visual approach.

"where an apprentice writer has difficulty with the formation of letters, with letter reversals and letter order problems, emphasis on putting spelling patterns unisensorily into kinaesthetic memory, excluding visual attention, is a promising way of proceeding."

Bradley and Bryant (1985) assert that children who are underdeveloped readers tend to rely on different strategies when they read. Such children tend to rely on a phonetic strategy when they spell, albeit with very little success. My 1995 investigation of the spelling ability of ten-year-old children and the analysis of the errors/miscues, tended to support this hypothesis as the children showed an almost total dependence on sound in word composition.

Advocates of a phonetic approach to spelling argue that when a child can spell '*at*', then the next stage would see him learn; *bat, cat, fat, hat*, etc., and by using onset and rime analogy, develop his/her spelling vocabulary. Those who advocate a visual approach would ask why the child should not also include such words as *eat, ate* and *what*, as these three words also contain the initial letter string '*at*.' The main argument being that spelling ought to transcend phonics, as there are too many exceptions to teaching the large number of phonic rules.

If the child's image and reproduction of the word are not automatic then there will be difficulties. Westwood (1993), states that ... "visual perception of word form is a vital element in the acquisition of spelling ability". By presenting spellings visually on spelling cards, white boards, sand trays or with magnetic letters, children may be trained to look meaningfully at words, pick out the difficult parts and get a mental picture of the word in question. Such training will move children away from a letter-by-letter copying habit and spelling words aloud letter by letter. Such training will also lead the child to decide whether a word looks right or not when it is written from memory. Spelling is also an associative skill which means that if children are familiar with the letter string *gar* as in *gar*den, then they can be trained to generalise to *gar*age, *Gar*y, and su*gar*.

I believe that children would benefit more from putting words into spelling categories based on letter strings, (d*one*, g*one*, b*one*, m*one*y) rather than into sound categories, which commercial spelling books usually do. It would also be beneficial if words were grouped according to spelling patterns, as this would allow them to explore words, and be trained in visual analogy. Thinking that children will be confused if we introduce analogy training that transcends phonics, (e.g. that there is an *ear* in B*ear*), is to underestimate their ability. This type of reasoning results in children not being trained to look at, or examine, word components. Rather than confusing children by telling them that every teacher has an *ache,* or that every street has a *tree,* it would be an incentive for them to look more intently at words. The concept of 'picture spelling' is crucial, but as it does not come automatically to those in need, drawing attention to the visual aspects of words should be done from as early as possible.

My (1992) spelling investigation of 1,185 children showed that 90% of the children could spell *teacher* correctly, but only 32% were accurate with *ache*. The fact that more than 700 children failed to use this letter string (*ache*) demonstrates that if words are not in the child's automatic spelling vocabulary, they tend to rely on sound to spell. This in turn is a consequence of not being trained in generalising or in visual awareness (R*ache*l, *ache*, re*ache*s, te*ache*r, or S*ara*h, c*ara*van, g*ara*ge, sep*ara*te,).

3

The Importance of Spelling

Spelling has always enjoyed a very high, if rather emotive, profile in education and in society in general. Recurrent protestations in the media assert that the standard of spelling is falling. Teachers are all too familiar with the criticism that schools fail to improve children's spelling. This criticism of inferior spelling is prevalent among parents, the general public and those involved in hiring secretarial or office staff. The debate about falling standards of spelling ability, first addressed towards the end of the 19th Century, still continues to the present. The proponents of the 'Back to Basics' movement in Britain have been very critical of the lack of spelling skills. Here in Ireland, the review of the Revised Curriculum (2005) found that teachers required more guidelines to enable them to improve children's spelling ability.

The study of reading has dominated the literature on literacy for many years and it is only in the past forty years that spelling has especially become a focus for researchers. Perhaps the dominant reason why spelling remained the poor relation in literacy research was the incorrect assumption that spelling was a skill that could be picked up incidentally from reading (See page 29). As a result of this supposition, the onus was thrown entirely on the pupil to learn how to spell. This assumption provoked differences of opinion in the past but the principal evidence of recent research indicates that spelling is a skill that has to be taught.

No longitudinal studies have been undertaken in Ireland to prove one way or the other whether children's ability to spell is deteriorating. What happens is that a weakness in spelling immediately brands a writer as incompetent. Spelling is considered by many to be a sign of full literacy and a good education. The tendency to pass unfavourable judgments about the writer's intellectual abilities or carelessness is all too prevalent. This is nothing new however, as similar judgments have been passed on written work ever since the introduction of the alphabetic code. Even Shakespeare was not sheltered from criticism. The often quoted fact that, in his last will and testament, he spelled his name in three different ways is to miss the point that prior to the introduction of the printing press, spelling was variable and such variation was accepted. This differs greatly to the present day where only correct spelling is acceptable.

It is evident from both national and international research that the acquisition of spelling ability poses enormous problems for many children and adults.

It is evident from both national and international research that the acquisition of spelling ability poses enormous problems for many children and adults. Teaching practices have varied from rigorous rote memorisation and testing of weekly spelling lists to informal study of words. There is plenty of research evidence to indicate that rote memorisation and informal approaches to spelling are not effective. The learning of isolated lists is not being transferred to creative writing. Words *learned* for a weekly test are not retained for any length of time. If there is evidence that children are not transferring these words to their writing and to other areas of the curriculum, then something is amiss. If the Friday test is the answer to spelling difficulties, then we ought not to encounter so many children with spelling problems! For many decades, common practice in Irish schools saw spelling being *catered for* when a particular book was purchased for the children. Traditionally, children and teachers *worked* their way through these books without an overall coherent plan. If children had the ability to *catch* spellings this practice was viewed as successful. However, the absence of such ability led to children receiving a consistent message of spelling failure and no assistance to improve their situation.

Profiling Inferior Spelling Ability

Cotterell (1984) argued that an 'inability to spell can be a crippling handicap because it restricts him from expressing his imaginative ideas and showing his knowledge in writing'. Arvidson (1989) maintained that 'the measure of a person's spelling ability is how well he spells in his writing.' Unless the child's spelling is automatic, predictable and reliable, s/he will lose confidence when writing and express herself/himself less competently. Jackman (1997) stated that

> 'the child who struggles with spelling, and realises that s/he is finding it difficult, is likely to be reluctant to expose this weakness by writing freely and confidently, no matter what the content.'

The child, who wants to inform us on paper that something is *gorgeous* or *beautiful*, will instead tell us that it is *nice.* Inferior spellers are inclined to choose words that are relatively easy to spell when expressing themselves in writing. Moseley's (1989) study supports this view when his research showed that

> 'poor spellers tended to avoid the use of long words, used fewer words outside a core 500 word vocabulary, and used more regularly spelled words'.

The same study contends that the fear of making spelling mistakes interferes with written expression for all except the best spellers.
Apel (2002) suggests that children

> 'choose words carefully; they avoid those they do not know how to spell so that their writing is very impoverished. They use short words. As their spelling improves, word choice improves.'

Both Dodds (1994) and Culligan (1997) assert that the child who finds spelling and writing difficult will avoid them as much as possible, will sense constant criticism and finish up feeling despondent about the whole process. Moseley (1989) suggested that,

> 'Pupils avoid using words that they may misspell and as a result tend to produce written work that appears linguistically impoverished or lacking in spontaneity.'

This suggests that children with spelling difficulties will utilise repeated words in writing rather than introduce variety. This conclusion is similar to Peters' (1985) when she declared that imperfect spellers might

> 'avoid the words they use in everyday speech because they are too difficult to spell, or they may not write at all.'

Persistence in trying to master difficulties is especially important for those who find the spelling process to be problematic. Dodds (1994) maintains that if the child 'is daunted by failure and gives up trying, then the chances of eventual success are thwarted.' In the same study Dodds also indicated that 'helpless children ... think they will fail regardless of what they try to do to prevent it.'

Spelling Knowledge

In order to eradicate this 'helplessness' and improve their 'impoverished' writing, it is important to recognise what is involved in the spelling process. Spelling should be seen as an integral part of vocabulary enrichment and communication through writing. Effective spelling is dependent upon the development of a number of closely associated skills. Vincent and Claydon (1981) described these as,

> 'essentially visual and include sensitivity to the appearance of words, and knowledge of the way letter strings and combinations provide the characteristic pattern and structure of English spelling'.

As a consequence, effective instruction has to involve a systematic examination of these skills rather than the rote memorisation of isolated sound related lists devoid of context. To enable children to move along the continuum of spelling development, teachers need to focus on four forms of spelling knowledge; *sound, vision, meaning* and *etymology.*

To enable children to move along the continuum of spelling development, teachers need to focus on four forms of spelling knowledge; sound, vision, meaning and etymology.

Research does acknowledge the role of *sound* as part of emerging spelling development. In Ireland, using sound to spell has been the traditional (and sometimes, solitary) approach to spelling. Although the Teacher Guidelines of the Revised Curriculum (pp.85-87), does propose a strategy for the learning of spelling (**Look**, **Cover**, **Write** and **Check**), spelling as a skill is undefined and its overemphasis on sound means that the other three knowledge categories continue to be neglected. (See page 27 for the role of vision and page 31 for the role of sound in spelling).

The function of meaning in the spelling process cannot be overlooked (Culligan, 1997). Because of a lack of morphological knowledge, children with spelling difficulties have great problems on certain type of word-endings, prefixes, suffixes, contractions and homophones. Children with spelling difficulties come to what I call a *spelling cul-de-sac,* when they are faced with words whose spelling is based on morphology rather than on sound. Focusing on meaning is a vital part of spelling instruction. A large portion of English spelling is built upon meaning and not sound e.g. ear – heard / push – pushed / there – their – they're. The meaning of homophones needs to be taught. The word *there* usually means *in that place,* while the word *their* means *belonging to them*. These meanings need to be constantly revised, as it is a very poor reflection that children are still leaving primary school not knowing how to use these words. Children need to be actively engaged in word study – learning how words are put together and learning about their meanings. Etymology is the study of the origins of words. Focus on derivations and etymologies can be of great benefit and fun to spellers of any ability.

Spelling is a written skill
Learning to spell should be finding about how words *work* and all spelling activities ought to involve written work. Oral spelling should be avoided as it does not assist the child's visual memory of words. Rather than have children involved in oral spelling they should be encouraged to *write words from memory*. Children frequently request the correct spelling of a word from the teacher when engaged in writing activity. If the teacher keeps answering these requests, the child will keep asking! Rather than the teacher providing the spelling orally the teacher has other options:

* encourage the child to attempt the word (approximate spelling) and continue writing the sentence

* the teacher writes the required word for the child on a piece of paper on his/her desk. When the child has finished writing his/her sentence, s/he may come and check the word. S/he is not free to take the piece of paper but rather to return to his/her seat and write the word from memory. The child is free to make more than one journey!

At home, children should also be encouraged to write their words. If parents adopt such practice then they will see an improvement in spelling ability. When the spellings have been written, the parent should look at the attempts, praise them and then get the child to check the words. It is the *child's responsibility* to check if his/her attempts are correct or not. If the parent tells the child that the words are correct, then the final part of the child's strategy (Check) has been rendered ineffective. Should some words be written incorrectly, then the parent should focus firstly on the correct parts and then on the problem areas. By emphasising what is correct and then finding out what still needs to be learned, parents are teaching their children *how* to look at their efforts. (Focusing on tricky/difficult parts is best done before the child 'learns' the words).

Spelling is a visual skill

There is plenty of evidence to indicate that spelling is a visual skill and that spelling words the way they sound is fraught with danger. Good spelling involves *looking intently* at words. The ability to visualise a word plays a huge part in determining spelling

> *Good spelling involves looking intently at words.*

accuracy. Westwood (1993), states that 'visual perception of word form is a vital element in the acquisition of spelling ability.' Gentry and Gillet (1993) state that 'the visual form of a correctly spelled word is the key to being able to spell it' and 'poor spellers cannot see the words in their mind's eye.' They are adamant that 'children must be shown strategies that will help them increase their capacity to store words visually.' They also add that 'expert spelling is a highly visual skill and expert spellers install words in their visual memory.' Vincent and Claydon (1981) also assert that learning to spell requires the ability to look closely at words, and the development of clear visual images of words in the child's memory. Sipe (2003) argues that 'competent spelling is a highly visual activity and schools need to utilise strategies that will encourage children to store and retrieve words visually.' While Makay (2003) states that competent spellers know a word is correct because it *looks right,* it is this good visual memory that is the key to confident spelling. As adults, if we are unsure of a spelling we write down different versions and then decide which one *looks right*. We don't go around the house sounding out the word! Rather, we base our judgment on vision not sound. However, a very common practice at home and at school is to ask children to break up the word and sound it out. This is completely at variance with the most common strategy currently in use in our schools (**Look**, Cover, Write and Check)!

Spelling is an associative skill

Using association or analogy to learn new words may be done through sound or vision. For children at the initial stages of spelling development, this association occurs primarily through sound. In the spelling books in use in our schools, word association is predominantly through sound to the detriment of the other areas of spelling knowledge. In the absence of specific teaching this gives children the message that spelling is chiefly sound based. It should be part of school policy to balance out auditory and visual association from as early as possible, so that by the time children leave primary school they are all predominantly visual spellers. To succeed at this, words ought to be grouped together because they have the same visual pattern e.g. *'My a̱u̱ṉt and u̱ṉcle are great f̱u̱ṉ.'*

Spelling is a hand - eye skill

The configuration of letters through the touch and movement of our fingers, even though our eyes may be closed, requires motor sense in recording the impression on the brain. Motor memory is important in spelling; the competent speller spells automatically, without even thinking about the letters, and can *sense* if the hand makes a mistake. The hand literally takes over. Writing your name and address with your eyes closed will demonstrate this. However, motor memory may be very strong and it may very difficult for the child to *unlearn* a word s/he has been miswriting because the hand may continue to write the word incorrectly because it continues to *feel right*.

Spelling is an 'all-or-nothing' skill

Spelling is generally perceived as 'an all or nothing' activity, where the child must choose all the correct letters and write them in proper sequence. In other words, it is an activity where the pass mark is always one hundred percent! For those children with difficulties, I strongly advocate that this should not be the case. In the past, the message children received was that if an error occurred, then the whole word is wrong. Templeton & Morris (1999) maintain that this is 'bad pedagogy because word knowledge is not an all-or-nothing affair'. Rather than marking the attempt as incorrect, we should first look at which parts of the word are correct and then talk about the part causing difficulties. For any child, who is struggling with spelling it should not be an 'all-or-nothing' affair.

For the child it is much more positive to be told that the attempt is almost right.

Children's attitudes to spelling change for the better when teachers move away from the all or nothing standpoint to one of accentuating the positive aspects of their attempts. For the child it is much more positive to be told that the attempt is almost right. Stewig (1993) argued that 'positive reinforcement (evidence of progress) produces greater learning than negative reinforcement (evidence of failure).'

4

Spelling and Other Language Skills

As every child is unique it is not good educational practice to have a class of children learning in the same way. Teachers are very aware that a 'one size fits all' approach cannot and will not be successful. As teachers, we need to provide different strategies as no one strategy will be *effective* for every child. Much has also been written regarding the relationship between spelling and the other language arts. How spelling relates to reading, phonics, handwriting, music and texting will now be examined.

Spelling and Reading

Reading and writing are essential aspects of literacy and they each necessitate their own dedicated teaching. It is a common misconception that all children are able to spell words just by reading plenty of books or being exposed to lists. Over sixty years ago, Nisbet's (1941) research estimated that a child is likely to learn how to pick-up (spell) only about 4% of words read. Stakes & Hornby (1996) asserted that 'learning to spell is not the same as learning to read'. Moats (2005) argued that that we clearly should not assume that progress in reading will necessarily result in progress in spelling. Reading, unlike spelling, affords the child opportunities to offer an acceptable choice of words (for example, *home* for *house*), which would not produce a loss of meaning. The efficient reader merges many sub-skills in order to understand the text. Such a reader skims over words using context and meaning. S/he is able to predict and anticipate vocabulary by using visual memory, and rarely is there any need to study the internal structure of words. The efficient reader will also utilise the title of the story and picture clues to his/her advantage. The efficient reader does not look intently at words unless he/she has a specific reason for doing so.

Spelling is a distinct and much more demanding skill than reading. It is an activity where less than one hundred percent accuracy is considered to be failure. It entails the sequencing of permissible assortments of letters (serial probability of letter occurrences) to encode words. The child must pay close attention to word structure and 'variation is not acceptable' (Peters, 1985). Spelling knowledge relates well to reading but not the reverse. Spelling requires a complete representation of letters in the correct sequence; whereas reading can be based on partial representation …sometimes only the beginning and the final letters need to be fully considered. This may be seen in the ubiquitous text/email message

Spelling is a distinct and much more demanding skill than reading.

'Aoccdrnig to rscheearch at Cmabrigde Uinervtisy, it deosn't mttaer in waht oredr the ltteers in a wrod are, the olny iprmoetnt tihng is taht the frist and lsat ltteer be at the rghit pclae. The rset can be a toatl mses and you can sitll raed it wouthit a porbelm.'

O'Sullivan & Thomas (2000) maintain that children who are good readers but poor spellers probably attend only to partial cues in their reading. When writing, they tend to adopt a mainly phonological approach in attempting to spell unfamiliar words. They argue that this is

> 'likely to be due to the fact that, as they are paying less attention to the whole of the word, their knowledge of other aspects of spelling is not highly developed.'

One may describe spelling as an isolated function, as previous or subsequent words do not, and cannot inform the child if the word in question has been written accurately or not. Spelling relies on the visual image of the word, recall of the word and relationship of letters.

> *Barr (1985) maintains that proficient readers, who pay little attention to word structure, are 'unlikely to gain much help with spelling from their experience of reading.'*

Barr's (1985) research reveals that 'most good readers are also good spellers, and the majority of poor spellers will also be poor readers'. However, it would be unsafe to assume that, just because children are proficient or avid readers that they will be proficient spellers (Culligan, 1997, Ehri 2000). It is not uncommon to encounter children who are good readers but are experiencing specific difficulties with spelling. Teachers frequently come across children who have no indication of reading difficulties but who are, according to Frith (1980) 'seriously handicapped by their inability to spell'. Barr (1985) maintains that proficient readers, who pay little attention to word structure, are 'unlikely to gain much help with spelling from their experience of reading.' The research findings of Peters & Cripps 1980, Barr 1985, Brown 1990 and Culligan 1997, clearly indicate that a child who has a weakness in spelling does not acquire the skill incidentally through reading. Gentry and Gillet (1993) argue that 'a poor notion' that abounds is that 'wide ranging reading and writing will miraculously result in high accurate spelling.' These findings are contrary to what Magic Spell (Educational Company, 2001) advocates when, without reference to any research evidence, it tells children that 'reading is good for learning new spellings'. Learning to read has only a minute effect on the acquisition of spelling ability.

The antithesis of this, i.e. that spelling knowledge could advance the development of reading, was suggested in the 1940s by both Fernald and Montessori. Fernald (1943) believed that children could be taught to learn to write before they learned to read, and she believed that movement played a central role in linking the visual and the spoken form of words. Montessori (1946) proposed closer links between learning to read and write, with her theory of write first, read later. Durkin (1966) maintains that the ability to read seems almost like a by-product of the ability to print and spell. Studies by Ehri and Wilce (1980) assert that invented spelling (where the child uses symbol-sound and sound-symbol association) may invaluably complement instruction in reading. Cataldo & Ellis (1990) are quite definite that 'experience in spelling promotes the use of a phonological strategy in early reading.' The spelling / reading relationship is a growth area in recent literature, where the available findings do suggest that the teaching of spelling has a significant role in early reading instruction.

Spelling and Phonics

Research shows (Smith 1971; Peters, 1985), that using phonics for spelling is very unreliable, and persisting with such an ineffective procedure is a major reason why children continue to fail. Cripps (1989), states that despite the evident problem of using sounds, teachers are so accustomed to equating spelling with phonics that they cannot think of the activity of spelling being other than that of sounding out a word.

The principal reason for confusion among the strugglers is the phoneme/grapheme (letter/sound) correspondence. When they invent/approximate spellings they seek a one-to-one correspondence between phoneme and grapheme. If such a one-to-one equivalence of letters and sounds existed, things would be different. One may see that, when there are 26 letters, which give 44 distinct phonemes, a sounding-out strategy cannot possibly be consistent. Although the role of sound at the initial stages of spelling development has to be recognised, Goswami and Bryant (1990), state that anyone who relies just on a phonological code will never properly spell words such as, *laugh*, *eyes* or *busy*.

Decoding and re-assembling words is beneficial in the reading process, but sound is most unreliable for spelling. Thompson (1970) asserts that phonic spelling is often wrong spelling. The disadvantage of the phonetic approach is most evident in those with deficient visual perception and memory and those who rely on sound to spell. In this latter group, the misspellings become phonetic analogies. Personal observation persuades me to believe that phonetic spelling in many instances may not be due to basic failure in visual perception. Rather, it may result from flawed practices that may have been adopted by the children themselves, as emergent spellers are very much dependent on their phonological awareness skills. This in turn may occur because of the 'lack of an initial strategy' (Culligan, 1997). Many come to school already proficient in their knowledge of the alphabet names but find it very troublesome to have to call them by something very different, i.e. sounds. Some find it extremely difficult to understand that sounds of letters are not always consistent, for example, l<u>oo</u>k / b<u>oo</u>t.

Webster and McConnell (1987), state that hearing impaired children have no problems remembering the visual patterns of words, which is why they are often proficient spellers. Ramsden (1993) endorses this opinion by stressing that 'profoundly deaf writers, for whom the phonic dimension does not even exist, are still capable of spelling words correctly.' Marschark (1993) notes that deaf readers are more likely to produce transposition/omission errors when spelling, suggesting that they rely more on visual codes than do hearing readers. These works strengthen the argument that as children move along the continuum of spelling development there is a need to accentuate the visual aspect rather than relying on sound. Henderson (1990) is adamant that 'children who rely on sound for spelling will be defeated.'

> *Henderson (1990) is adamant that 'children who rely on sound for spelling will be defeated.'*

Spelling and Handwriting

Another crucial factor, which emerged in the 1960s, again from Peters, was the relationship between handwriting and spelling. The clear message emanating from research at this time was that learning to spell ought to involve the writing of words, not merely the chanting out of letters and sounds. Peters' work is supported by Sipe (2003) who states that 'the maximum impact for spelling improvement comes from integrating spelling and writing.' If teachers and parents accept this, then the next issue to be considered must be the type of writing instruction or style to which children need to be exposed; should the children use manuscript (print), or should they use cursive (joined) writing? (See Chapter Fourteen on the *Importance of Writing*).

Spelling and Music

Many children who have difficulty with spellings are often quite proficient in other curriculum areas. Music is one such area where children benefit from teachers who can match their teaching to the musical ability of the children. When asking adults if they remember singing off spellings while in school, two spellings are usually mentioned, namely, *Mississippi* and *difficulty*. (Children were recently exposed to the latter in the film 'Matilda'). Such musical mnemonics motivate children, help improve recall and add great variety to the spelling lesson. In my years in the classroom I made use of the well known football anthem 'There's only one David Beckham' (sung to the chorus air of Guantanamera, guajira Guantanamera). These three examples indicate how it was used;

× There's only one /l/ in always

× There is no /h/ in water

× There are two /p/s in stopping

Spelling and Texting

Texting is a system of sending short messages either by using predictive text or through the deliberate use of abbreviations, misspellings, acronyms and figures. In its original format, space was at a premium as one had only 160 character spaces to get one's message across. Therefore, the use of abbreviated language was encouraged in order to include more information. Recent reports indicate that Ireland is one of the world leaders in mobile-phone use. The quantity of messages is an ever increasing phenomenon but now their educational quality is being questioned. While it is unlikely that texting will have a negative effect on language as a whole, its effect on children's spelling, grammar and punctuation is a major concern for educationalists both here and abroad.

Research from Harvard in 2001 warned that text messaging was ruining the English language. In 2004, research from the University of Coventry found that children, who were better at spelling and writing, used more 'textisms'. The same study found that children wrote significantly less and it expressed concern about the quality and expressiveness of children's writing. The Irish Examination Commission's report (2007), which was based on the results of Junior Certificate English, expressed similar concerns. Its findings appear to suggest that our fifteen and sixteen year olds are becoming increasingly poor spellers and writers (these teenagers would have been seven or eight years old when the Revised Curriculum was introduced). The report from the Examination Commission labelled these teenagers as being

> 'unduly reliant on short sentences, simple tenses and a limited vocabulary… choosing to answer sparingly, even minimally'

The Commission concluded that texting has encouraged poor literacy, stating that

> 'text messaging, with its use of phonetic spelling and little or no punctuation, seems to pose a threat to traditional conventions in writing.'

This problem is not an exclusively Irish one. Texting is popular wherever people have access to mobile phones. Some see and welcome texting for what it is - an evolving language, a short way to give meaning, a wonderful way to have 'disengaged' students reading and writing more. However, others see it is becoming a problem with serious implications for conventional writing. To date, the consensus appears to be that this intentional misspelling will negatively influence spelling ability. Without adequate research there is little or no evidence to demonstrate that this perception is a reality. For children who have a strong foundation in grammar, punctuation and spelling, texting is merely non conformity to written language rather than incompetence. These children are able to distinguish textisms from conventional writing and have the ability to switch easily between both codes. Research is needed to determine if texting impacts differently on the good and weak speller. My chief concern would be for those children who struggle

> *Texting, as a method of instant communication, is here to stay and we must find ways of accommodating and using it wisely.*

with the various aspects of conventional writing. For those children who struggle with spelling, research is needed to determine if texting prevents them moving along the continuum of spelling development.

Texting, as a method of instant communication, is here to stay and we must find ways of accommodating and using it wisely. The vast majority of texters know that they are engaged in the use of non-standard spelling (whether or not they know the correct spelling of the word in question, is another question)! Texting does motivate some children to '*write,*' so rather than trying to prohibit its use in classrooms, it should be used positively and comparatively. Passages of text could be '*translated*' from conventional writing to text-speak and vice versa. For example;

'It's great to know that there won't be anyone in school tomorrow. Fortunately, someone forgot to fix the heating system.'

'Its gr8 2 no tha thr wnt b ny1 n skul 2moro. 4tun8ly sum1 4got 2 fx d hetn systm.'

Such '*translations*' would benefit the exploration of the use of vowels, consonants, and serial probability. This would also support discussion on the visual aspect of words, how words *work* and how they are *formed*.

5

Spelling as a Developmental Process

Frith (1980) and Gentry (1981) stated that learning to spell is not simply a process of memorising words, but rather a consequence of developing cognitive strategies. The child who was failing at spelling could now be introduced to these step-by-step strategies. This research added a new dimension to the spelling process. Both Gentry and Frith revealed that as children learned to spell, they passed through distinct stages of spelling development. Since then, various researchers both in Britain (Peters and Smith,) and in United States of America (Bissex, Lerner, Templeton & Henderson) have endorsed this. They also argue that these different stages predict the type of errors that children will make. Knowledge of these developmental stages allows teachers to notice and adjust their teaching.

However, any stages of development, although important and helpful, only provide guidelines. As there are always exceptions, it is not always possible, or indeed advantageous, to regularly compartmentalise children. When a child moves from one developmental stage to the next, it doesn't necessarily mean that the old stage has been forever completed or mastered. The inferior speller may not fit neatly into a specific stage of development and more likely than not, with some children there will be an overlap of developmental stages. Gentry stresses this when he states that spelling development is gradual and samples from more than one stage may exist at any one time. Bentley

it may be unwise to predict that a child should move along the stages of development at a certain age

(1990) also advises that children move through these stages at different rates. It is important to remember this as it may be unwise to predict that a child should move along the stages of development at a certain age. Just as teachers do come across very young children who are at the correct stage of development with words they use, teachers also encounter teenage children who have not succeeded in passing through the phonetic stage. What follows is an in-depth look at both Gentry's and Frith's stages of development.

Gentry's Model of Spelling Development

The Pre-communicative Stage

Gentry suggests that from early on in their life many children take to the pen and with marks or scribbles indicate to us that they are *'writing'*. They may have watched their parents, or older brothers or sisters involved in the writing process and they too wish to be part of it. If these young children are being read to, and exposed to stories, they will identify a relationship between their "scribbles" and the language of books. They are intrigued with print and are willing to experiment with the written word. At this stage they are aware of stories, they are aware that print carries a message, they know that writing differs from drawing pictures, although their marks may or may not look like letters as we know them.

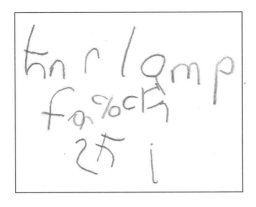

'*(Everywhere that Mary went,) the lamb was sure to go*' (Age 3).

Spelling attempts appear to be a random stringing together of letters of the alphabet, which the speller is sometimes able to produce in written form. The child may or may not know the principle of left to right directionality for writing. Gentry (1982) states that this stage of development 'is the natural early expression of the child's initial hypotheses about how alphabetic symbols represent words.' This lays an important foundation for their concept of the pattern and function of the written word. Home environment is an important factor at this stage of development as children need to be encouraged to experiment with writing. If children do not get the opportunity to experiment with these early attempts at '*writing*', they are at a huge disadvantage.

Pre-Phonetic Stage
As they move to this stage their letter formation is still very underdeveloped. They may know the names and patterns of some of the alphabet but their concept of a word may not be developed. Pre-phonetic spelling is abbreviated and one letter may

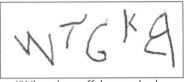

"*When the gruffalo came back...* (Age 5).

represent a word, e.g. *M* for Mammy. There will be a noticeable absence of vowels, and capital letters *HS* may represent *horse* (Culligan, 1997).

Although this may be done consistently until the child begins to name and form letters correctly, it does demonstrate left to right sequential skill. These children are able to copy letter by letter and are aware of left/right and top /bottom orientation of print. As they progress through this stage, alphabet knowledge and mastery of letter formation become more complete but in many instances the introduction of vowels may not be accurate.

I waNt It ni fah has aud wt ra baNt
and tl WaNt a yats Dan

'*I went to my friend's house and we are playing and it was a great day*'. (Age 6)

Phonetic Stage

This stage of development is also known as the Invented Spelling Stage and the Approximate Spelling Stage (Revised Curriculum). As children's awareness of letter – sound correspondence increases, they move to the Phonetic Stage. This stage is an extremely important step as it is an indicator of the child's spelling ability and what spelling knowledge still has to be developed. Bradley and Bryant (1985) state, 'it is a growing awareness of the spelling system, necessary but not sufficient for good spelling.' This 'good spelling' *cannot* be a direct derivative of phonic knowledge, because children are now relying solely on their auditory skills to produce an almost perfect match between letters and sounds, and visual perception of word form is not utilised. These children have little or no regard for letter strings or patterns. Thompson (1987), states that inferior readers, especially boys, persist with a phonic approach to spelling, relying almost completely on this strategy to the detriment of speedy recall of common visual patterns.

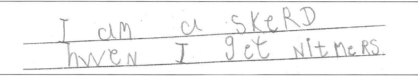

'I am scared when I get nightmares'. (Age 5)

Much research has been done on this particular stage of development. One finds those who strongly support and those who strongly disagree with the theory that the *Invented Spelling Stage* is a temporary one from which children move on to the next stage. Studies from both United States of America and Canada show that those children who invented spelling outperformed those who didn't. Clarke's (1989) study found that traditional spellers (those who learned lists of words) made fewer spelling mistakes, but tended to write shorter stories than those who invented spelling. This difference is due to the strength of the child's phonemic analysis and those inventors who outscore their traditional peers are more likely than not to be at a more advanced phonemic and linguistic level. It is interesting to note however, that both groups in this particular study experienced considerable difficulty with common irregular words.

Within this phonetic stage of development there will be a huge divergence of inventions, ranging from the use of just the initial consonant, to the use of the initial and final consonant, and where vowels are selected they will more than likely be incorrect. One will also encounter attempts that are reasonable alternatives, e.g. 'skar' for 'scar', and attempts that are totally bizarre, e.g.

When my tooth fell out, the tooth fairy came to my house. (Age 5) 'hafllat' for 'headache'. Those children who tender bizarre/random spellings have 'no internalised knowledge of letter strings/patterns and require individual spelling programmes' (Peters & Smith, 1993).

Chomsky (1979) maintained, 'once you have invented your own spelling system, dealing with the standard system comes easy. A considerable amount of the intellectual work has been done.' Intellectual is an interesting choice of words as it presupposes that the child is capable of doing this. The reality is, that the problem will continue to linger if these invented spelling attempts do not progress and become more recognisable.

The favoured children have the ability (linguistic skills) to proceed from stage to stage even without specific teacher intervention. Conversely, the child who is struggling with spelling and who may have reached this stage of development may find it extremely difficult to progress as s/he is still looking for a one to one phoneme and grapheme correspondence. Children do not seem to have a problem if the name of the letter contains its sound, whereas they experience great difficulty with vowel digraphs. This is because the spellings of vowel sounds are more numerous. For example the long /a/ sound may be represented in so many different ways, namely; **a**ngel, g**a**te, p**ai**d, d**ay**, pers**ua**de, **ei**ght, b**ea**r, th**ey**, or wh**ere**, etc. Vowels are the greatest cause of difficulty, as Moseley (1986), states 'there are more than two hundred vowel spellings associated with the eighteen basic sounds.'

This phonetic stage of development is primarily a system, which allows children to use their phonic knowledge to invent words they need, but cannot spell. Moats (1995) states that 'phonetic spelling is a desirable but brief stage of early spelling development.' As Gentry (1982) states 'letters are assigned strictly on the basis of sound, without regard for acceptable English letter sequence or other conventions of English orthography.' By continuing to do this, the inferior speller will not automatically pass on unaided to the next stage. In all probability, without prescribed support, his/her spellings will deteriorate and his/her self-esteem as a speller may be irrevocably damaged.

The child who continues to rely on sound will not become a competent speller.

Peters and Smith (1993) assert that with developing phonological awareness comes the need for intervention in the form of the teaching of spelling. They stress that such a strategy will need to be consistent, systematic, and visually based, as spelling is a visual motor skill. The child who continues to rely on sound will not become a competent speller. As Smith (1985) argues, the worst spellers are the *'wuns hoo spel fonetikly.'* He argued that training children to look for common letter strings and patterns is crucial. Unless the children are trained to look at words within words, and compare letter strings regardless of their sound, inferior spellers will continue to fail. It is by comparing letter strings and putting together letters that look right or that appear in our spelling system that marks the passing on to the next stage of development.

Transitional Stage

At this stage of development, the favoured children move away from the heavy reliance on phonics and present the first evidence of a new visual strategy. For the favoured children, the moving on to this stage occurs incidentally whereas the strugglers will unquestionably require teacher intervention and continued support. This new visual strategy is not yet integrated to the point that the speller automatically recognises what *looks right*, and Bissex (1980) asserts that children at this stage may still transpose letters as a result (e.g. *wiht* for *with*). Children become very alert to serial probability of letter occurrences. They will know what letter strings go together and they begin to use visual analogies and meaning. They also begin to take responsibility for their progress by self-checking and self-correcting.

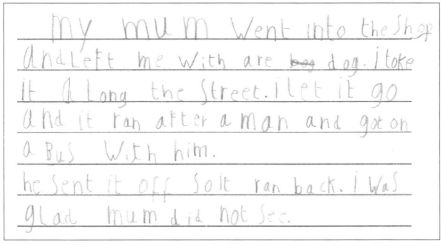

Age 7

Correct /Competent Stage

Children reach the Correct/Competent Stage when they are mastering phoneme - grapheme relationships. (A phoneme is the smallest unit of sound that may be spoken or heard, such as 'a' in apple. A grapheme is the smallest unit of written language, for example each written letter of the alphabet is a grapheme). Children at this stage are now very aware of word structure/patterns that are characteristic of the English spelling system. Such children have the ability to recognise when a word does not look correct and propose alternative spellings. Spellers at this stage of development will also have accumulated a large automatic spelling vocabulary. The competent speller, according to Gentry (1982),

> 'shows an extended knowledge of word structure…and is able to think of alternative spellings and employ visual identification of misspelled words as a correction strategy.'

Frith's Model of Spelling Development

Frith (1980) saw progress in literacy as 'an alternating shift of balance between reading and spelling. She referred to reading as the pacemaker for the logographic strategy, writing for the alphabetic, and reading again for the orthographic one.' Frith's model proposed four stages, which were symbolic, logographic, alphabetic, and orthographic.

The symbolic (pre-literacy) phase

This compares to Gentry's pre-communicative stage, where children may use *scribble* writing to tell a *story*. Children are alert to the fact that print carries a message, although their *letters* have little or no correspondence to our alphabet.

The Logographic Phase

Frith suggested that children at the earliest stages of learning to read and spell can retain the visual image of a written word sufficiently well to read it, but not to spell it. She argued that the child learns to read and spell by visually imaging the whole word. Frith also concluded that reading ability would be superior to spelling ability at this phase because logographic representations of words are used first for reading and later for spelling.

The Alphabetic Phase

Frith maintained that at this stage the child establishes the connection between phonemes and graphemes and uses this knowledge first for spelling and then for reading. Attempts at spelling are based primarily on how a word sounds. Just as there is crossover in Gentry's stages of development, Frith also declares that a child may be reading logographically but writing alphabetically.

The Orthographic Phase

Frith concluded that this is the phase where the child acquires spelling proficiency due to increasing experiences with spelling and its rules. Irregular spellings are accurately represented. Spelling by sound is phased out as the children become more aware of recurring letter strings. They now commence to process these letters as orthographic patterns and as units of meaning (morphemes).

Frith connected her four-stage model to methods of teaching reading. She connected the logographic phase to the 'look and say' method, whose aim is the acquisition of a sizeable sight vocabulary. She equated the alphabetic phase with the 'phonics' approach, arguing that the phonics stage of reading 'is of great importance and can not be simply skipped.' The orthographic phase was equated with the morphemic approach, in which the acquisition of meaning is determined.

The evidence that spelling is a developmental process is indisputable. As teachers, we must embrace this knowledge and familiarise ourselves with characteristics of the various stages of development. If spelling is breaking down or not progressing across the continuum of development, teachers need to be spelling 'mechanics' who will be able to look under the spelling 'bonnet', diagnose the problem and adjust or modify instruction.

6

Spelling and the Revised Curriculum

For the first time in Irish Primary Education, the Revised Curriculum (DES, 1999) acknowledged that it is necessary to teach spelling. The increase in the amount of space devoted to spelling in the revised curriculum is a welcome departure from the 1971 document. Much experience of providing in-service on this topic throughout the country leaves me in no doubt but that this 1971 document failed to improve the spelling ability of many children. Unlike its predecessor, this 1999 document has finally recognised that spelling is a skill that is not picked up incidentally. It is therefore a welcome departure to observe such comments as 'progress in spelling is most likely to be achieved if it is *taught* (my italics) systematically' (Teacher Guidelines, p.14), and … 'progress takes place when children experience a consistent and systematic approach' (Teacher Guidelines, p. 86). Unfortunately, as with handwriting, the document does not present any satisfactory clarification as to how these tenets may be achieved. In the absence of specific intervention strategies, it is doubtful if this document will change the plight of a child struggling with spelling.

Spelling Development

The Curriculum makes no reference to the models of spelling development advocated by Frith and Gentry in the early 1980s. Instead, teachers are presented (Teacher Guidelines, p.85) with three developmental stages that are rather disappointing. Although not credited, they do appear to loosely resemble the work of Schlagal (1989).

Much recognition is given to encouraging children to approximate spellings. This approximate or invented spelling stage is an important step in the developmental process. Bradley and Bryant (1985) assert that, 'it is a growing awareness of the spelling system, necessary but not sufficient for good spelling.' This 'good spelling' cannot be a direct derivative of phonic knowledge, where children rely solely on their auditory skills to produce an almost perfect match (a one-to-one correspondence) between letters and sounds, and where visual perception of word form is not utilised. Many of these 'inventors' have little or no regard for letter strings or patterns. Thompson (1987) states that poor readers, especially boys, persist with a phonic approach to spelling, relying almost completely on this strategy to the detriment of speedy recall of common visual patterns.

With their knowledge of the names of the alphabet letters and an emerging awareness of sounds within spoken words, children approximate their spellings as they write. Research shows that it is the consonants which emerge first in children's invented spellings. Over the course of time children move away from using sound to using vision and learning how spelling represents meaning. The trouble is of course that not all children move away from approximating. While we encourage children to approximate spelling, we must also provide systematic spelling instruction at their developmental levels. Approximate spelling must never be seen as a substitute for instruction. Fresch (2002) argues that

> 'unless there is direct instruction other than in the memorisation model, students may get 'stuck' at the predicting stage as they do not have the tools to look at words in any other way than as isolated units.'

Allowing children to invent spelling is an important stage of spelling development. At this particular stage of development, phonics and spelling are very closely aligned. The invented stage of development is primarily a system that allows children to use this phonic knowledge to invent words they need, but cannot spell.

Czerniewska (1992) stated that the term *invented spelling* became popular as it turned attention away from children's errors and focused instead on children's experiments. The advocated use of approximate spelling will be nothing new to children! This is, and has been the usual procedure adopted by children when confronted with words not in their automatic spelling vocabulary. In what must be one of the most educationally flawed comments in the Revised Curriculum, this approximate stage of development is described 'as an interim measure' (English Curriculum, p. 28). Not every child has the ability to pass through this stage of development unaided. This comment stands alone without any explanation how to guide children, who do not have this ability to surmount this specific developmental stage. One may only speculate why there is an absence of guidelines to deal with those children whose inventions / approximations are so unstable that they change from word to word. McGuinness (1997) aptly sums it up by stating that 'no one should ever be encouraged to write misspelled gibberish he cannot read.'

Current research provides evidence that many children do not pass through the various stages of development without adequate guidance. This document fails to address the question of intervention by globally stating that 'the teacher's input will come at the conferencing stage.' (Teacher Guidelines: 86). The reality is that the problem will continue to linger if children's spelling attempts do not progress and become more recognisable. Unless teachers are to be trained in how to utilise invented spellings / approximations to determine how a child is applying information about our spelling system, we will continue to encounter many children for whom invented spelling has not been 'an interim measure.'

Current research provides evidence that many children do not pass through the various stages of development without adequate guidance.

Spelling Rules

Approaching spelling through the mastering of spelling rules is not to be recommended. Hanna et al (1966) argued that 'trying to teach spelling by rules is one of the least effective approaches one can take.' Gentry (1987) asserts that by teaching spelling through rules, 'children are ignored in favour of teaching fixed and ready-made sets of facts and formulas.' For many children, memorising spelling rules is unproductive and rarely influences spelling development. Again, there is much research evidence available to question the effectiveness of spelling rules and to demonstrate that when children eventually memorise them, they are seldom applied in the spelling process. For children, who have short-term memory problems, rules present many problems. Does the child understand the rule? Some rules are pretty straightforward, for example, the letter /u/ is always written after the letter /q/. However, some spelling rules may be quite complicated.

> *memorising spelling rules is unproductive and rarely influences spelling development.*

'monosyllables and words of more than one syllable with the accent on the last syllable, which end in a single consonant preceded by a single vowel, double the final consonant when adding a suffix beginning with a vowel.'

Once the rule is understood, can s/he remember it? Can s/he apply the rule? Is s/he aware of exceptions to the rule? The Revised Curriculum states that when words end in 'e' we drop the 'e' when adding the suffix '*ing*' but what about b*eing*; s*eeing*; glu*eing*; dy*eing*; fre*eing*; ag*eing*? If adults were asked to remember a rule they may have learned in primary school, it is most likely that '*i before e, except after c,*' will be recalled and yet, this rule is so seldom called upon. Words which contain the /ie/ or /ei/ letter strings account for less than two percent of Fry's one thousand instant words! Rather than subjecting children to the memorisation of rules, time would be better spent in training them in generalisation or analogy. There are methodologies available that are particularly effective for developing spelling as an associative skill, but these were not included in the document.

Spell-checkers

The ability to spell, even in this ever expanding technological age is, and will be as crucial as it has been in the past. As children need to be free to write what they want and when they want, the acquisition of spelling and writing skills will remain essential. The advent of voice activated writing technology will not terminate the basic need of written skills, any more than the advent of television destroyed reading habits. Graham (2000) argues that

'spell checkers have not replaced the need for children to understand how to spell words correctly. Such technology assists in proofreading, but is not a substitute for spelling knowledge.'

There have been some calls for mandatory provision of word processors for all children with specific learning difficulties. However, it is important to note that spell-checkers are not the answer to spelling problems. Those children who over depend on spell checkers are unlikely to improve their spelling ability. For example, a spell-checker will not assist the child who has flawed pronunciation and writes/types, '*Are* horse is dead.' Neither will it assist the child who writes '*Eye lead the too buoys two the sighed of the rode*!' McAuthur (1996) asserts that spell-checkers do not identify twenty five percent of all errors because the misspelled forms are the correct spelling of other words. For example, the child who transposes some letters and writes/types, 'I got a sweet *form* my teacher,' will not be corrected. Montgomery et al (2001) as cited in Moats (2005) reported that spell checkers usually catch just 30% to 80% of misspellings overall.

> *Children who over depend on spell checkers are unlikely to improve their spelling ability.*

Spell checkers are also limited in their ability to suggest a correct spelling, as this is dependent on the severity of the misspelling. For example, if the child writes '*nitaes*' for '*aunt*' s/he will not be given any assistance. In the same study by Montgomery et al, it was found that spell-checkers 'identified the target word from the misspellings of students with learning disabilities only 53% of the time.' To date, spell-checkers may be of use in assisting the writer or compensating for weak spelling, but they cannot be a substitute for the child's spelling knowledge and command of strategies. Graham (2000) concluded that

> 'spell checkers are ineffective in facilitating the type of knowledge children must develop to become accurate and consistent spellers.'

List Learning
The document advocates word lists as an aid 'to improve his/her command of spelling,' (English Curriculum, p. 40). Gentry (1997) argues that

> 'a spelling curriculum that requires seven or eight years of memorising word lists and remembering isolated facts is not likely to deepen children's knowledge .'

The legacy of such a process is that learning isolated lists of words (more often than not phonetically grouped) is confused with *learning how to spell*. Templeton and Morris (1999) stress that teaching spelling should not consist merely of presenting students with lists of words without explicit teaching of spelling knowledge. Moats (2005) stresses that

> 'lists are unmotivated, unappealing and difficult to learn. Lists without a logical framework or set of principles must be learned by rote rather than by reason.'

> *Rote memorisation of word lists is of little value.*

Rote memorisation of words doesn't lead to long term spelling effectiveness or teach children how words *'work'*. Rote memorisation of word lists is of little value. However vague the 1971 Curriculum was, it did nevertheless caution against 'cultivating skills in isolation from their purpose' (Part 1, p. 95). My research (Culligan 2000) confirms that when spelling is well planned, individualised and taught, there are benefits for the child, the parent and the teacher (See Chapter Nine). By altering attitudes and practices, teachers may improve children's spelling without depending on phonically based word lists and weekly tests.

Word Searches and Anagrams

The proposed use of word searches and anagrams (English Curriculum, p. 40) is also a source of worry. Words in such activities ought to be presented in a left to right format. Word searches, where words are presented top to bottom may be acceptable, but those presented right to left or diagonally should be avoided for inferior spellers. If they are presented in this format, then at least the child should be alerted to the fact. Anagrams do present the superior spellers with an opportunity to use their spelling knowledge. However, they ought not to be given to poorer spellers who have not acquired adequate knowledge of the spelling system. Most teachers will acknowledge that this is what the weak speller does anyway!

Spelling Methodology

The fact that a methodology for *teaching* spelling is advocated has to be highly commended. The prescribed strategy (Look, Cover, Write and Check) is one, which is currently part of spelling policy in many schools. Despite much research evidence, which forcibly demonstrates that visual perception is a vital element in the acquisition of spelling ability, it is rather curious however, that the one recommended strategy is predominantly a visual one as no reference is made to visual perception of word form, or visual awareness training anywhere else in the document. (The word *visualise* is used once, but only in relation to the proposed strategy). The unfortunate overemphasis on the use of *sound* and *sound based patterns* (Teacher Guidelines, p.86) negates the importance of the visual dimension and gives further credence to the belief that the function of spelling is to represent sound. Researchers in the past twenty years have consistently warned that it is wrong to equate spelling and phonics. The samples of regular letter patterns that are presented in the Teacher Guidelines (p. 86) may add to this misconception.

Various strategies ought to have been included, as no one method will meet every child's needs. It is critical for teachers to be aware of alternative methodologies, which may suit these different learning styles. Whichever strategy is utilised, it is also imperative that it is a 'living strategy'. This means that children need to both understand and implement it, especially in the home situation. An assumption that their methodology is always understood and utilised may have serious implications for both teachers and children alike.

Far from being a 'radical' document, as it was once described to me, it is quite a disappointing one. It is rather disingenuous to suggest that its limitations may be accredited to lack of preparatory time and limitations of space. As already stated, spelling as a skill is undefined and neither is any reference made as to how spelling may assist reading. It is difficult to comprehend why so much of current research findings and literature both on the development of spelling and cursive writing have not been embraced. As it stands, it is unlikely that the document will further the development of spelling which our children deserve. Cripps (1999) summarises the situation when he states that 'if the spelling of Irish children does improve, then this document will either have earned its place, or teachers will have developed their own strategies for teaching spelling. I believe the latter will be the case.'

> *It is difficult to comprehend why so much of current research findings and literature both on the development of spelling and cursive writing have not been embraced.*

Review of the Revised Curriculum
In 2005, the National Council for Curriculum and Assessment (NCCA) published a review of the primary school English curriculum. The findings of the report were based on responses from 719 teacher questionnaires, interviews with parents, children and teachers, and principals in six schools. Unfortunately, the findings did not come as a major surprise. It reports (p. 76) that 'a concern with spelling, phonics and grammar appeared consistently throughout the responses provided by teachers'. Not surprisingly, one of its main recommendations urges 'detailed direction and guidance should be provided for teachers concerning the teaching, learning and assessment of spelling, phonics and grammar.' One can only speculate why these were not addressed adequately at the planning and writing of the document.

The treatment of spelling in the Revised Curriculum is very flawed. 'Detailed direction and guidance' ought to have been clearly presented. The inconsistencies in the initial in-service programme for its implementation, where in many instances spelling was not referred to at all, would tend to endorse the belief that a wonderful opportunity has been squandered. Gill and Scharer (1996) found that 'many teachers express concern that they do not have a strong foundation either in how to teach spelling or in the nature of the spelling system.' In 1998, Mountford asserted that teachers were not professionally equipped for the teaching of spelling. Regrettably, as the results of this NCCA review indicate, the 1999 Revised Curriculum did very little to counter this assertion. An excellent opportunity for combining the teaching of both handwriting and spelling has been missed. Our children and teachers certainly deserved better.

47

7

Assessing Spelling

The Bullock Report (1975) states that spelling should be a part of the fabric of normal classroom experience, neither dominating nor neglected. School policy and teachers' work schemes state the level of attainment and competence to be achieved in the various curricular areas. In order to check if these targets are being reached, teachers assess the children, either formally or informally. The two main functions of assessment are to assist and improve learning. Assessment *of* learning and assessment *for* learning are ongoing processes and the foundation stones of effective teaching, but only if the test findings are acted upon. Goulandris (1996) argued that assessment is not simply a process of identification but is a vital prerequisite of effective teaching. It enables the teacher to pinpoint precise strengths and weaknesses and so provide appropriate learning experiences and instruction for that individual child.

Assessment may be used to determine the range of ability in the class, to determine if teaching objectives have been attained, to identify difficulties, and to plan to overcome these. This may be achieved informally or formally. Informal assessment predominates, as the teacher is constantly observing all aspects of the child's development. The I.N.T.O. Education Committee Report (1989) states that observation is not confined to what one can see; it also involves questioning, discussion, and exploration of pupils' perceptions. Formal assessment is carried out by using one of the many standardised / normative tests which are commercially available. Such tests will indicate how the child is performing in relation to his/her own age and also in comparison to his peers, whereas diagnostic assessment (formal or informal) identifies the strengths and weaknesses of the individual pupil.

With the possible exception of mathematical tables, no other area of curriculum seems to be tested as much as spelling

With the possible exception of mathematical tables, no other area of curriculum seems to be tested as much as spelling (Culligan, 1997). Todd (1982) asserts that 'in many schools the ritual weekly test is common practice.' In Ireland, current practice sees children's spelling progress assessed in two ways: – performance in written work or the weekly test. The "Five-a-night and Test on Friday" fits into the latter category, and although these weekly tests are not normative or standardised, they are usually used to compare performance and judge progress of one child to that of another. These tests are not of enormous value to the deficient speller. The traditional Friday Test is rarely accompanied by direct teaching/instruction. (See Chapter Eight). There is a tendency for misspelled words to be abandoned or presumed to be 'known,' and apart from getting children to correct their errors a number of times, 'no further work is done in school upon these words' (Todd, 1982).

The purpose of teaching spelling is for the children to be free to use, in *all* writing situations, the knowledge and skill gained during these spelling periods. Assessing children on standardised/normative tests and thereby acquiring a spelling age may not be of significant assistance to the teacher. Procuring information that a child has attained a spelling age of 8 years 2 months may be of minimal benefit to the teacher. For example, in terms of spelling ability and progress, it is difficult to differentiate between a spelling age of 8 years 2 months and one of 8 years 8 months.

Such tests are of limited value in planning a programme, as they are just an indication of how the child performed on a particular day. Pain (1980) acknowledges that while such tests may be useful for comparative purposes they are 'not helpful when planning remedial teaching for individuals.' Sipe (2003) agues that 'standardised spelling tests represent the worst practice for challenged spellers.' It is regrettable that intervention decisions are often made on the basis of results from isolated word tests. These tests do not diagnose his/her strengths or weaknesses. Vernon (1963) questions the validity of spelling tests as 'testers regard the spelling test as measuring spelling ability in general.' Teachers regularly encounter children who achieve an average or above average score in such standardised tests, and yet present with inferior spelling ability in free – writing.

An invaluable method of assessing spelling is to use diagnostic assessment procedures. In these, inaccuracies may be categorised according to type, and individual mistakes as well as prevalent tendencies may be evaluated. Although diagnosing children's spelling is very time consuming, not every child's spelling needs to be analysed. Analysis is a valuable tool and Goulandris (1996) maintains that the understanding gained from embarking on such a diagnostic procedure should, in the long run, save time for practitioner and student alike. It is by examining what the children are writing, that teachers can determine how and when to intervene.

> *An invaluable method of assessing spelling is to use diagnostic assessment procedures.*

Intervention ought to be gradual and teaching approaches will need to be modified if the child progresses or fails to progress. Diagnostic assessment will show if a child has failed to grasp basic spelling principles, or has developed an over-reliance on using sound. Teachers may also determine if deficient spellers are likely to become improved spellers, while capable spellers may be directed to more efficient ways of learning, and towards independent methods of study. Being acquainted with the causes of spelling difficulty and the stages of spelling development, it is possible to predict if the child is going to be 'a good or potentially good speller, and plan accordingly,' Torbe (1977).

Whether the teacher analyses a passage of free writing or uses a standardised test as a diagnostic tool, it will be advantageous to categorise the child's spelling attempts. The value of a Spelling Error Analysis Grid (Culligan, 1997, p68) cannot be overstated. Once diagnosis of strengths and weaknesses has been made, positive and relevant programmes should be planned and introduced. According to Thompson (1991), these programmes ought to be structured, sequential, cumulative and multisensory, allowing the pupil to build one skill upon another.

In another diagnostic grid, Peters and Smith (1993) refer to three kinds of errors (miscues), plausible, invented, and random.

Peters & Smith Diagnostic Spelling Grid.

Error	Analysis
Plausible	Words that conform to English spelling, e.g. 'appel' for apple.
Invented	Words are written as they sound to the child, e.g. 'shuger' for sugar.
Random	Words that show neither visual nor phonological awareness, e.g. 'clnt' for galloped.

Employing such a grid, the child's strengths and weaknesses may be profiled by comparing the child's incorrect attempt with the correct spelling and individual programmes may be planned accordingly (See Chapter Nine).

> *...when spelling is well planned, individualised and taught, there are benefits for the child, the parent and the teacher.*

8

The Friday Test

The card below was sent to me some time ago. Before this, Jack's mother described the terrible tension in the home caused by the Friday test. She talked about all the time and effort the family invested in improving Jack's spelling, but to no avail. The entire family dreaded Thursday nights when after long periods of effort, Jack might eventually 'know' his spellings. However, during the test the next day he would get so anxious that he could not perform, and consequently scored very poorly. His teacher indicated on many occasions that Jack's spellings were getting worse. Jack eventually developed stomach pains on Friday mornings and it was a struggle to get him to go to school.

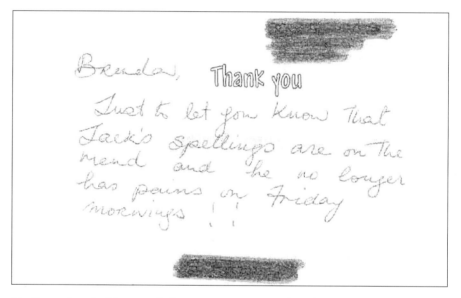

I believe that Jack's story is by no means an isolated one. For children such as Jack, a different approach to both teaching spelling and to classroom management is necessary to impact more positively on their self-esteem and automatic spelling vocabulary. When Jack's writing was analysed, attention was focused on what he could already achieve; on his strengths rather than his weaknesses; on the type of errors he was making rather than on the quantity. His developmental stage of spelling was identified and he followed an individual programme based on my 'Corewords' dictation exercises to activate his visual awareness and move him to the next stage of development.

Impact of research on weekly spelling tests:
One has to ask why this particular area of curriculum may cause children to become physically ill. Is the emphasis on correct spelling too early in the child's school life the cause of such high anxiety? Browne (2001) believes this to be the case and concludes that such anxiety can 'inhibit the valuable insight into the principles of spelling.'

Has research influenced methodology in any way? It is reasonable to assume that the publication of major international spelling research from the 1960s onwards has had little impact on the Irish education system and has not influenced thinking on spelling. The traditional approach (phonetic list learning) continued as before. Change only occurred in the switch from one list source to another. Spelling publications of the time, some of which are still in use, were organised upon the principle of getting children to learn daily or weekly groups of words of similar sound, with usually the week's words tested on Friday. (The relevance of such books to the spelling needs of children requires careful consideration when whole school policies are being formulated.)

> *It is common practice that children are required to learn lists of words regardless of whether these are relevant to their writing needs.*

There is evidence in the literature to suggest that some teaching practices e.g. an over reliance on programmed lists/kits, may contribute to children's spelling difficulties. Ramsden (1993) insists that 'we need to realise that that the structures of spelling have never really been taught … spelling has only been corrected and tested.' It is common practice that children are required to learn lists of words regardless of whether these are relevant to their writing needs. It may be argued that lists do indeed serve a purpose, as research shows that the best spellers need lists of some sort (Peters, 1970). However, research also indicates that these lists do little or nothing for children struggling with spelling as more often than not they are required to 'learn' these words without context or purpose (Culligan, 1996). Influential factors in learning to spell include teachers' attitudes and practices, teachers' knowledge of the subject, and classroom management. Sheahan's (1998) research findings indicate

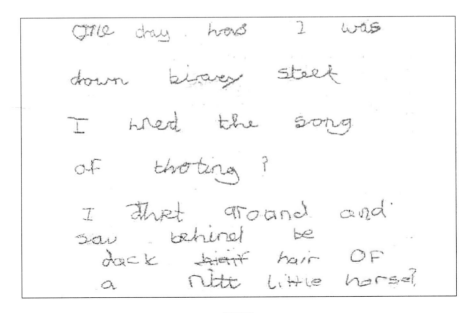

that the majority of the teachers surveyed stated that they had not found any effective approaches to teaching spelling.

If one examines this writing sample from a nine-year-old girl (see case study four, page 89), it is obvious that the traditional approach to spelling has not worked. For such children, this Friday test is inappropriate. Sheahan (1998) found that 'some teachers are accustomed to giving such tests, but they may not be totally convinced of their usefulness'. Parkinson et al (1994) concluded that 'the benefit arising from the weekly test of phonically related words is likely to be short lived'. It is obvious that utilisation of such lists and procedures has its roots in tradition rather than in educational theory or research.

Although its origins are indeterminate, the concept of the Friday spelling test may be traced back to the beginning of the last century and it still forms a part of Irish school life to this day. The legacy of this process has resulted in 'success' in the Friday test being confused with spelling improvement, and learning lists of words confused with learning how to spell. One cannot assume that children are improving at spelling just because they may get a good result in Friday's test. Once used and perhaps corrected a number of times (a very dubious practice in itself), the words are rarely revisited as Todd (1982) states 'no further work is done in school upon these words'.

> *One cannot assume that children are improving at spelling just because they may get a good result in Friday's test.*

Barone (1992) stated that the rote memorisation of spelling lists is of doubtful value. Gentry & Gillet (1993) maintained that the notion that spelling is simple memorisation has resulted in many failures in the classroom. Frequently, the words the child may have spelled correctly in his/her Friday test may be written incorrectly later the same day or during the following week. Gentry & Gillet(1993) assert that by

> 'sheer effort and rote memorisation they can do well on Friday, but they lack the ability or training to internalise/generalise letter/word pattern knowledge. It is this training that leads to long term spelling effectiveness.'

For many children the Friday test hinders long-term mastery of words. These children's objective is to try to memorise a specific list of words for short-term gain or accuracy on Friday. As teachers, our objective is for the child's long-term mastery of words. Children need to be shown that their responsibility for learning spelling does not end on a Friday. The teacher's objective must take precedence by focusing on high frequency words and by targeting word study activities relevant to each child's needs. Makay (2003) states that

> 'it can be very daunting for strugglers to have to learn 20 words every week (and fail miserably in the Friday test). This only helps to

convince them of their inadequacies as spellers and will turn them off their spelling even more.'

Short-term gains of rote memorisation are not permanent and soon diminish over time. Fresch (2002) argues that 'a post-test on Friday does not necessarily ensure carry over into a student's writing'. These words have not moved into the child's long-term memory (automatic spelling vocabulary). From a professional viewpoint, a weekly spelling test tells the teacher nothing that s/he does not already know about the children in her/his care. It is more beneficial to judge spelling improvement from their own personal or creative writing. As Arvidson (1989) maintains 'the measure of a person's spelling ability is how well he spells in his writing.' What this system of the weekly test does is to continue to isolate spelling and separate it from the rest of the curriculum. Peters and Smith (1993) assert that spelling

> 'should be seen by the writer as an aspect of communicating ideas, feelings and information to the reader, rather than as a separate skill which is teacher initiated and taught as a discrete exercise.'

Spellings are best done in context, with words that children need and these in turn should not be grouped together just because they happen to sound the same (Culligan, 1993). If there is a need for words to be grouped, then as Cripps (1990) asserts, it is necessary to group words according to visual structure, thus enabling children to employ associative skills to facilitate learning. There are no exceptions to visual patterns. The sourcing of lists ought to comprise both children's own writing vocabulary and frequency of use.

To assist teachers, who utilise weekly tests, Bell (1970) developed the 'Test - Study - Test Method.' With this approach, the children are given all the week's words in the form of a pre-test on Mondays (Formative Assessment). Undoubtedly, the teacher will get the same 'class picture', i.e. the superior spellers will perform well and the inferior spellers will not. This allows teachers to see exactly which words the children already know, and those that will have to be learned. More importantly, however, is the fact that the teacher and child have now got the remainder of the week to do something about teaching/learning these words.

it is crucial that teachers focus on the type of spelling errors children make and not on the quantity.

From an assessment perspective, although it is clear that spelling is frequently tested, the type of children's errors is not focused upon. There is evidence that a diagnostic evaluation of children's writing is more beneficial than merely administering a spelling test (Culligan, 2000). I believe that it is crucial that teachers focus on the type of spelling errors children make and not on the quantity. Sheahan (1998) concluded that 'the current state of spelling depends very much on the initiative of the individual teacher.' Wilde (1996) asserted that 'many teachers pick and choose practices that do not reflect a common underlying philosophy.' Cripps & Peters (1978) believed that progress in spelling occurs when teachers' attitudes are consistent and when they are rational and systematic in their teaching. This involves a diagnosis of children's writing to determine strengths and weaknesses, profiling the needs of the child and planning an individualised programme. The case studies (See Chapter Thirteen) demonstrate that, despite the high pupil teacher ratio, it is possible to plan and implement an individual spelling in a whole class situation (Culligan, 2000). This viewpoint is supported by the work of Anderson and Lapp (1988), who concluded that 'spelling instruction must be well planned, individualised as much as possible and effectively implemented'.

As already stated, I believe the Friday test is of very little benefit to the child, teacher or parent. The weekly spelling test has its roots in tradition rather than in educational theory or research. It is true that some children 'enjoy' such a Friday activity; these are usually the children with little or no difficulty with spelling. Those children with spelling difficulties usually dread spelling tests. There is plenty evidence in the literature to indicate that weekly spelling tests are commonplace, and that correction takes the form of asking the child to write out the correct form of the word a number of times. Unless errors are analysed, little benefit accrues. It is also true

> *The weekly spelling test has its roots in tradition rather than in educational theory or research.*

that many parents expect a weekly spelling test. This is a throwback to their own school days and they expect similar for their children. It would be far more beneficial if good practice was explained to parents and if they were shown how to help children get these words into long-term memory. Teachers need to provide parents with the necessary expertise to assist their child. The stages of spelling development need to be explained to parents in order to help them interpret writing behaviours through the various stages. When educational liaison between home and school is active, attempts to eradicate difficulties will be successful. The development and dissemination of procedures, which would assist parents in promoting the spelling development of their children, ought to be at the core of every school policy (See Chapter Twelve).

9

Managing Individual Spelling Programmes

Research literature clearly confirms that many children continue to experience difficulty with spelling long after their language and reading skills have improved. Although individualised reading programmes are now a fairly common part of the language curriculum, individual spelling needs of children do not seem to have been afforded similar attention. There is plenty of evidence in research literature to indicate that the real solution to spelling difficulties lies in individual help. Because of this research evidence, there is a growing awareness that for instructional models to be effective they must be tailored specifically to meet the needs of the child.

...an individualised approach to spelling is most successful.

Gentry & Gillet (1993) are quite adamant that learning to spell is an individual process and that 'spelling is a complex individual accomplishment.' Torbe (1993) states that 'spelling instruction should always acknowledge the uniqueness of the learner and so an individualised approach is always best.' This supports Anderson & Lapp (1988) who argued that an individualised approach to spelling is most successful. In Ireland, the traditional approach to learning spellings is usually whole class teaching (a one size fits all approach) where the 'struggler' is required to learn the same words from the same book or list as the proficient speller. It is not best practice to have every child in the class learning the same list of words (Culligan, 1997).

Westwood (2003) queries how this individualisation of spelling programmes may be accomplished and states that 'in classrooms containing twenty eight or more students it is virtually impossible to find the necessary time to devote to such a personalised approach.' If there is a need to 'differentiate/individualise spelling instruction,' and research evidence strongly supports this, then teachers need to be empowered as to how to plan and implement such instruction in classes with a high pupil-teacher ratio. With this in mind, my research (with eight and nine year old boys and girls) was carried out to determine if the good practice of instruction with a small group of children in a learning support setting could be transferred to a whole class situation of more than twenty-eight pupils. I also wished to demonstrate that a consistent, rational and systematic approach is necessary if children are to overcome their spelling difficulties and that by following a carefully constructed programme, children would spell more accurately because they are motivated to do so. The high pupil / teacher ratio in classes and an overloaded curriculum are repeatedly cited as major obstacles in supporting children with learning difficulties. To overcome these barriers it may be best to adopt a twin approach. Firstly, the best methods for dealing with these strugglers are effective teaching practices, i.e. observing, diagnosing, planning, teaching and evaluating. Tasks should be clearly defined and these children should, according to Westwood (1993) receive as much direct guidance and support as necessary to ensure success. Everyone in the class will benefit from effective practices, and these should not be seen solely as the property of the strugglers. Secondly, the children in the classroom do not only learn from teacher, but they also learn from each other. Goldstein (1994) stated that the teacher in the classroom is the 'environmental engineer who can facilitate the environment and the experiences, so the students benefit and learn.' It is important for the teacher to realise that he/she is not the only teacher in the room.

As already stated, my research was to determine if the good practice of instruction with a small group of children in a learning support setting could be transferred to a whole class situation of more than 28 pupils and also to ascertain if a move away from the traditional use of phonic lists and the 'Friday Test' to a more individualised approach would enhance the spelling ability of the pupils. I will now outline procedures followed to individualise the teaching of spelling over a period of thirty weeks. This will comprise the testing materials selected, the intervention, its implementation and correcting techniques. Attention will also be focused on the measures and criteria employed to formulate three distinct classroom groupings (the Independent, Semi-independent and Dependent groupings).

I used the following materials in the research;
- a standardised spelling test, (Daniels and Diack, 1958)
- a graded dictation exercise (Dictation 2, Peters & Smith, 1993)
- 'Corewords' lists and dictation exercises based on these lists (Culligan, 1997)

The Daniels and Diack Spelling Test
The Daniels and Diack spelling test was chosen because it comprises four lists of ten words, each of which would be in the speaking and reading vocabulary of the 'average' eight or nine year old child. Two of these lists contain regularly spelled words, and two contain irregularly spelled words (these spellings cannot be reliably worked out on the basis of the sounds heard in the particular words). The Daniels and Diack Spelling test converts raw scores to spelling ages but does not present results in quotient form. Although Young (1983) warns that such a calculation 'can grossly confuse assessments,' I decided on calculating a quotient by dividing the child's spelling age by the child's chronological age and multiplying the result by one hundred. (A spelling quotient of 100 indicates that the child's spelling is developing commensurate with his/her chronological age).

Peters' Graded Dictation Exercise:
Pain (1980) stressed that

> 'Although tests of general spelling ability may be useful for comparative purposes they are not helpful when planning remedial teaching for individuals. Diagnostic tests are more useful.'

In order to diagnose specific errors and determine the developmental level of spelling of each child, I also administered Peters' graded dictation exercise (number 2) to all the children. A profile each child's strengths and weaknesses was then attained, using the spelling error analysis grid. The Peters' diagnostic dictation comprises one hundred words. I read it out a phrase at a time and the children were encouraged to write *something* for each word. When the passage was completed, it was reread to allow for self-corrections.

'Corewords' Dictation Exercises

Much has been written about the advantages and disadvantages of using dictation sentences or passages. Westwood (2003) asserts that unless they are used diagnostically that there is little to support the continued use of dictation exercises. This is a valid argument but it also true to say that dictation may be the bridge between isolated list learning and the child's own personal and creative writing, and is a far more realistic way of assessing spelling ability. In practising dictation, the child gains experience in many elements. S/he must attend to various functions simultaneously, e.g. attention, memory and motor skill. Mudd (1994) urges that teachers 'should include spellings in sentences, and if possible in continuous text so that the children experience flow of writing.' It is only when a child can produce a word in written work can we say that the child is improving. It is of little benefit if s/he gets five out of five in her/his isolated spelling test and then cannot produce the same words correctly when next s/he needs them in his/her written work.

Dictation is a controlled instrument, which enables the teacher or parent to guide the child through these high frequency but troublesome words. Arvidson (1977) argues that these commonly used words are difficult to master and they cannot be learned once and for all in one given week of a child's school life. They must therefore be continually learned and relearned. Roberts (1989) urges the teacher to ensure that,

> "the child be required to return to the word after a very short
> interval and subsequently at frequent intervals, so that his memory
> of the word is refreshed and his learning reinforced."

Gulliford (1985) concurs with this and adds that spelling needs to be taken to the point where the correct response is automatic. He argues that this is a point at which much learning of spelling breaks down since it is not easy to arrange for effective revision and to ensure frequent use of words. My dictation exercises were specifically devised to fulfil this role, as the high frequency words are constantly being revisited and reinforced, a point validated by Mudd (1994) when she emphasised that it 'helps to reinforce and revise children's knowledge of spellings if past work is included in dictated texts.' The compilation of dictation sentences based on phonic patterns of the *'the pin is in the bin'* variety was avoided. Although this is not normal use of written language, this approach is still common practice in many schools. By adhering to such a programme, some children will never complete study on the high frequency words s/he requires for personal writing. Apart from increasing a child's awareness of phonemic characteristics of words, I believe that these phonic based dictation exercises are of little benefit to the struggling speller. For example, the P.A.T. Programme (Phonological Awareness Training) is currently being used as a spelling scheme in many schools but it comprises about 39% of the most common occurring words.

The Teacher's Role

There is plenty of research evidence that shows that the influential factors in learning to spell include teachers' attitudes and practices, teachers' knowledge of the subject, and classroom management. Peters' (1974) stated that the 'behaviour of the teacher determines more than any other single factor whether a child learns or does not learn to spell.' Westwood (2003) stressed that 'it is important for teachers to be aware of the normal stages of development through which children pass on their way to becoming proficient spellers.' Templeton & Morris (1999) agree that the classroom teacher needs to have knowledge of both the spelling system and spelling development.

In order to plan effective instruction, the teacher must know not only where the child is on the spelling development continuum, but also how to take him/her on to the next stage of development. Teachers who understand where children are in this developmental continuum will be able to provide the explicit teaching necessary to move them forward to the next stage of development. Teachers need to understand the kind of spelling mistakes that are being made by the child in order to set meaningful targets. Gentry and Gillet (1993) stated that 'a thorough understanding of invented spelling reaps rich rewards for practical use.' They also add that many teachers feel that they are not confident of their expertise in this area. Sheahan's (1998) study indicates that two-thirds of the teachers surveyed stated that they had not found any effective approaches to teaching spelling. She suggests that teachers may not have kept pace with recent developments in spelling. Sheahan found that 'it was common practice among teachers surveyed to use a phonically – based spelling book with their pupils.'

Children do not learn to spell with equal ease or in the same way. If a child's spelling is ineffective s/he can become greatly confused and disheartened. This is especially so if the child's writing is met with reproach because not enough has been written or because the spelling attempts are so unacceptable. Children who find spelling difficult will need a strategy if they are going to be successful with the learning demanded of them. Spelling programmes for these particular children need to contain step-by-step strategies, exposure to spelling patterns, and guidance in checking and self-correcting. As with sight vocabulary in reading, an automatic spelling vocabulary is too important to be left to chance.

Selecting Spelling Groups

Classroom management is a key component in assisting the strugglers to overcome their difficulties. In many classrooms, children are arranged in different groups for Mathematics, English, and perhaps Irish. Such groupings are usually formed as a result of teacher's own informal evaluations, standardised screenings or assessments. Within any of these groups one would inevitably find other subgroups. If the children are grouped according to reading ability there will be children within that group with diverse language, comprehension and writing needs. More often than not such groupings are not changed accordingly if a lesson involves any of these particular areas. For example, when the lesson plan turns from reading to a writing exercise, one will find some children within the group at an immediate disadvantage. Any such inflexible system would need to be reviewed in order to take individual differences and needs into account.

In any class, one will find many different ability levels. Spelling is no exception, although it is a part of curriculum that constantly seems to be viewed in isolation and often assessed devoid of context. If one were to group children according to their spelling development, one would find a huge diversity of ability. Over forty years ago, Tansley (1967) stated that in any class, even in large streamed schools there would be a wide range of spelling ability and attainment.

First of all are the very proficient spellers, those who have no difficulty in learning, retaining and reproducing with speed any words they require. The next grouping will be the proficient/competent spellers. Any mistakes within this group may be attributed more to 'slips of the pen' than to anything else. These children have the ability to self-correct and retain correction. These two groups, covering the upper levels of spelling ability, fall into Peters' category of 'favoured' spellers. Those who are not 'favoured' may also be subdivided into two groups. Firstly, there are those who desperately try to improve their lot, but for one reason or another do not achieve a level of success commensurate with their efforts. They continue to the best of their ability, more often than not without a 'living' strategy to assist them. Secondly, there are the 'strugglers', those who rarely see any success at all and who seem to move through the educational system totally frustrated with spelling/writing. Certainly there are others within this latter group who take absolutely no responsibility for their own progress or may come from what is now called a disadvantaged environment and may not have any learning support at home. Positive and meaningful intervention is crucial if we want to ensure that these children do not reach the age of eleven or twelve and continue to be inaccurate with words that caused difficulty when they were seven or eight years old.

The procedure for selecting the three groups (Independent Spellers, Semi-independent spellers and Dependent Spellers) will now be examined in the light of their attempts in both measures of ability (Daniels and Diack Spelling Test and the Peters' Dictation Exercise). Spelling attempts in both the standardised spelling test and graded dictation exercise were individually analysed to profile each child's strengths and weaknesses. The research literature suggests that there are many benefits to be obtained from carrying out a diagnosis of children's difficulties before devising a spelling programme (Cripps 1983; Carless 1989; Peters and Smith 1993; Reason and Boote 1994; Culligan 1997). Such individual diagnosis allows for the profiling of the child's strengths and weaknesses, thus enabling identification of the stage of spelling development achieved, and where the spelling process is breaking down. It has been suggested by Corley (2001) that miscue analysis of spelling is a more useful assessment tool than establishing a 'spelling age', because it leads into appropriate 'remedial' measures.

Such a diagnosis will provide information pertaining to the developmental stages of spelling the child has attained. This information cannot be gathered from spelling ages/quotients alone. Although Young (1983) indicated that spelling ages are 'more easily interpreted in practical terms and they more accurately suggest viable groups for remedial work,' their use necessitates caution in interpretation, as the chronological age of the child is not taken into account. For example, it is possible that the youngest child may score below the class average when compared to his/her classmates, but a different perspective of the child's ability may be attained if he/she is compared to children of exactly the same age. To incorporate an age allowance, I used spelling quotients as a more appropriate instrument of gauging progress. A spelling quotient automatically judges progress in relation to the child's chronological age at the time of the test. Young (1983) asserts that comparison of tests is easier if the results are in quotient form. This is demonstrated in the cases of Josephine and Emmet, as shown below.

Profile of some of the Independent Group at Pre-test Stage:

	C.A. September	S.A. September	S.Q. September	Peters' Dictation
Noel	9.0	11.6	129	100%
Máirín	8.9	11.0	124	100%
Jenny	8.3	10.2	123	86%
Cora	8.9	10.5	122	94%
Josephine*	8.3	9.8	118	89%
Emmet*	8.5	9.8	115	80%
Killian	9.2	10.5	114	90%
Hugh	9.0	10.2	113	72%

(Key: C.A. = Chronological Age: S.A. = Spelling Age: S.Q. = Spelling Quotient)
* Examples of where quotients are more suitable indicators of success

Of all the children in this group, Hugh presented with the most conflicting results. He attained a spelling quotient of 113 in the standardised spelling test but only 72% accuracy in the graded dictation exercise. Although he was less accurate than some other children, his errors were qualitatively nearer the correct spelling than children in the semi-independent group (below). This indicated that his spelling knowledge i.e. his developmental level and understanding of the spelling system was superior to that of Stephanie, Ciara, or Malcolm (see below). The type of errors from these three children determined their position in the semi-independent group.

Profile of some of the Semi-independent Group at Pre-test Stage:

	C.A. September	S.A. September	S.Q. September	Peters' Dictation
Stephanie	8.6	9.5	110	78%
Austin	8.2	8.7	106	74%
Ciara	8.8	9.2	105	81%
Anthony	9.1	9.5	104	73%
Kate	9.2	9.5	103	71%
Malcolm	8.5	8.5	100	77%
Ita	8.3	8.3	100	70%

The third group – the dependent group, comprised six children (four boys and two girls). The quotients obtained from the standardised spelling test indicate a huge disparity, ranging from 110 to 77. However, a miscue analysis of their attempt at the graded dictation exercise, throws up an entirely different picture of their spelling ability, with scores ranging from 71% accuracy to 51%. The incidence of more boys than girls in this particular group supports my earlier work (Culligan, 1997) that boys tend to experience more difficulties with the spelling process than girls.

Profile of the Dependent Group at Pre-test Stage:

	C.A. September	S.A. September	S.Q. September'97	Peters' Dictation
Jane	8.6	9.0	105	68%
Jack	8.9	9.8	110	68%
Aidan	8.4	7.6	90	71%
Joan	8.5	8.8	103	71%
Bernard	8.8	7.3	88	Incomplete
Andrew	8.8	6.8	77	51%

Although the quotients for Jane, Jack and Aidan were superior to every other child in this group, the type of errors they made in the graded dictation suggested that they be positioned in the dependent group.

Spelling Strategies
From the initial testing and analysis it was apparent that the Look / Cover / Write / Check / methodology may not meet the individual needs of all the children in the class. As a consequence, the Simultaneous Oral Spelling strategy and the Cued Spelling strategy were used. Mnemonics were also used.

Class Management – Modus Operandi

Once the groups were selected, every child got a notebook which was alphabetically ordered, and which was used as a dictionary of personal errors. If a child was really struggling with spelling, (as was the case with Bernard and Andrew) it was used as a 'positive notebook' into which s/he entered words s/he knows or controls). The National Guidelines in Scotland (English Language 5 –14) state that 'a personal spelling book for words causing difficulty becomes both a reference for the pupil and a record for the teacher.'

Each child received a copy of my 'Corewords 1' list, which was kept for one month. When errors were made, the words were highlighted on the child's list of 'Corewords.' A different colour highlighter pen and marking system were used each day, thus enabling me to know what day and week the error was made. The child compared his/her effort with the correct one in the 'Corewords' list in order to find the 'good part(s)' and the 'bad part(s).' This would reinforce the visual imagery of the word as well as emphasising the '**_Check_**' element of their strategy. The child then wrote the word into his/her 'personal dictionary,' using his/her 'Corewords' list as a reference for the correct spelling. Collecting errors in personal dictionaries enabled the children feel responsible for their own spelling development. At the end of each month, I retained each child's 'Corewords' list in order to note the common uncertainties of each group and plan accordingly. Beard (1993) indicated that such classroom practice was vital to promote spelling improvement. By providing a 'clean sheet' of the same 'Corewords 1' each month, it was possible to get an overall picture of the class and detect areas of weakness and types of errors still being made.

Unlike Westwood's belief (2003) that children should study the dictation before they write it, each sentence was dictated without any prior study. The children listened to it while it was read twice, and then they wrote it. When the sentence was written, time was allowed for the child to check and self-correct his/her written attempts. This was to initiate the practice of proofreading, which Torbe (1977) describes as 'a good spelling habit.' Initially, only one sentence was dictated, but as time went on and the children achieved success, more sentences were added. By the end of the first term (12 weeks), even those in the dependent group were coping with three sentences. By observing these efforts I could establish how each child was learning.

Misspelled words formed the basis of the child's spelling homework. I was very conscious of the amount of spelling homework to be given and ensured that the no child had more than three spellings to revise at home. The purpose of the dictation exercises is to help the child improve, not to be given additional homework. The idea of 'poor' spellers being assigned *more* work is poor practice. Before s/he went home, the child was <u>taught</u> how to overcome the bad part(s). For example, if the word 'holiday' is written as 'hoilday', the child is praised that all the letters chosen are correct; the child is asked to compare the correct version with his/her own attempt and correct the 'good parts' (the initial and final letters). Attention is finally drawn to 'lid', and the child was asked to remember that there is a '**lid**' in 'ho**lid**ay'. If many children in the class were inaccurate with the same word, such an occurrence led to a 'troublesome word' time, e.g. 'What do you do to remember that word? Do you know any parts already? Does it look like any other word that you know? What are the tricky parts to remember?' Having children listening to each other was a very valuable teaching aid. The next time the child met this word and wrote it correctly, it was 'highlighted out' of the child's personal dictionary. This was a vital part of the approach as the child could see this progression and his/her self-esteem was enhanced.

Each child progressed at his/her own pace dealing with words that were troublesome to him/her. We worked through Set A of 'Corewords 1' dictation exercises and then moved on to Set B. This approach to teaching spelling has been adopted by many colleagues in different schools. Some teachers opt to complete the first set of exercises before moving to the second. Others prefer to move freely between the two sets of dictation for more immediate revision.

Programme of Intervention

The programme for the three groups in the table below will now be explained. The independent grouping consisted of the very proficient spellers. The second grouping comprised those mainly at the transitional stage of development. These children were moving away from the heavy reliance on phonics and were presenting evidence of visual awareness. The third grouping consisted of those children who were struggling and clearly 'stuck' at the phonetic stage of spelling development.

Programme for the Ability Groupings within Class

Independent Group	Semi-independent Group	Dependent Group
1 Visual awareness training	1 Visual awareness training	1 Visual awareness training
2 Dictation exercises	2 Visual Discrimination exercises	2 Visual Discrimination exercises
3 Games / ICT	3 Dictation exercises	3 Stile Programme
4 Activities	4 Games / ICT	4 Dictation exercises
5 Mnemonics	5 Activities	5 Games
	6 Mnemonics	6 ICT programs
		7 Activities
		8 Mnemonics

The first groups to be organised were those at the top end of the scale - the skilled spellers (the independent group). These competent spellers independently worked their way through the various sets of 'Corewords 1' and 'Corewords 2'. The children were broken into two groups. These groups used cardboard cards, which were numbered according to what dictation sentences were in use, e.g. 1 to 36. The relevant number of cards was shuffled and put them face down on the table. The children decided who was going to start. The first child lifted the top card, and then dictated that sentence twice to the others, (suppose it was number 24, 'Our teacher ran around the school after a little dog'). Only after listening to it for the second time were they supposed to begin to write. Time was allocated to those who wished to self - correct. The next child then followed suit so that in a group of five, each child would write four sentences.

Evidence suggests that competent spellers do derive benefits from lists but rather than being constantly subjected to formal list learning, these children could be more gainfully employed in playing spelling games or performing word study activities. Torbe (1977) pointed out that a good spelling game is one that stresses visual patterns and makes it clear to the children that there are predictable patterns, which they can anticipate. Activities such as Name Sorts (see below), Word Sorts, and games such as Upwords, Scrabble, Boggle, Beetle (Hangman) Shannon's Game, Kim's Game, Snooker, Spelling Software, Stile Spelling and Gotcha (Sparkle), which allow them to use their spelling ability, were used to further assist them with word structure, letter patterns and serial probability.

The semi-independent group needed to be carefully structured and monitored, as they did not initially have the ability to work independently. A similar system of dictation to that outlined for the independent group was used. (Meanwhile, children in the dependent group were working on the Stile Spelling Programme). Correcting these sentences was always done in the child's presence. It was possible after a while to have this group totally autonomous and discussing their strengths and weaknesses.

With these groups engaged, I could then focus more attention on the 'strugglers.' They attended to their 'black-spots' within troublesome words, reviewed or refreshed words from their personal dictionary or considered words they feel they may need for some upcoming story or topic. With this teacher dependent group, much use was also made of the Stile Spelling Programme (Cripps, 1985). This is a self-checking aid designed to enforce a visual approach to spelling. It consists of eight books, which deal progressively with the letter patterns in words used by children aged seven to nine years. These words are based on Catchwords (Peters and Cripps, 1978). The strength of this programme is that trains children to look intently at the structure of words, select common letter patterns/strings and self-correct.

In the course of the research the children completed the sets of dictation exercises related to 'Corewords 1' (180 of the most common words). By Easter, the dependent group had moved on to 'Corewords 2', (comprising 156 of the next most common words).

Visual Awareness
Visual awareness training involved numerous activities to stimulate the memory and recall of sequences of shapes, colours and objects; to stimulate the recall of an increasing number of shapes or objects; to teach attention to detail; to recall different attributes such as size, colour and shape; and to

develop the ability to recall information over an increasing time span. Spot the difference pictures; what's wrong pictures; finding 'hidden' objects in pictures; Where's Wally? Where's Duck? Kim's Game, Configuration activities and sequence cards and blocks (Learning Development Aids) were used for these activities.

As spelling is predominantly a visual skill, it would be more beneficial if words were sorted by visual patterns.

Word Sorts
Much research has been carried out on the effectiveness of word study activities, such as word sorts. Westwood (2003) describes these activities as helping the child to 'compare, contrast and categorise two or more words based on the discovery of points of similarity and difference.' In the United States of America, there are many strong advocates of such type of word study. However, I believe that one big disadvantage of these word sorts is the overemphasis on sound as the words presented are more often than not, meant to be sorted because they share some phonic element.

Name Sorts
As spelling is predominantly a visual skill, it would be more beneficial if words were sorted by visual patterns. As previously stated, there are no exceptions to visual letter patterns! In order to counteract the phonic dependency of word sorts, I worked extensively with children's names at three distinct stages.

➤ Firstly, the child is asked to examine his/her Christian (first) name for one letter words e.g. **Caroline** (*a, I*), two letter words (*in*) three-letter word (*car*), etc. These two, three and four letter words in their name *must be in sequence*. Anagrams are not allowed. If the child does not have a word in his/her name, draw attention to the letter string/pattern in the name, e.g. Edel (/ed/; /del/). In doing such activities, I am training the child to **LOOK** with intent. When this has been done they may use surnames, family names, names of famous people, pets' names, addresses, etc.

➤ Secondly, children compare a group of names and pick out the letters they have in common, regardless of sound. (**Mar**k / **Mar**y: Marg**are**t / K**are**n: Br**enda** /**Brenda**n / **Enda**). The bigger the 'chunk' of letters the better the answer! "I want to put M**icha**el and R**icha**rd together because they both have /***icha***/."

➤ The third stage of my 'name sorts' involves the child associating a name with a 'real' word because they have letters in common, e.g. **Gar**y /su**gar**; **Rach**el / te**ach**er; **Rita** / B**rita**in; **Mar**y / gram**mar**; Br**enda**n / cal**enda**r, etc. When formal work with name sorts was completed, the children then began to use the Stile Spelling Programme, (L.D.A).

Further examples of what may be achieved with names appear in **Appendix Five**. These letter strings/word associations were formulated to show what the teacher might do with a child's name. As teachers, we have to train ourselves to look differently at names / words, before we pass this visual training to the children. I have found that by working in this way with name sorts, children progressed through the Stile Spelling Programme at a faster rate.

Mnemonics

A spelling mnemonic is a device that makes a link between the word and the spelling, even though the device has no connection with the spelling to be learned. This helps a person remember 'seemingly illogical and random spellings', (Phenix & Scott – Dunne, 1994). The best mnemonic device is the one the child thinks up for himself/herself because it will be of specific personal meaning and will be retrieved from memory when it is needed.

Arguments to validate or invalidate the case for mnemonics are scarce in the principal literature on spelling. Mnemonics are certainly useful to some children, but we cannot *teach* spelling through their use alone. Too many mnemonics may cause confusion through an overload of short term memory. Todd (1982) stresses that mnemonics 'might be useful as an aid to overcoming a hitch, but not as general method to teach spelling.' Jackman (1997) argues that

> 'whilst the use of mnemonic trickery cannot seriously of itself underpin a spelling programme, in its place it can have a useful, if limited application, especially with those one-off problem words.'

Feiler & Gibson (1997) are dubious about the effectiveness of mnemonics, and speculate that children will with time, forget a large proportion of them. Merry (1991) also warns that mnemonics are rather more complex and difficult to use than other strategies but 'they can sometimes be highly effective, particularly with older children.' Picture mnemonic cards, similar to those below, are also very useful.

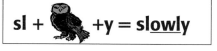 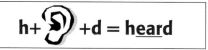

(See Appendix Three for further examples of picture mnemonics)

There are many words that are not so straightforward to spell, for example, 'would' or 'sure'. There are no concrete pictures (words within words) to attract meaning. There are common letter strings however, e.g. ould and ure. I have taught the word 'would' by using the mnemonic O U Love Doughnuts. Resulting from this, other 'Doughnut' words were built up, e.g. could, should, shoulder and mould. Other devices such as syllabification or phonological distortion may be used. For example, many people remember the spelling of

/Wednesday/ as Wed / nes / day. The following mnemonics have been successful with older children and indeed adults!

Sep**arat**e: there is **a rat** in separate!

Ne**cess**ary: we have one **c**aptain and two **s**ubs on our team.

A**cc**o**mm**odation: Two **c**hildren and their two **m**others looking for somewhere to stay.

O**cc**a**s**ion: Two **c**offees but only one with **s**ugar!

Results of the Intervention

> The teacher's role is crucial in diagnosing children's difficulties and establishing the level of development attained.

> Diagnosing children's spelling attempts to determine their strengths and weaknesses is more advantageous than relying merely on the results of a standardised spelling test. Such analysis enables the construction of more precise homogeneous groups.

> Successful grouping of children for spelling instruction is essentially dependent on the teacher's own awareness and understanding that spelling is a developmental process through which each child progresses differently.

> Structured classroom management enabled children to embark on an individual programme of learning words that were relevant to their own specific needs.

> Those children experiencing the most spelling difficulties achieved more long-term benefit from an individual programme (see case studies).

> Results suggest that a move away from phonically based word lists and the 'Friday test,' improves long term spelling ability.

> Some children's needs were not being met by using a single spelling strategy (L. C. W. C.) and therefore other strategies had to be used.

> Evidence suggests that from a handwriting viewpoint, the practising of letter strings based on frequency of occurrence, in the context of their individualised spelling programme, was advantageous.

In conclusion, there does not appear to be any reason why individualisation of spelling programmes should not occur in a normal classroom setting and I suggest that the adverse pupil/teacher ratio can no longer be cited as justification for retaining the traditional approach to spelling.

...the adverse pupil/teacher ratio can no longer be cited as justification for retaining the traditional approach to spelling.

10

Children's Attitudes to Spelling

Children have often told me that spellings are done solely so that they will not be caught out by, or be in trouble with the teacher during next day's test. This is a rather negative message that children receive and it results in the whole spelling process being perceived in isolation to the rest of the curriculum. I believe that a more positive and effective learning environment would be created if teachers and parents were seen as helpers rather than 'checking up or catching children out'. Rather than treating spelling in such a way, it should be regarded as a part of writing development. It is an integral aspect of curriculum, which frees the child to be able to write confidently and happily. Arvidson (1963) asserts that 'the child should be encouraged to adopt a particularly determined attitude towards words that persistently give him trouble.'

Although children spend a great deal of time doing / learning spellings, they are seldom asked how they perceive themselves as spellers, or why they think they spell some words accurately and others inaccurately. Dodds (1994) studied sixty-four adolescents to determine attributions of success or failure in a spelling task. These 'attributions' were defined as 'indications of a child's beliefs about whether he has control over the outcomes of attempting a challenging task,' Dodd's findings showed that inferior spellers are more likely than expert spellers to explain their failure as a lack of ability. This has implications for teaching, as Dodds (1994) comments, 'helplessness, resulting from prolonged feelings that whatever they do, will end in failure, gives rise to negativity and performance deterioration.'

As part of my research into spelling attitudes, I used a questionnaire to elicit children's views and more importantly, to identify those who lack a positive self-image as spellers. Vincent and Claydon (1981) suggest that

> 'children who regard themselves as bad spellers are more likely to be bad spellers. In the absence of any intervention they are likely to perpetuate this concept of themselves.'

Children's Questionnaire

For the design of the questionnaire, I settled for the format devised by Vincent and Claydon (1981) in their Diagnostic Spelling Test (sub-test 7). I rephrased some of the ten statements. For example, 'I am rather careless over my spelling' was changed to 'I am careless with my spelling.' I also appended six different statements in the final questionnaire. All sixteen statements were read aloud twice and the child had to do was tick a box to indicate if the statement was 'like me', 'not like me' or 'not sure'. A profile of the child could then be built up, as Vincent and Claydon (1981) assert 'this is an important consideration for the teacher who proposes to develop a remedial programme for poor spelling.' The additional statements that I included were to deal with memory, (when I learn a word I remember it for a while but then

I forget it); attitude to writing, (I like writing stories); how they learn spellings at home, (I always write out my spellings at home); a future projection of spelling ability, (As I get older, my spelling will get better); and if spelling was viewed as a fun activity, (I think spelling is fun and I enjoy it).

Discussion of Children's Questionnaire

The results of the children's questionnaire suggest a number of discussion points on how children think on areas such as their self-esteem, how they learn spellings, their attitudes towards writing and a future projection of their ability. Of all subject matters in the questionnaire, it is with writing that the most positive outcomes are witnessed. Although half of the children were unsure whether they possessed 'nice' handwriting or not, practically all of the children indicated that they enjoyed writing stories. This is of vital importance because if a child is not motivated to write, then spelling is no longer a point at issue (Carless, 1989). Fundamental to this willingness to write is their perception of spelling as a task. It was most encouraging to discover that the vast majority of both boys and girls perceived spelling as a fun activity. The teacher's role is to actively encourage this eagerness to write, while at the same time to supporting his/her spelling development in such a way that it does not stultify this enthusiasm.

Gender Issues

Half of the group asserted that they were proficient spellers. From a gender perspective it was clear that boys were more confident of their ability. Girls, on the other hand, were very unsure of their spelling proficiency. This would support research literature, which suggests that as early as middle childhood, girls begin to evaluate themselves less favourably than boys do. However, this does not reflect the reality of the situation where there was almost the same number of girls and boys in the Independent and Semi-independent groupings. This uncertainty of one's ability may have had something to do with the phrasing of the question, for when they were asked to identify with the statement 'my spelling is rather poor,' a different picture is presented. Not only did the vast majority of children reject this statement, but also the same uncertainty was absent. The significance of this may be that they are more certain of the term 'poor speller' but are not totally sure what constitutes a 'good speller.'

Discrepancies are also evident on the question of being 'careful' or 'careless' with spelling. No child stated that s/he did not take care with spelling, whereas five children (one girl and four boys) stated that in fact they were careless. Another significant area where the majority of girls were more confident is how effortless they found learning new words. In contrast, boys had almost an even distribution across the options of 'yes', 'no', and 'not sure'. When words were 'learned,' boys stated that they had less difficulty in retaining them over time, which also did not reflect the reality of the situation in the classroom.

Despite the evidence that an individual approach to spelling had significant benefits for the group as a whole, it was interesting to discover that only slightly more than half of the children adhered to their strategy of always writing spellings at home. This percentage is at variance with a greater number of parents who indicated that the child spelled words aloud at home. From a spelling perspective, the self-esteem of the group was quite high. The majority saw themselves just as capable as anyone else in the group. However, they were quite unsure as to how they performed against similar aged boys and girls in other classes. The vast majority believed that as they got older their spelling ability would improve.

My earlier research (Culligan, 1996) found that girls were superior spellers to boys. An examination of Dependent group in this study would also indicate that more boys were experiencing difficulty. However, the notable trends arising from the children's questionnaire are the positive attitudes emanating from the boys' responses and the great uncertainty the girls possess of their ability.

> *...only slightly more than half of the children adhered to their strategy of always writing spellings at home.*

The positive self-esteem of the children and their confident future projection of ability, do not reflect Dodds' (1994) findings, which assert that children, who fail in spellings, think they will fail regardless of what they try to do to prevent it, and they devalue any success they do have, still predicting failure in the future. The evidence that the most challenged spellers did not possess a lower self-esteem than proficient spellers mirrors the findings of Gildea (1991) who found that children with a learning difficulty did not possess lower self-esteem than their classroom counterparts. This is significant from an age perspective. They have not yet come to believe that they are experiencing failure, or that any failure they do encounter is the result of their own inadequacies. France et al (1993) stress that a positive 'feel-good factor' is important as it is widely recognised that a positive self-image and confidence are critical to success.

11

Parents' Attitudes to Spelling

In an educational climate driven by the continuing demand to raise standards and to address the literacy levels of the population, parental involvement in education is imperative. Effectiveness of parent/teacher partnerships is a recent growth area in educational research. This research is very clear and consistent in its findings that when parents are involved in the education of their children the benefits are multiple (Pape, 1999). Templeton & Morris (1999) state that 'opportunities for child/parent partnerships increase the potential for growth.' Jowett et al (1991) stress that work with parents should be central to the ways schools function. In schools where parent/teacher co-operation is evident, research is clear that gains are made. Topping (1986) concluded that even greater achievements are attained when parents become involved as tutors. The work of Epstein (1989, cited in Swap, 1993) indicated that although parents wanted to assist their children, they felt that they needed the assistance of school and teachers to do so. Parental involvement in their child's education begins with regular association with teachers not merely for common school activities such as helping on school tours or organising fund raising activities, but in participation in assisting with teaching objectives. Although the Plowden Report (1967) concluded that there was an association between parental encouragement and the child's educational performance, Topping (1986) asserted that the practice has not flourished. Spelling is one particular subject, which lends itself to the establishment of teamwork involving the child, the parent and teacher. This teamwork allows for the development of a sense of mutual trust and appreciation.

Although much has been written on the role of parents in the reading situation, evidence of direct parental involvement in spelling programmes is very scarce in the literature. Daw et al (1997) agree and maintain that very few schools hold any meetings with parents on the subject of spelling. To this extent, this parental spelling questionnaire is innovative in Irish research. I have previously alluded (Culligan (1997) to the traditional role of parents in the spelling process to one of signing the Friday test or overseeing the writing of corrections. To determine the effectiveness of parental involvement in spelling, I also conducted a study in association with parents. The development of such involvement comprised an examination and discussion of the parents' personal views of the spelling process, school meetings to provide an explanation of the proposed programme and how they may assist the child at home.

Topping (1986) concluded that if schools apply themselves to developing parental involvement, greater achievement is possible, even in disadvantaged areas. His research indicates that when parents were involved in their child's programme, greater performances were evident. This correlation between parental involvement and improvement in children's performance is also witnessed in the work of Kramer (1996) and Daw et al (1997).

Parents tend to be quite concerned about the functions of spelling. The teaching of spelling may perpetuate these concerns and parental definitions of effective spelling greatly vary. Two parents (cited in Redfern, 1993) comment that 'schools should have clear and consistent aims, and schools need to let parents know the areas where they can help.' Unless this is accomplished, the parent is usually unaware of the role s/he may play. Humphreys (1993) emphasises that parents are

> 'not experts in how best they can provide for the intellectual development of their children. Teachers can provide them with that expertise.'

By involving parents from the beginning of the school year, it was my intention to demonstrate that a more active role than the traditional one of 'listening' to spellings or signing the corrections from the Friday test would result in a much stronger collaborative approach. Daw (Daw et al., 1997) indicated that positive home school links are crucial and superior results accrued in schools where an effective partnership with parents was established. Their findings also maintained that few schools held any meetings with parents on spelling. However in those schools, which regularly offered meetings to parents, feedback was extremely positive. Kramer (1996) experienced that the 'parent response had been overwhelmingly favourable, with many parents expressing how sensible and practical the spelling programme was.'

An introductory meeting with parents was held before the beginning of the planned thirty week intervention. An overview of the year's work was presented. Parents were also informed of the intended survey to be undertaken on spelling ability. I informed the parents that a different approach rather than traditional approach (phonetic list learning) to teaching spelling would be employed. The main difference for the parents would be the moving away from 'five words a night and test on Friday,' to a more individualised approach. The reasons for using cursive writing and its relationship to spelling were also explained.

The rationale for an individualised approach was explained and I detailed the methodology that was to replace traditional approach. Details of the initial spelling strategy (Look / Say / Picture / Cover / Write / Check / and / Use) to be employed were explained. I emphasised both the Look (see visual awareness training above) and Check stages. Combined with 'Look', this Check stage is of utmost importance. By glancing at the child's attempt, the teacher/parent will see if it is correct or not. I believe that the child verifying the accuracy of his spelling for himself is much more advantageous than having others (teacher or parent) disclosing how s/he performed. If the teacher/parent crosses out the child's incorrect attempt and writes the correct version above it, then the important process of checking has been ruined. Checking his/her own attempt puts the responsibility for progress firmly back on the speller. It is essential both to develop the habit of checking his/her own work and to give responsibility for testing his/her own progress.

Parents were encouraged to keep spelling sessions short and to incorporate a fun element into the work. Follow up meetings were proposed throughout the duration of the thirty weeks. In the interim, it was explained that they would receive a questionnaire, the purpose of which was to determine parental views on spelling.

Proposed scheme of work at home

1. Parent and child to discuss the known parts and the 'tricky bits' of words to be learned.

2. Parent calls out words and **child writes** them.

3. Parent looks at written attempts. Parent does not inform child how many are correct / incorrect. Parent praises the efforts and then asks **child to check** them.

4. Child reports back to parent stating how many are correct.

5. If child makes an error, the parent asks about the letters that are correctly written and then draws attention to the incorrect part(s).

6. The process is repeated for words that are written incorrectly.

Parents' Questionnaire

This questionnaire was constructed in such a way to yield the necessary information and facilitate ease of completion. Most questions required a 'yes / no' type answer. Two were multiple choice and the others were open-ended questions. Although acknowledging that open-ended questions are more difficult to complete, their inclusion was crucial in determining opinions on their perception of, and role in the spelling process. The final open-ended question offered the opportunity for queries or comments. The children in the class distributed the questionnaire to the parents. Having completed the questionnaire the parents returned them in a sealed envelope. To ensure respondents' anonymity the children placed these envelopes in a box in the classroom. All thirty-two envelopes were returned. One envelope did not contain a completed questionnaire. Anonymity was preserved in all but three cases. These three respondents considered it necessary to express their delight at being so closely involved in their children's education!

The first five questions dealt with the purpose of learning to spell, the perception of their role, how they viewed their child's ability, and how often they assisted their child in the spelling process. The format for the first two questions was open-ended questions, (e.g. Why does your child have to learn spellings?). The other two were multiple choices; (e.g. Do you spend time with your child on spelling? Always / frequently / sometimes / never). The remainder of the questionnaire involved 'yes / no' type answers, (e.g. Does your child spell aloud words he/she has just learned?). These questions were grouped to elicit information relating to knowledge of their child's spelling strategy, the relationship between spelling and reading, the role of sound and vision in spelling, the relationship between spelling and handwriting, correcting spelling, and finally if spelling ought to be given specific time in the curriculum.

Discussion of Parents' Questionnaire

From the answers received in the parents' questionnaire, it is evident that spelling is a topic of great concern. These findings support those of Stubbs (1980), Graves (1983). It was notable that without exception, parents were emphatic that it was the school's function to provide specific instruction time for spelling. This too, mirrors the findings of Westwood (1994) and Chandler (2000). The results indicate that all parents spent a great deal of time assisting the child at home but their responses suggest that they were unsure of their role. The majority saw themselves as helpers or supporters, but almost one fifth believed their role was to teach spelling. It is interesting to note that these were the same parents who believed that children should be spelling words aloud and that corrections ought to be written a number of times. It is quite likely that these parental attitudes may have originated from experiences of their own schooling.

Hannon (1995) maintained that 'most parents find involvement in their child's development intrinsically rewarding and fulfilling.' Wolfendale (1985) asserted that parents may be highly effective teachers of their own children. However, there is a danger that unless this teaching complemented that of the class teacher's, this would lead to further confusion for the child. To overcome this dilemma, Humphreys (1993) maintained that it was the teacher's role to provide parents with the necessary expertise to enhance the intellectual development of their child. The results of this study are consistent with Merttens' (1996) evidence, which suggests that what parents do with their children can have an enormous influence on pupil achievement. I believe that where teacher and parents are partners, and educational liaison between home and school is active, attempts to eradicate difficulties will be successful.

It is quite likely that these parental attitudes may have originated from experiences of their own schooling.

Although the limitations of generalisability of such a small study are acknowledged, it nevertheless poses important questions as to type of support schools offer parents to assist their child at home. This is evident from the fact that although the vast majority indicated that they were familiar with their child's spelling strategy; nevertheless they stated that most children spelled words aloud after learning them. These findings suggest that schools need to develop and disseminate a list of procedures, which would assist parents in promoting the spelling development of their children. Such procedures could include a definition of their role, guidelines as to how to implement the intervention in conjunction with the teacher and how to evaluate progress.

The vast majority of parents agreed that spelling is linking letters to sounds. However, a sizeable minority expressed doubts about whether it was more advantageous to sound words out rather than to look closely at word structure. Such parental doubts increase the importance of teacher/parent communication to prioritise the development of visual awareness with the aim of training children to look more closely at words. Differences in methodologies at home and at school could have wider implications and not just in spelling alone.

Parents were not aware of the relationship between handwriting and spelling.

One important finding reveals that the vast majority of parents believe spelling is a skill that is picked up from reading. The majority of parents also believed that although different skills are needed for reading and spelling, both are linked. It is evident that parents are not aware that spelling aids reading much more than reading helps spelling. The school has also a crucial role in differentiating between the skills utilised both in reading and spelling and disseminating this information to parents, as Cripps (1983) asserts that there is no evidence that spelling will come naturally if the child reads enough.

Parents were not aware of the relationship between handwriting and spelling. In one of the most striking findings of the survey, over half of the respondents did not believe that spelling and handwriting ought to be linked. It was not surprising therefore, to discover that these same parents did not believe that cursive writing ought to start as early as possible in the child's schooling. There is much evidence in research literature to support the introduction of cursive writing from the beginning (Cripps & Cox, 1989; Peters, 1985 and Ramsden, 1993). For the successful introduction of cursive writing at infant level, parents need to be part of what Merttens (1996) refers to as a 'learning triad' (child, parent and teacher), where they could be made aware of the importance of observation of correct letter formation and pencil grip. Cripps and Cox (1989) stress that the role of parents is central to the success of such innovation. Teachers also need assistance to extricate them from the belief that it would be confusing for the child to write cursively and to read from print. Such an opinion is not evidenced in research but is based on tradition and underestimation of children's ability (Culligan, 1997).

Finally, a majority of parents believed that the child writing a correction a number of times was effective spelling practice. It was noteworthy that all parents who disagreed with this practice were also insistent that learning lists of words was not the key to success in spelling. This suggests that some parents were very aware of what efficient spelling practice entailed. However, because of the anonymity of the questionnaire it was not possible to discern in which group their children were positioned.

12

Developing a Whole School Policy

Effective schools place huge emphasis on developing, implementing and reviewing their policies. These policies should result in children having common expectations, methodologies and practices. Sipe (2003) argues that this will allow both the pupils and teachers to 'work as a unit to promote spelling development for all, including those who have been struggling.' She also agrees that the absence of a spelling policy 'will result in children experiencing different approaches and teacher attitudes as they progress through the system.'

Byers and Rose (1996) state that the development of any policy ought to contain the following elements: - planning, formulation, implementation and review. Successful policies depend on consistency of implementation by the whole staff. This consistency ought to be much more than the selection of one particular spelling book, resource, strategy or practice over another. It is important that policy making is seen as both an opportunity to review and build upon existing good practice, and an opportunity to utilise staff experience and expertise.

Before considering the planning stage, an audit of current school practice is crucial. Fundamental to this would be the teachers' observation of what they perceive the current situation to be. If a spelling policy exists, is it a *living* one? How effective is it? Is it policy that all members of staff comply with, execute and review its effectiveness, or does it just gather dust in the Principal's office awaiting the inspector's visit or Whole School Evaluation? Spelling policy will specify what each member of staff is expected to do in relation to learning, teaching, approximating, writing, proofreading and correcting. Policy will also enable children to recognise the difference between composition and secretarial writing skills, and when correct spelling is vital (expanding the sense of audience) and when it is less important (personal note-taking).

If teachers observe a significant proportion of children from second class upwards experiencing spelling difficulties, then it is reasonable to assume that spelling development has not occurred and that present practices need review. Goulandris (1996) stated that children who have excessive difficulties in the early school years are likely to have even more severe difficulties as they move up the school if appropriate intervention is not provided as early as possible. Encountering similar errors year after year means that pupils' knowledge of spelling is not progressing. Alternatively, if spelling development is evident then it is just as important that current practices be retained and updated.

An examination of current practice is not only specific to middle and senior classes, it is perhaps more important for those in junior classes. The focus at this level ought to be on the support strategies available to assist emergent writers. How does the school cater for the development of children's fine motor skills? How does the school encourage children to write independently from as early as possible? Are children given the opportunities to play with, experiment with and look intently at words? What strategies or resources are used to improve visual memory?

How policy is intended to improve the standard of spellings within the school depends on teachers' knowledge of spelling development and perceptions of children's spelling approximations. How do teachers encourage spelling approximations? What messages can teachers extrapolate from these approximations? How can teachers ensure that they are always trying to build on what the child already knows? Arising from these approximations, teachers must ask what they need to change if they feel that change is necessary. How does the school foster careful spelling? How does the school cater for individual differences? How does the school cater for the challenged speller? What criteria will be used to define *poor* spelling? How does the school react to *poor* spelling? Is spelling being valued more than content or organisation of ideas? Does the method of correcting spelling lead children to be apprehensive about making mistakes?

> *It is important for staff to draw up a list of obstacles that may prevent intended change.*

Having reviewed existing practice, focus should switch to formulating the purpose and the contents of the policy. What does the whole staff need to do to improve the standard of spelling in the school? This may require a rethink of instruction, practice, materials and resources. It is important for staff to draw up a list of obstacles that may prevent intended change. This will encourage dialogue as to how these difficulties may be overcome. For example, what are the obstacles that prevent teachers from focusing on the systematic development of the child's spelling? What are the obstacles that prevent the introduction of a cursive style of writing from as early as possible in the child's school life?

What spelling aids, games, visual exercises will be used? Are the children going to work from spelling books or workbooks? If so, how are these books going to be used to increase children's automatic spelling vocabulary? Is the importance of handwriting stressed throughout the book(s)? What criteria will be used for selecting one particular book over another? What is the rationale behind the selection of words in these books? How are the high frequency words introduced? Not only should teachers examine how the words are selected and presented, but also they must ask who will benefit from using a particular book.

Will the chosen book(s) support *all* children develop their spelling ability? Are there written exercises that link spelling to real purposes and audiences, or are words exclusively presented in isolated lists based on phonic patterns? If furnished, how suitable or relevant are suggested activities? How do activities such as 'word searches, anagrams, cross words and jumbled words' relate to the child's stage of development? Does the staff opt for a particular book or a series of books? If a series of books is used, do the activities vary or are these very similar throughout? Do the exercises promote the writing of words from memory? Are these exercises or activities conducive to improving children's spelling ability, or could they just be defined as 'busywork'?

Schools should also include the role of ICT in their policy. However, before software is purchased some questions may need to be addressed, e.g. does the program allow for the installation and saving of personal word lists? Does it permit the teacher/parent to monitor and review progress? How quickly can one access/exit the program? Will it allow the printing of worksheets or progress charts? Unless spelling software may be personalised with words that are problematic to the individual child, its value is diminished.

The role of the Principal is to foster an approach to change, whereby the focus is on the staff to perhaps change attitudes and methodologies rather than on the failure of the child. From the outset, it is important that collective responsibility is determined and clear workable targets are established. This means that the principal, a number of teaching staff and parents need to be involved in formulating policy. If for some reason, parents are not involved in formulation of policy, how will policy be disseminated to them? How are parents going to be informed of practices and strategies? How do teachers demonstrate ways of creating a positive spelling environment to parents? Jackman (1997) states that great consideration is required when briefing parents but 'most parents are only too willing to accept guidelines when professionally provided.'

Effective schools will have a policy of correcting children's written work that all staff members have discussed, endorsed and observe. Positive marking offers both support and encouragement to the child by recognising errors as 'developmental signposts' and trying to eliminate such errors in the future. Torbe (1977) comments that the teacher's job is not to correct mistakes the pupil has already made, but to help him/her not to make the same mistake next time the word is written. How will the teacher respond to spelling errors in an individual child's work? How will the teacher correct a child's written work? All staff members need to discuss what implications these questions have for classroom management and organisation. Effective correction means that the child responds to it and for this to occur it must be perceived to be both positive and meaningful.

Each staff member must be accountable for the implementation of policy and it ought not to be the responsibility of a few enthusiasts. Little change will occur unless the achievement of all pupils is seen to be the responsibility of *all* staff members. Once collective responsibility for the achievement of all pupils has been agreed, each teacher must be very certain of his/her role. Teachers will know the common errors that occur and the words most likely to be troublesome. Teachers may plan discrete or mini-lessons to *teach* these words, as spelling needs to be taught to those most in need. Teachers' objectives should endeavour to:

➤ remove the child's fear of writing a word incorrectly

➤ encourage the child to have a go and experiment with words i.e. to approximate/invent spelling and to write the *bits* they know

➤ encourage the child to look intently at words

➤ develop the child's visual memory

➤ encourage the child to write from memory

➤ review the effectiveness of the child's spelling strategy

➤ encourage the child to bring his/her prior knowledge and understanding of spelling to bear on the word

➤ promote an interest in words, their meanings and origins

➤ provide for individual/small group discussions on troublesome words

➤ encourage the use of personal spelling logs/dictionaries

➤ ensure that the child becomes more responsible for his/her spelling development

➤ share expertise with parents so that they may consolidate strategies at home.

Effective policies contain aims and objectives that are clearly designed, attainable, and measurable. Effective policies are monitored and reviewed. When it comes to reviewing policy, the principal and staff members need to be quite specific in determining how they will evaluate the 'success' of their new/revised policy. What set of criteria will be used to make this judgment? Within what time frame will the policy be reviewed? Throughout the school year, time needs to be set aside at staff meetings to review policies by obtaining feedback from individual teachers. Focus sheets may be displayed on the staff-room notice boards for this purpose. If staff members feel that assistance or further training is required in order to implement policy, the Principal / Board of Management must ensure that this is provided. A whole school commitment to training teachers in understanding spelling and in teaching it in an explicit and systematic way will help teachers to apply these understandings in the classroom.

A school policy on spelling must be a *living* one and all teachers must be aware of their responsibilities. The contents of the policy must be disseminated to parents/guardians. The importance of having a spelling policy is summed up by Sipe (2003) when she asserts that

'Perhaps the greatest benefit of a school policy is the emphasis it places on really understanding the problems children encounter, an understanding of how to solve the problem and consideration of methodologies/practices to support implementation. We need to impart the knowledge that spelling is important; but we also need to emphasise when and where it is important.'

13

Case Studies

ase studies showing the work of six children will be examined in this chapter. These case studies are intended to give a picture of how the children in question responded to their intervention over a thirty-week period. Each child's pre-test and post-test scores will be compared. A pre-test and post-test sample of spelling errors will be examined to detect the relevance and success of intervention techniques.

Examining case studies is one way in which active learning strategies can be applied in class. Such studies give valuable insight into the problems and type of errors in children's writing. Assessing children's progress by keeping work samples or portfolios is an increasingly popular form of assessment and has a central role in developing skills and knowledge. The Revised Curriculum (1999) asserts that such assessment 'can highlight some of the more persistent difficulties s/he may be experiencing.' I hope that by discussing these cases, you will be encouraged to consider your own teaching methods and whether this approach, or aspects of it, is appropriate to your own classroom practice.

CASE STUDY ONE: Stephanie (Semi-independent Group)

With an above average spelling quotient of 110, Stephanie would appear to be an independent speller. However, the quality of some of her errors in the dictation exercise indicated that she would need careful monitoring. For this reason she was placed in the semi-independent group. In this first case study there is an in-depth analysis of Stephanie's strengths and weaknesses. A worthwhile activity for teachers would be to conduct a similar analysis on the other case studies presented in this chapter, or preferably on a child in their own class, who may be experiencing spelling difficulties.

Stephanie's Attempt at Peters' Dictation Exercise (pre-intervention)

One day as I was walking down brige
street. I heard the sound of chooting.
I truned around and saw behind me
The fined fitined little house.
I new where he belongs.
I looked in me langhe bed box
for a apple and gave it to him.
I scoted for a prise of robe to
tie around his neck.
then I lead him back.
I opened the gate of he own fide and
gluped in.

When examining this piece of writing it is important to remember a few important points. Teachers ought to

- ✓ focus on whether or not we can get meaning from the piece of writing. If we cannot, is it due to illegibility or lack of meaning obtained from the spelling attempts?

- ✓ focus on the child's strengths

- ✓ focus on whether or not the child has any specific needs, which need urgent attention (fine motor skills, letter formation, reversals, etc.)

- ✓ focus on the type of errors (whether a pattern of errors exists)

- ✓ focus on how we may help the child to remember the spelling of words that cause difficulty

Strengths

By examining Stephanie's writing and focusing on her strengths, one may compile the following list. Rather than concentrating on what she cannot do, it is much more positive to be able to praise her for what she can achieve;

- ✓ she completed the piece of dictation – she did not give up

- ✓ she is willing to attempt words she doesn't know

- ✓ her writing is legible

- ✓ her letter formation is adequate and uniform

- ✓ she writes on the line (fine motor skills are adequate)

- ✓ she writes from left to right

- ✓ her spacing between words is good

- ✓ there is no interspersing of upper and lower case letters

- ✓ she can spell some high frequency words

- ✓ she always uses vowels

- ✓ she uses blends and digraphs

- ✓ she has knowledge of morphological structures (e.g. /ed/)

- ✓ her serial probability of letter occurrence is strong

- ✓ she uses her phoneme / grapheme knowledge

- ✓ she uses punctuation (capital letters, full stops and the capital letter /I/)

- ✓ she uses all the correct letters (but sometimes transposes these)

- ✓ she is very strong on initial, medial and final letters

Weaknesses

× she transposes letters

× she inverted b / p

× she produces some bizarre spellings

× she confuses homonyms

× she omits letters

× many errors are associated with auditory analysis skills

Stephanie's Test Results

	Age	Daniels & Diack Spelling Age	Daniels & Diack Spelling Quotient	Peters' Dictation Exercise
Pre-test	8.6	9.5	110	78%
Post-test	9.2	12.3	134	84%
Increase		2.8	24	6%

Sample of Stephanie's Errors

	No. of Errors	Daniels & Diack Spelling Test	No. of Errors	Peters' Dictation Exercise
Pre-test	6	tin (thin) sem (seem) dard (dart) don (done) anwer (answer) buteaful (beautiful)	22	chroting (trotting) truned (turned) uitl (until) langhe (lunch) sroted (searched) prise (piece)
Post-test	0		16	bidag (bridge) toting (trotting) frendind (frightened) shuch (searched) tracfk (traffic)

An initial comparison of Stephanie's spellings in her two attempts at the Daniels and Diack test would tend to confirm that she made significant progress. Her spelling quotient increased and the number of errors decreased from six to zero. Her quality and presentation of handwriting improved and she also exhibited signs of proof-reading and self-correction.

However, this development was not reflected in her attempts at the dictation exercise. The majority of her errors in the post-intervention dictation exercise did demonstrate that she was moving towards the transitional stage of development. Her knowledge of serial probability improved. However, her random errors, such as 'bidag' and 'shuch', would be still a cause of concern. She did become more responsible for her work and this is very much reflected in how she developed her style of handwriting. This may be judged by the sample below.

Stephanie's Attempt at Peters' Dictation Exercise (post-intervention)

CASE STUDY TWO: Jane (Dependent Group)

With a spelling quotient of 105, one would have expected to position Jane in the semi-independent group. An analysis of her spelling test errors did not indicate any significant problems. However, an examination of her dictation attempt indicated a child with many difficulties. This is another good example of where the dictation passage was a more valuable assessment tool than just relying on a spelling age.

Jane's Test Results

	Age	Daniels & Diack Spelling Age	Daniels & Diack Spelling Quotient	Peters' Dictation Exercise
Pre-test	8.6	9.0	105	68%
Post-test	9.2	11.0	120	92%
Increase		2.0	15	24%

Sample of Jane's Errors

	No. of Errors	Daniels & Diack Spelling Test	No. of Errors	Peters' Dictation Exercise
Pre-test	8	hear (here) fier (fire) fome (from) I (eye) fith (fight) grate (great) wimen (women) butiful (beautiful)	32	sowed (sound) droding (trotting) tuded (turned) aronud (around) pec (piece) robe (rope) calluped (galloped) dutres (dangerous) tasic (traffic)
Post-test	2	grate (great) buatiful (beautiful)	8	brige (bridge) beld (belt) serched (searched) lead (led) calopped (galloped) noisey (noisy) dangerst (dangerous)

In the pre-test spelling test her eight errors were plausible. She demonstrated an awareness of letter strings and patterns and her attempts were readable. The decision to position her in this group resulted from her performance in the pre-test dictation exercise. The quality of her errors indicated that she was experiencing many difficulties. The samples above, taken from her 32 errors, depict problems ranging from random spellings to those with inverting the letters /b/ and /p/. She also displayed complications in auditory discrimination finding it difficult to distinguish between the sounds of initial /c/ and /g/, and also /d/ and /t/. Her handwriting showed immature letter formation.

Jane responded very positively to her intervention strategies and received great parental support. In the post-intervention tests she showed considerable progress. She was not making random guesses, had achieved confidence and by and large, was moving to the transitional and correct stages of development. On the negative side, she still exhibited difficulty with auditory discrimination. Her handwriting style and neatness also improved as may be seen in the second and third samples overleaf.

Jane's Attempt at Peters' Dictation Exercise (pre-intervention)

one day as I was walking
down brige street I herd the
sowed of draging. I luded aroun
and saw behind the dack
hare of a Frined tittel hor
I new he beronged. I looked in m
Luch box for an appel and gave
it to him. I suched for a pec of
rope to tie aronud his neck
Then I lied him back. I

Jane's Attempt at Peters' Dictation Exercise post-intervention)

One day as I was walking down brige street
I heard. I turned and saw behind me the dark
hair of a frightened little horse: I know where
you should be. I serched in my luchbox
for an apple and gave it to him I remov
the beld of my rain coat and tied it around
his neck. Then I lead him back. I opened the
gate of his own field and he caloppd
in. I laughed with pleasure because he was
was now safe far away from the noisey
and dangerst traffic.

Sample taken from Jane's writing booklet three months after intervention

How do you know that paant grow there. ✓
We didnt take any cream on our cake. pie ✓
Why does your dog keep running across the
road.
He was caught coming through window. ✓

CASE STUDY THREE: Jack (Dependent Group)
Jack is another example of a child scoring well in the spelling test and exhibiting many difficulties in the dictation exercise.

Jack's Test Results

	Age	Daniels & Diack Spelling Age	Daniels & Diack Spelling Quotient	Peters' Dictation Exercise
Pre-test	8.9	9.8	110	68%
Post-test	9.5	11.6	122	87%
Increase		**1.8**	**12**	**19%**

Sample of Jack's Errors

	No. of Errors	Daniels & Diack Spelling Test	No. of Errors	Peters' Dictation Exercise
Pre-test	5	Hear (here) Geart (great) Ansr (answer) Wimin (women) Belatful (beautiful)	32	Briode (bridge) Sorud (sound) Aunrd (around) Strod (searched) Galtet (galloped) Lannted (laughed) Bders (dangerous)
Post-test	1	Tin (thin)	13	Brighe (bridge) Sruted (searched) Apeelp (apple) Gludet (galloped) Ticttit (traffic) Peser (pleasure)

In the pre-test, Jack's spelling quotient was above average. An analysis of his errors in his spelling pre-test showed that his attempts were plausible and readable. However, in his pre-intervention attempt at the dictation exercise, he engaged in a large amount of invented and random spelling as shown above. His parents were extremely anxious about his spelling difficulties and were very supportive. This was evidenced in the many parent/teacher meetings that were held.

Jack himself was very conscious that he had difficulty and was reluctant to write. In creative writing he would choose words that were in his automatic spelling vocabulary. For example, he would use 'nice' rather than 'beautiful.'

Although he greatly reduced the number of errors in his post-intervention dictation exercise, some of his errors demonstrated that serial probability of letter occurrences was still a problematic area for him (e.g. sruted). The sample from his writing booklet demonstrates that his skills and general presentation had also improved.

Jack's Attempt at the Peters' Dictation Exercise (pre-intervention)

Jack's attempt at Peters' Dictation Exercise (post-intervention)

Sample take from Jack's writing booklet three months after intervention

How long is it since you brought yourself a new pair of shoes.

The city air made many people sick.

Do you think he knows anything about horses.

CASE STUDY FOUR: Joan (Dependent Group)

Joan's profile is interesting for many reasons not least for the great disparity between her attempt at the spelling test and the dictation exercise.

Joan's Test Results

	Age	Daniels & Diack Spelling Age	Daniels & Diack Spelling Quotient	Peters' Dictation Exercise
Pre-test	8.5	8.8	103	71%
Post-test	9.1	11.0	121	84%
Increase		2.2	18	13%

Sample of Joan's Errors

	No. of Errors	Daniels & Diack Spelling Test	No. of Errors	Peters' Dictation Exercise
Pre-test	5	Oho (who) Fit (fight) Gamin (women) Anser (answer) Bountiful (beautiful)	29	Biarey (bridge) Hred (heard) Song (sound) Jhrt (turned) Nitt (frightened) Srhet (searched) Clunt (galloped) Lunght (laughed)
Post-test	2	Frie (fire) Bueaiful (beautiful)	16	Fightend (frightened) Fleid (field) Laued (laughed) Noice (noisy) Daougld (dangerous) Galped (galloped)

A comparison between Joan's errors in the pre-test dictation exercise and spelling test displays a totally different picture of her ability. While the five errors from her spelling test are plausible and readable, a similar opinion cannot be expressed regarding her errors from the dictation passage. The latter exercise displays a child with great spelling difficulties. Some of her efforts (see the sample of eight above in the pre-intervention dictation) would place her in the pre-phonetic stage of development. Difficulties with serial probability are witnessed with attempts such as 'jhrt' and 'srhet.' Although her letter formation and handwriting were immature, on occasions she did attempt to use cursive writing.

Her post-test results demonstrate that she made considerable improvement. She demonstrated an awareness of letter strings and patterns. She reduced her dictation error count by 13%, but more importantly, an examination of these errors shows a child who has moved towards the transitional stage of development.

The main error category was that of omission of letters, for example 'brige' for bridge, and 'shoud' for should. Such omissions accounted for 44% of her total errors. Her random efforts diminished although there was still one example present ('daougld' for dangerous). The great care and responsibility she discharged with her letter formation and handwriting influenced the post-intervention improvement which is shown below. The sample from her writing booklet indicates a continued difficulty with omission of capital letters but it nevertheless displays an improvement from her pre-test ability.

Joan's Attempt at Peters' Dictation Exercise (pre-intervention)

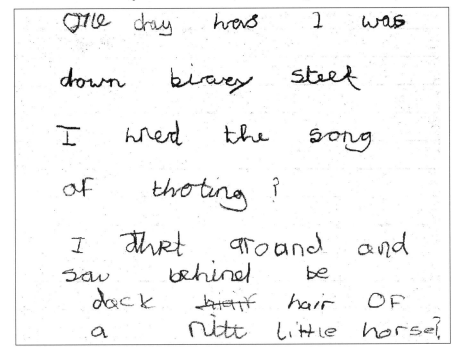

Joan's Attempt at Peters' Dictation Exercise (post-intervention)

one day ~~bus~~ I was walking down ~~the~~
street I heard the ~~sound~~ of ~~tatting~~ I ~~turn~~
and saw behind the dark hair of a
~~frightened~~ little horse. I know ~~were~~ you
~~should~~ be I said. I searched in my
~~lunch~~ box for an ~~apt~~ apple and
gave it to him. I removed the
belt of my rain coat and ~~tried~~ it
around his neck. then I led him
back. I opened the gate of his own

Sample taken from Joan's writing booklet three months after intervention

when the chair hit the floor the
leg fall off.

who caught him coming through
the window.

last winter there wasn't any
snow ice in the school yard.

At the beginning of the study Joan presented as a child at the early stages of spelling development. An analysis of her post-test results confirms that she progressed to the transitional stage. The care and responsibility she adopted with her spelling is also mirrored in her letter formation and handwriting.

CASE STUDY FIVE: **Bernard** (Dependent Group)

Bernard exhibited difficulties in both his spelling test and his dictation exercise. He did not complete the latter and only attempted twenty-three words.

Bernard's Test Results

	Age	Daniels & Diack Spelling Age	Daniels & Diack Spelling Quotient	Peters' Dictation Exercise
Pre-test	8.3	7.3	88	Not completed
Post-test	8.9	8.2	92	82%
Increase		**0.9**	**4**	-

Sample of Bernard's Errors

	No. of Errors	Daniels & Diack Spelling Test	No. of Errors	Peters' Dictation Exercise
Pre-test	19	How (who) Frme (form) Ftie (fight) Wimin (women) Lawd (loud)	Not completed	Waiking (walking) Brig (bridge) Stee (street) Drack (dark) Hir (hair) Arurond (around) Lved (lived)
Post-test	12	Stit (sit) Beag (beg) Hear (here) From (form) Sorre (sure) Waman (women)	18	Seetre (street) Wilking (walking) Trued (turned) Fitnt (frightened) Srite (searched) Dadris (dangerous)

In the pre-intervention spelling test, Bernard presented as a very inferior speller in comparison to the rest the class. His confidence in his ability was practically non-existent, and this was borne out in the dictation exercise where he ceased writing after attempting twenty-three words. He was the only child in the study who did not attempt all the pre-test dictation.

An examination of his errors from his spelling pre-test would indicate that his spelling was developing, although they do display evidence of omissions and transposing letters. During the course of the study Bernard was frequently absent from school due to illness.

Bernard did not respond to the initial strategy of Look & Say, Picture, Cover, Write, and Check (Horn, 1919; Arvidson, 1963; Peters 1967). He found the Simultaneous Oral Spelling Method, adapted by Bradley (1981a) more successful. It may be read that he made fewer errors post-intervention, but some of these would still be a cause of concern, for example '*srite*' for searched and '*dadris*' for dangerous.

He did become more responsible for his handwriting, which showed progress in letter formation and presentation. Bernard remained a cause of concern throughout the study. Evidence of transpositions persisted during the intervention period. Some of his post-test attempts indicate that serial probability still was problematic, for example '*srite*' and '*fitnt*'. On a more positive note, his style of handwriting demonstrated improved letter formation and presentation.

Bernard's Attempt at Peters' Dictation Exercise (pre-intervention)

Bernard's Attempt at Peters' Dictation Exercise (post-intervention)

CASE STUDY SIX: Andrew (Dependent Group)

Andrew's Test Results

	Age	Daniels & Diack Spelling Age	Daniels & Diack Spelling Quotient	Peters' Dictation Exercise
Pre-test	8.8	6.8	77	51%
Post-test	9.4	8.3	88	64%
Increase		**1.5**	**11**	**13%**

Sample of Andrew's Errors

	No. of Errors	Daniels & Diack Spelling Test	No. of Errors	Peters' Dictation Exercise
Pre-test	23	Ho (who) Our (are) Shour (sure) Wiman (women) Fit (fight) Off (of) Beag (beg)	49	Woking (walking) Send (sound) Lukt (looked) Wurte (worried) Anw (away) Fritin (frightened)
Post-test	11	Hear (here) Feid (fire) Fiet (fight) Grate (great) Shere (sure) Boeauieful (beautiful)	36	Dowe (down) Brige (bridge) Hered (heard) Sowend (sound) Troting (trotting) Shued (should) Apelp (apple)

Andrew attended the Learning Support Teacher for help in literacy. The results of a psychological assessment carried out on Andrew two years before this study, indicated that he was performing at quite a low level of intellectual ability. Andrew's pre-test scores indicated that he was spelling at a level two years below his chronological age and he attained at 51% accuracy in the dictation exercise.

These results would tend to support the psychologist's viewpoint that Andrew was what is commonly referred to as a 'slow learner.' His pre-test endeavours indicated that he was experiencing difficulty with high frequency words (both regular and irregular). As may be seen from his sample below, letter formation was immature and poorly presented. Words 'ran' into each other, which could be interpreted that he may not have the concept of what a word is.

Andrew's Attempt at Peters' Dictation Exercise (pre-intervention)

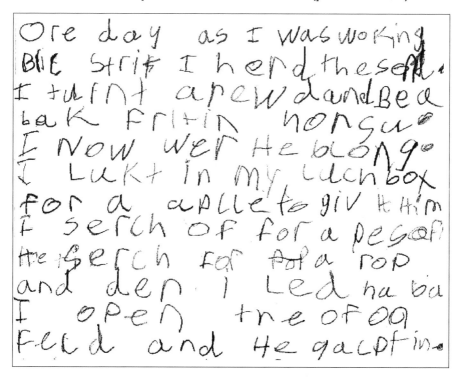

The initial part of Andrew's recovery programme was designed to increase his visual awareness. Foremost in this was the utilisation of 'what's wrong' pictures and visual recall cards. To increase visual awareness of words, he began by examining his name for 'real' words (for example, 'and' and 'drew'). He moved on to other family names (Stephen = 'step' + 'hen'). He was next placed on the Stile Spelling Programme to develop his ability to look intently at word structure.

In his post-test he exhibited both an increase in spelling quotient by more than halving his inaccuracies. His error count on the post-intervention dictation decreased by 13%. Although his quotient (88%) and his error count in the dictation (36%) still indicate that he was functioning at a rate below his chronological age, he gained considerable experience of the spelling process. His attempts at unfamiliar words indicated that he was gaining a superior understanding of serial probability of letter strings and patterns. The number of random spellings also decreased giving him a strong basis for future improvement. He became more responsible for his handwriting, which also displayed some improvement.

Andrew's Attempt at Peters' Dictation Exercise (post-intervention)

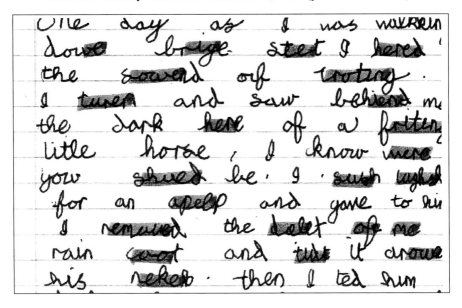

These samples of children's work clearly demonstrate the noticeable development of spelling skills. The vast majority of the children progressed from the phonetic to the transitional stage of development, i.e. they were now developing 'spelling knowledge.' Although some children still offered random spelling attempts after the thirty-week intervention period, there was a noticeable improvement in the reduction of letter reversals, letter transpositions, and an improvement in serial probability of letter occurrence. Their post-intervention attempts are effective pieces of meaning, something that may not be said of their initial attempts. This would suggest that the prescribed intervention based on their individual strengths and weaknesses was successful.

The post-intervention writing samples also clearly demonstrate that the vast majority of children improved their quality of handwriting, which presents them with a basis for future development. This is particularly evident in letter formation, spacing and uniformity of letter size.

> *In order to plan effective instruction, the teacher must know not only where the child is on the spelling development continuum, but also how to take him/her on to the next stage of development.*

> *'Individualising handwriting and spelling is hard work; but it can be done.'*

14

The Importance of Handwriting

Handwriting and Spelling

There is a huge correlation between handwriting and spelling and this relationship is well documented in research literature. The overwhelming consensus is that since both skills are so closely connected, their teaching ought to be combined. Peters (1985) stated that the quality of handwriting is highly correlated with spelling attainment. Ramsden (1993) states the reason handwriting affects spelling ability is because 'we have a tactile movement memory by which we learn word formation and the reproduction of words in writing.' Blumenfeld (1997) also argues that cursive writing assists spelling 'since the hand acquires knowledge of spelling patterns through repeated hand movements.' Barr (1985) summed up the importance of writing in the spelling process when he stated that fluent handwriting 'is crucial in helping children build clear memories of how particular words are written.' This implies that, as teachers of spelling, we need to remember that children ought to be involved in the writing of words not merely just chanting out letters or sounds.

> *Despite current technological advances, there will always be a need to teach children in a systematic and explicit manner to write legibly.*

Does handwriting matter?

Towards the second half of the last century, television was proclaimed to be the death knell for reading. Nowadays, computers and short messaging systems (texting) are perceived as end of the road for legible handwriting and spelling. However, I believe until such time as all children in the education system are equipped with laptops and voice recognition software, the pencil/pen will remain very much to the fore! As long as parents, guardians and teachers value effective communication through the written word, the answer to the above question is an unqualified *yes* and the development of handwriting will continue to be a major part of school curriculum. Despite current technological advances, there will always be a need to teach children in a systematic and explicit manner to write legibly. If we want our children to devote their full attention to elaboration and organisation of ideas in creating stories, then their handwriting/penmanship needs to be automatic.

According to Teodorescu (2001) the process of writing involves 'a complex co-ordination of motor, perceptual and cognitive skills.' Handwriting as a skill takes a great deal of time and practice to perfect and unfortunately it is a skill that children seldom acquire spontaneously. Lerner (2003) states that competent writing

'requires many related abilities, including facility in spoken language, the ability to read, skills in spelling, legible handwriting or skill with computer keyboarding, knowledge of the rules of written usage, and cognitive strategies for organising and planning the writing.'

Although handwriting takes up much of the child's school day, it has a very low profile in literacy.

As the child progresses through school, the requirement to write quickly, legibly and fluently increases significantly. Conversely, the cost of being unable to do so also increases as poor quality handwriting can negatively impact on school performance in relation to content, organisation and elaboration of ideas. Handwriting is a vital skill and a rational and systematic approach is essential if we want children to develop their penmanship and creative writing ability. A school's handwriting policy should exist to encourage and develop emergent writing skills and to ensure that children develop these correctly from the beginning. The objective of handwriting instruction should be to develop the ability to write legibly in a relaxed way at an acceptable speed.

Although handwriting takes up much of the child's school day, it has a very low profile in literacy. The Revised Curriculum (1999) completely ignored the emergent writer and did not offer any guidelines on handwriting instruction to teachers. It is not surprising then that many children find handwriting difficult to master and that some teachers find it difficult to teach. Two thirds of teachers would ask for a 'carelessly written piece' to be rewritten and three quarters of teachers take account of handwriting when assessing creative writing (*INTO Statement on Handwriting in the Primary School, 2003*). Another interesting observation from the same Statement on Handwriting is that although seventy percent of teachers believe that the use of workbooks in schools has negatively affected handwriting, they are still widely in use! Chief among teachers' concerns about handwriting would be inadequate pre-service training and lack of guidance in the Revised Curriculum as to how to teach it. Manning (1988) argues that handwriting instruction 'usually has been based on personal opinions and tradition, rather than on research.' It is very evident from research findings that children do benefit from a consistent, systematic approach to the teaching of handwriting. Before examining how this may be done, let us look at how writing develops.

Emergent Writing
Each child moves through various stages of development on the road to becoming a writer. However, it is important to remember that they do not all achieve these developmental milestones at the same pace. Many children experience problems along the way and these writing difficulties will be discussed later. From their first day in school, do children need to master certain skills before they begin to write? Do they need to be able to form all their letters correctly and 'know all their sounds' before they put their thoughts on paper? Let us step back from written language for a moment and contrast what happens with a young child's emergent oral language.

From the moment of the child's first words, s/he is encouraged to talk. S/he is treated and acknowledged as a speaker. Expressions such as '*Me goed shops*' are accepted, responded to, encouraged and built upon. Young children are not prevented or discouraged from using spoken language until they can *speak properly*; the same ought to apply to the written word. Just as the child, who is learning to speak knows what s/he wants to say; the emergent writer will also have a message or story for us even before s/he can write conventionally. Teachers of young children regularly encounter children who can write 'meaningful text' before mastering penmanship.

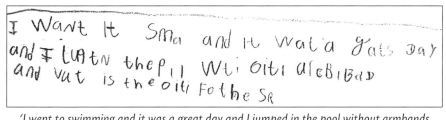

'I went to swimming and it was a great day and I jumped in the pool without armbands and that is the end of the story.' (Age 6)

There is plenty of research evidence to indicate that children, who are encouraged to experiment with words and 'write' their own stories very early in their school life, will later learn to create more easily and with greater self-belief than children who are only engaged in copying exercises. This emergent writing conveys the important message that writing is not merely handwriting practice and children are encouraged to use their own drawings and words to communicate meaning to others. It also gives the clear message that there is more to writing than correct spelling and correct syntax. How teachers promote and react to emergent writing and approximate spelling will determine what kind of writers the children will become later on in their school life.

'Once upon a time he was going to his room to get. (Age 5)

'Once upon a time he was going to his room to get his dinosaurs.'
(Same boy, continuing his story)

Teachers of young children usually introduce creative writing by asking them to draw a picture (of an event, feeling or happening). They engage the children in an oral rehearsal of what they could write by asking them to talk about their drawing. Getting the child to talk first is one of the most established pre-writing strategies that teachers use. This talking is important since at this stage they may not be able to write whole words and their writing may consist of just scribbles, lines, letters or letter strings that represent words. As Schickendanz and Casbergue (2004) state, 'their writing simultaneously resides in two worlds, the oral and the written.' Some teachers consider it important to record the child's story as dictated on the child's page, as this models the act of writing for the child and allows for later referencing and rereading.

Some teachers also use 'scaffolding' to assist the emergent writer. Bruner and Vygotsky argued that 'scaffolds do not make the task any easier, but rather make it possible for a learner to complete the task with support.' Using highlighters in rehearsing / practising what the child wants to write (Bruner's *Materialisation and Private Speech*), the teacher and child repeat the message together as the teacher draws a line to stand for each word in the message/story. When the child starts to write, these highlighted lines are intended to act as memory aids. As may be seen below, lines may be of different length to represent the number of letters present in each word.

'The crocodile is eating a fish.' (Age 5)

To promote creative writing from the beginning, a special centre/corner should be an integral and part of every Infant Classroom, where children will be encouraged to experiment and write for a purpose (in different genres) through using real situations and play. The writing corner should be inviting and attractive with access to a wide variety of paper and writing implements, typewriters and a computer. It should be seen as an enjoyable place where their writing attempts will be respected and that they do not feel that they have to be always correct. Finally, the writing corner should be a 'living' area where activities are reviewed and materials frequently changed.

As with language and reading, some children are ready for formal handwriting instruction before others. Research (Lamme, 1979 and Amundson, 1994) indicates that the child must acquire certain skills before formal instruction begins. These skills include; fine motor development (See Chapter Sixteen); hand-eye co-ordination; correct pencil grip and the ability to form basic shapes; vertical and horizontal lines; a cross; an 'x' shape; slanted lines (bottom left to top right / top left to bottom right); a triangle; a square and a circle (clockwise / anticlockwise).

Stages of Writing Development

Just as in the case of spelling, research (Schickedanz and Sulzby, 1986) also indicates that there are certain developmental stages that the child passes through on his/her journey to becoming a writer.

* **'Scribbling' stage:** Scribbling with pencils/crayons represents this phase where the child reproduces forms and shapes. This 'babbling' of the written word may only consist of lines and squiggles and be incomprehensible to the adult. However, the child will be able to talk about the 'picture/story/message.' Long

'My tree in the park' (Age 3)

before her/his stories become legible, s/he is acquiring information about this thing we call writing. At this stage, the child understands that the marks used for writing are different to those used for drawing pictures.

* **Alphabetic stage:** The child now progresses to linear/repetitive drawing. This involves making controlled marks (straight and curved) that resemble letters of her/his own language system, but not necessarily accurate.

'I fed the hens and...' (Age 4)

* **The stage of using letter-like forms:** The child proceeds to making marks that almost look like letters; the child is experimenting with the visual appearance of letters/writing, and it is quite common that some of these are still reversed. S/he is more

comfortable using capital letters. At this stage, letter size and neatness ought not to be the focus of attention. It is quite common to have children experiment with the directionality of letters / words, write from right to left and from bottom to top. Some left-handed children have a tendency to do this. It is necessary to monitor this as this sample shows that a child has reached the age of seven and is still experiencing problems with directionality.

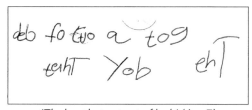

'The boy that got out of bed.' (Age 7)

* **The stage of making letters and symbols that represent entire words.** The child has now progressed to using one letter to represent an entire word, for example, the initial consonant /M/ may represent mother. The

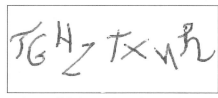

'The Gruffalo has tusks and paws.' (Age 5)

101

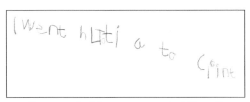

'Teddy I love you, I think you are gorgeous.' (Age 5)

child may write a string of random letters or the letters from a familiar name to represent the ideas s/he wishes to share. Later on, /HS/ may represent house/horse, but one still notices the absence of vowels.

'I went on holidays to my cousin.' (Age 6)

* **The stage of using approximate / phonetic / invented spelling:**
The child's writing demonstrates knowledge of sound/letter relationships and word structure. S/he realises the permanency of words (r-u-n always spells run). S/he seeks one to one correspondence between phoneme and grapheme. S/he has the concept of word (uses spaces between words). S/he spells familiar words correctly. S/he starts at the left and moves to the right and back again to the left to start a new line. S/he moves from the top to the bottom of the page.

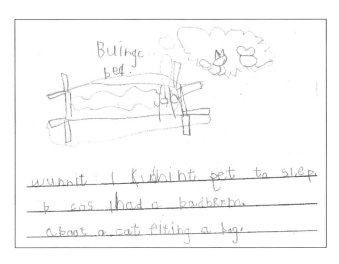

'One night I couldn't get to sleep because I had a bad dream about a cat fighting a dog.' (Age 6)

*'I could not sleep when I was two because I was scared of the dark and
I could not find my special teddy bear.'(Age 6)*

* **The stage of using conventional / standard spelling:** the child's writing demonstrates that s/he has attained required skills of letters, words, sentences, meaningful text, and standard spelling. S/he uses capital letters, basic punctuation and has a coherent sequence of sentences.

Assessing Writing
Any assessment of writing (penmanship) should include inspection of letter formation, legibility and speed. The vast majority of teachers use observation of 'how' children form letters as a method of assessing handwriting. When assessing legibility, teachers focus on the readability of letters, spacing, uniform letter size and uniform slant. Teachers should observe pencil grip, paper position and posture because if poor habits are developed in these areas, they are very difficult to eradicate.

In the process approach to writing, assessment will need to focus on each stage of the process i.e. are the child's strengths in planning, drafting or editing? Attention should focus on meaningful content vocabulary used including descriptive language, organisation, command of syntax and grammar. For the assessment of handwriting and secretarial skills there are many checklists available. (See Appendix Two for my checklist). To ensure consistency throughout the school, it is crucial that assessment is included in the policy on handwriting.

Writing Difficulty Indicators
The following factors may impair a child's writing and in some extreme cases there may be need for specialist assistance from an occupational therapist. These indicators are worth taking into consideration:

* Generally illegible writing even when sufficient time and care is given.

* Slow or laboured writing – even when result is neat and legible

* Inconsistency of position on page; irregular spaces between words and/or letters; mixture of print/cursive, interspersing upper/lower case letters; inconsistency of size/shape/slant of letters

* Letters, syllables (or even words) omitted

* Cramped or unusual grip, e.g. holding the pen/pencil too low, or holding thumb over two fingers and writing from the wrist

* Unusual position of wrist, body or paper

* Uses whole arm movements to write

* Talking to self while writing, or carefully watching the hand that is writing

* Content, which does not reflect the child's other language skills

Left – Handed Children

All right handed people write in a movement away from the body whereas left handed people write towards the body. Many left-handers write with their hand above what they write, and in order to see what is being written on the page some of them develop a hook. These hooks range from being insignificant to quite severe. To overcome this problem, left-handed children need:

➢ to hold the pencil further up from the point

➢ to have the paper/copy to the left of body

➢ to have the paper/copy angled

➢ to be seated so that s/he is not obstructing or being obstructed by a right handed child.

Writing left to right is more difficult for left-handed children, so we need to be watchful that they do not develop bad habits of poor pencil grip, paper position and posture.

Paper position for left-handers

15

Handwriting and the Revised Curriculum

I f one examines the document from a creative writing viewpoint, the writers are to be praised for the way that the 'Writing Process' is clearly outlined and promoted. This section is very well explained and it draws on current thinking and research. However, it is a major disappointment that the Writing Process itself has not been fully embraced by all schools. Results from the review of English, by the NCCA and DES (2005), found that it was only being implemented in 50% of the schools surveyed. Research done by Medwell and Wray (2007) also indicates that 'the writing process has had little impact on classroom practice.' Perhaps this is another indication of what Manning (1988) asserted that traditional methods and personal opinions are still very much to the fore.

Examining the Revised Curriculum document from a handwriting/penmanship viewpoint, the opening paragraph of the Teacher Guidelines (p. 15) is to be lauded for its clarity of purpose. It states that cursive writing 'can have a significant influence in improving spelling since letter strings are connected when the child is writing a word'. However, apart from this, there is little else praiseworthy to be found. The whole issue of the emergent writer is ignored. There is no guidance on the actual teaching of handwriting, and what is presented to teachers is rather deficient and confusing. There are no guidelines on how to assist children to form letters with speed and accuracy.

There is no guidance on the actual teaching of handwriting...

Information on the style of handwriting to be implemented appears to be contradictory. It states (p.14) 'the early style of handwriting that is most accessible to children will be based on the print style of their reading material'. It then goes on to state (p.15), that 'from the start they should be encouraged to form letters in a way that will facilitate the introduction of a cursive script later on.' Regrettably, my fear (Culligan, 1997) that teachers would be presented with a global statement on cursive writing has materialised. Children in middle standards are to be enabled (suddenly, miraculously and without any guidelines as to how it may be achieved) to 'write in a legible joined script with confidence and fluency' (p. 40). The ambiguity doesn't end there however, as the curriculum itself appears to have been modified by the in-service provided to primary teachers nationally by the Primary Curriculum Support Service. Slide 16 (Writing) clearly states

> 'the introduction of cursive writing should be done before the child develops fluency – as early as Senior Infants in exceptional instances, but it certainly should happen during first and second class.'
>
> *(These exceptional instances are undefined)*

Such inconsistencies are clearly confusing and most unhelpful to the classroom teacher. Once again our policy makers seem to have taken the easy option of not providing either the literature or in-service training for the teaching of handwriting. This dearth of provision is in total contrast to France, where Thomas (1997) found that the teaching of handwriting is a high priority in the French system. Thomas found that French teachers and education professionals displayed a high degree of knowledge of the principles underlying the teaching of handwriting and that

> 'there is a wide range of literature available to teachers that
> supports their understanding and the development of their
> teaching of handwriting'.

According to Cripps & Cox (1989), 'good handwriting and good spelling go together and it would seem logical and more economical to teach them together.' If teachers accept this, then the next issue to be considered must be the type of writing instruction and style to which children need to be exposed; should the children use manuscript (print), or should they use cursive (joined) writing?

Print or Cursive Writing

While whole school policies on writing do exist, the contentious issue still remains as to when cursive (joined) writing should be introduced. The concept of teaching cursive writing to children on school entry has been both promoted and opposed by teachers for various reasons. In Ireland, the shift from cursive to print occurred around the beginning of the nineteen sixties. Prior to this, all children learned a cursive style, not only for written English but also for Irish. Interestingly, many letters of the 'old' Irish alphabet were completely different to their English counterparts. The absence of any research from this period makes it impossible to ascertain if there were similar cries back then that children were being 'confused' by using two distinct writing alphabets or that they did not possess the required fine motor skills or ability to write both.

It appears that the decision to move away from cursive was taken to reduce confusion between reading and writing alphabets in order to enhance the former. If the decision to abandon our distinct Irish alphabet was taken to prevent confusion by providing a common writing alphabet, then the past forty years ought to have seen an improved standard in competency of written Irish. This, sadly, does not seem to have materialised.

Teachers who believe that teaching cursive writing to be impracticable may agree with Roberts (1989) when he states that

> 'the change from separate letters to some form of connected
> handwriting usually occurs at the age of approximately nine years.
> There is no need to rush into this and there is no reason why all
> the class should transfer immediately.'

McGuinness (1997) takes this anti-cursive argument further when she states 'books are not printed in cursive, so it makes no sense to have a child write in one way and read books printed in a different way.' Those who advance the argument of teaching children to print, assert that its advantages are, firstly, it is easier to teach, and secondly, as McGuinness argues, it is similar to the printed form that children are exposed to in books, therefore children will not be confused by two different styles. It is interesting to note that in today's world, children are exposed to an ever-increasing variety of print and fonts (on logos, billboards, shop fronts and food-packaging) and they seem quite proficient in reading them! The absence of guidelines, programmes and materials for cursive writing is also cited as a reason for not teaching it from as early as possible.

Those in favour of teaching cursive from the beginning, find solace in studies by Brown (1990), Cotton (1992), Cripps (1989), Sassoon (1983) and Jarman (1979), who all advocate that this practice ought to be the norm. In order to advance the argument in favour of cursive writing, Brown (1990) states that the aim of any support to handwriting should be to

> 'allow maximum use of kinaesthetic memory for words and letter strings, with minimal visual control.'

For Lerner (1985) the arguments for beginning with cursive are that,

> 'it minimises spatial judgment problems for the child and that there is a rhythmic continuity and wholeness that is missing from manuscript writing.'

Reason and Boote (1994), argue that children with lesser motor control or little stamina need a cursive model that makes minimum demands on their physical abilities. Cotton (1992) states that cursive writing should be seen as

> "a contributing factor to the whole writing process which enables children to both enjoy writing and communicate freely. Where creative writing, spelling and handwriting are not seen as three separate activities, but are perceived as three very important stages in the development towards a piece of finished work."

Over thirty years ago, the Bullock Report (1975) stressed the importance of the teacher's role in helping to create a 'running hand', that is, the ability to write easily, quickly and legibly. Printing cannot create this 'running hand'. To argue that a cursive style is more difficult for children to both use and read is not supported by research evidence. According to Brown (1990), there is

> 'no significant confusion, even in children with quite severe literacy difficulties, of printed with cursive letter forms. Therefore there seems little point in teaching children to print first.'

For the past decade or so, Ireland's strong economy has resulted in the arrival of immigrants from many different countries. Because of this, the children in our schools today are more disparate in their backgrounds, experiences and abilities than those we taught in the past. Many teachers of infants are now marvelling at the high standard of cursive writing evident in many of these immigrant children. However, despite this evidence from European Countries and despite research evidence, many teachers still consider that cursive writing is too confusing and difficult for young children. It is somewhat mystifying and indeed disappointing, that traditional practice still prevents research from impacting on Irish classroom methodologies. For whatever reason, there appears to be unwillingness on the part of policy makers to embrace research findings thereby retaining the status quo. Tradition has schools in Ireland preferring to begin with print to avoid confusion with reading.

> *...many European Countries begin cursive writing in reception classes and what research proves is that this has not led to confusion and hence a decline in literacy rates.*

As mentioned earlier, many European Countries begin cursive writing in reception classes and what research proves is that this has not led to confusion and hence a decline in literacy rates. Do European children, for example, possess superior motor skills to Irish children? In effect, children in Irish schools are guided and trained to perfect their print for four years and then change to a different style. This traditional practice of children learning a style of writing and then later in their school life unlearning it in order to acquire a different style seems to be questionable time management and practice. Gladstone (2000) states that we do not

'allow this artificial split to be created in any other area of Education. It would be considered ridiculous to teach Maths entirely in Roman Numerals up to third grade, and then drop it all for modern Arabic numerals!'

Advantages of Cursive Writing
I believe that cursive writing should be taught from as early as possible in the child's schooling. Cursive writing from the beginning would mean 'leading in and out' of letters – what Cripps and Cox (1989) call 'separate flowing letters'. It would be during the child's second year at school where I would advocate the joining of letters. Having said that, if the child has the capability of joining letters together, then let him/her at it!

Among the advantages of using cursive writing are: -

➢ Creating a 'running hand' or a 'flowing continuous pen movement' is a more natural process

➢ This continuous movement enables the child to form words as units

➢ There is scope for revising flowing/continuous patterns in pre-writing and directly associating them with correct letter formations

- ➤ It allows for faster and more automatic writing
- ➤ It assists left to right movement through each word
- ➤ All letters begin at the same starting point
- ➤ It is characterised by a rhythmic fluency and continuity of the movement of pen-in-hand, which is missing from print (Lerner, 2000)
- ➤ It makes more sense that children begin with a writing scheme that will not have to be changed later on in their schooling. Changing from one 'embedded' style to another can cause many problems. Why teach something that has to be unlearned?
- ➤ It helps to prevent the interspersing of capital letters among lower case letters.
- ➤ It minimises spatial judgment problems for the child (Lerner, 2000)
- ➤ It makes minimum demands on the children's physical abilities (Reason and Boote, 1994)
- ➤ Cursive is a fluid style and it ultimately improves the fluency and speed of the child's writing and therefore helps spelling
- ➤ Letter formation is supported since the ligatures lead naturally into the starting point of the following letter
- ➤ Confusion between letters is prevented (especially between /b/ and /d/)
- ➤ Cursive is the preferred style for children with difficulties
- ➤ Print can make words look disjointed and thus lessen legibility/readability
- ➤ Printing is not only inefficient, but it also fragments the writing of words. (Ramsden 1993)
- ➤ Each time the pencil is lifted from the paper, the potential for error increases
- ➤ In many European Countries, print is seen as an unnecessary step in handwriting development
- ➤ Teaching children print script or always allowing them to write in capital letters, delays their orthographical development (Brown, 1990)

Fluent handwriting helps children to build clear memories of how particular words are written. This point is also emphasised by Taylor (1996), as she states that cursive is essential for automatic, legible handwriting and should be incorporated into every teaching programme. Teaching children print script, or allowing them to write in upper case letters, according to Ramsden (1993) will,

> 'hinder their orthographical development... the connection with spelling suggests that real handwriting should be characterised by fluency and continuity of the movement of pen-in-hand.'

Most cursive joins are relatively straightforward and just involve the joining of the leading in/out strokes of letters already practised. However, there are some joins (depending on chosen style) that do cause difficulty and may require a great deal of practice e.g. b / o / w / v / r / and / s /. These letters do not involve going down to the base line to form the join to the next letter.

Advantages of Teaching Print

➢ It is easier to form letters

➢ No connectives / joins

➢ It is similar to that found in textbooks

➢ It is easier to discriminate visually (although this is not always the case!)

➢ It is needed for filling in forms / applications

➢ Many choices of books / materials commercially available

The French Connection

In France, teachers consider the teaching of handwriting as high priority as soon as children enter the educational system. Thomas (1997) was impressed with their 'unanimous commitment' to the development of handwriting and, as stated earlier, she concluded that this is due in no small part to the 'wide range of literature that is available to support their understanding and development of their teaching of handwriting.'

French children are exposed to *l'écriture cursive* as soon as they begin school (Cotton, 1992). It is also common for those attending nursery school to be visually exposed to cursive writing for their names and classroom labels. Lurçat's research in the 1980's, found that a cursive style helps the writing flow, and that exposure to it in classroom surroundings is extremely important. This contrasts sharply to Irish classrooms where charts and other aids are usually printed.

Before any letter practice takes place, teachers constantly reinforce the concept of both a reading alphabet and a writing alphabet. Children are exposed to what Lurçat calls *static* and *moving models* of cursive writing. The former being what children see on their classroom walls and charts, and the latter requiring children to observe the teacher as he/she actually models the letters. In the French system, great emphasis is placed on fine motor skills at the nursery stage. Once a child can hold a pencil correctly and there is no physical impairment that may interfere with fine motor control, then children are exposed to much pattern work to emphasise 'the running hand'. As may be seen from this example taken from a *pre-school* handwriting exercise book where child is expected to replicate the patterns in an identical blank template, these exercises can become quite complex. These contrast sharply with some of the exercises presented to children in Junior Infants in Irish schools, where they are expected to join dots or 'channel' a dog to its kennel.

The French system also recognises the important role of Art, Physical Education and Music in handwriting acquisition. Children are explicitly taught how to write and are given plenty of time to practise their handwriting skills. However, the French system and some American systems are not flawless and a significant disadvantage is that *dans l'ecole primaire*, individualism appears stultified. A personalised style of handwriting, which should be evident around the age of seven or eight, is notably absent, and this makes it quite difficult to differentiate one child's writing from another.

I believe that it is not a question of whether children should use cursive writing, but rather when it should be introduced. As argued above, this should be done from as early as possible once fine motor skills have been developed. The introduction of cursive writing from the beginning would see children being trained to always begin a letter at the same starting point, to *lead in* and *lead out* of letters. In other words, the Junior Infant teacher's role is to prepare them for joining letters together. **The introduction of cursive writing in third/fourth class, as the Revised Curriculum suggests, is too late.** Joss (2001) argues that this is bad timing as not only does the child have to master two successive styles of writing, but 'the changeover occurs at a time when the child is expected to put expanded thoughts into writing.' There is also evidence in the literature (Mudd 1994; Culligan 1997) that children, who initially learn to print, revert later to the disconnected letters they first learned.

Teaching Letter Formation – (lower case letters)

If children's writing skills are to be improved, then teachers need to be explicit and systematic in their modelling and teaching of correct letter formation. Teachers also need to be very vigilant in observing the child's attempts. Instruction should be short, precise and individualised as much as possible. In the absence of any guidance from the Revised Curriculum, it has been left to individual schools to develop policy on letter formation. In many instances, this merely entails opting for a particular scheme over another. As a child demonstrates that s/he can manipulate a pencil, pattern work begins. The teacher will explain the rationale of the various pattern exercises, so that the child may see why s/he has to practise them (e.g. the anti-clockwise circular movement for the letters, c, d, g, and o). The teacher will then model the making of the letter, the child will then 'channel', trace and copy the letter. (With regard to tracing activities, it is common practice in many handwriting books to 'fade away' the letter and just leave the starting point).

When pattern work has been satisfactorily completed, the child then moves on to practise / copy the relevant letters. Initial emphasis should be on developing the motor patterns required for correct letter formation (size, uniformity and slant come later). The most common method in Irish schools is to introduce/practise letters according to shape/letter families, as mentioned above. A less common method is for teachers to introduce/practise the letters in alphabetical order. The choice between the former and the latter usually depends on school policy and the commercial material chosen. Provided fine motor skills have been developed, there is no research evidence to suggest that one is more advantageous than the other. Using either of these two methods can be very limiting, as children are not introduced to many letter strings/patterns. This viewpoint is supported by Webster and McConnell (1987) who argue that 'it is pointless practising patterns and letter blends which are unrelated to writing itself.'

However, a third method to consider is teaching letter formation based on frequency of occurrence (Culligan, 2005). If teachers have developed the children's fine motor control, if children can control and manipulate the writing implement and if pattern work is satisfactory, then what are the obstacles in preventing them from beginning to form letters according to their frequency of occurrence? The letter /e/ is the most commonly used and therefore I believe it should be the first one practised. When children have reached the stage of joining letters, they would then be trained to join two together /ee/. It is not advocated that children laboriously complete lines upon lines of the letter /e/ (or any other letters). When teacher is satisfied with progress, they then move to /t/, /tt/. Now both of these letters may be united into various combinations of common letter strings/patterns */et/, /te/, /eet /, /tee/, /teet/, /ete/, /ette /*. The advantages of using frequency of occurrence is that with just two letters practised, the children are already writing letter strings that appear frequently in writing. Joining newly acquired letters with those already mastered, allows the child to write in a meaningful context. With the practice of the next letter /a/, the child is already writing whole words and additional common letter strings */ea/, /ae/, at/, /eat/, /ate/, /atte/, /ta/, /tate/, /eta/, /tea/*, etc. This approach contrasts sharply with one of the commercial writing schemes currently in use, where the most frequent letter in the English language is the third last practised!

Teaching Letter Formation – (upper case letters)
The practising of upper case (capital) letters also needs to be examined. Children are mostly exposed to upper case letters in environmental print. At home, many parents begin teaching their children to form upper case letters. Olsen, in her Handwriting without Tears (http://www.hwtears.com) advocates the teaching of capital letters before lowercase letters. As lower case letters require more finger dexterity, Olsen argues that capital letters are easier to make, the vast majority consist of straight line movements, they are all the same size (height) and they are easier to identify and recognise. However, this model does not sit easily with practice in Irish schools, where both upper and lower case letters are traditionally practised together.

While much research has been done on frequency of lower case letters, the same attention has not been given to the frequency of upper case (capital) letters. Perhaps this is as a result of assuming that there would be total equality of occurrence. This may also explain why children have traditionally been expected to practise writing upper and lower case letters together. I established frequency of occurrence of upper case letters (see below) from the study of various children's novels, picture books, 'Corewords', and all of the first books of both the Sunny Street and Starways schemes. While examining these books, each upper case letter was recorded with the exception of proper nouns. When both lower and upper case letters are contrasted in tabular form below, it is obvious that exposure to both forms differs greatly.

e	t	a	o	i	n	s	h	r	d
l	u	c	m	f	g	y	p	w	b
v	k	x	j	q	z				

I	T	W	S	H	A	B	Y	N	M
O	D	L	F	C	G	E	P	R	J
U	K	Q	V	X	Z				

Arising from this limited research sample, there is evidence that is a questionable custom that children would simultaneously practise a lower case /e/ (the most common letter) with an upper case /Ɛ/ (the 17th most common). During the course of their school day, how often would children use a capital /Ɛ/ to begin a sentence? For example, in this chapter on handwriting, comprising almost 5,500 words, only one sentence commences with /Ɛ/! I believe that it would be more beneficial to children if they practised the most frequent upper case letters from the start. The most common capital letters used in children's writing are /I/ and/T/. Perhaps the next capital they should learn is the one in their own name, and from then on it may be more beneficial to follow frequency of occurrence, as presented above.

In creating a whole school policy on spelling and writing, discussion should focus on the school's aim / objectives for handwriting; on prioritising the development of fine motor skills; on the type of writing implements; on the type of paper to be used, and on the style of writing. The advantages of using one commercial writing scheme as opposed to another should also be discussed. Short handwriting practice sessions should be an inherent part of the daily timetable throughout all classes.

16

Fine Motor Skills

As the development of handwriting is a central part of school curriculum, this chapter will focus on the mechanics of handwriting and on the skills required for its development. Fine motor skills are essential for writing, for without them the child's ability to form letters quickly and efficiently may be severely affected. Factors that contribute to illegible writing are incorrect letter formations or reversals, inconsistent size and height of letters, variable slant and poor alignment, and irregular spacing between words and letters (Alston & Taylor, 1987).

The importance of developing fine motor skills before handwriting training begins has long been emphasised in the literature. Alston & Taylor (1987) argue that children who begin formal writing instruction before they are ready may develop poor writing habits. Beery (1992) suggested that formal instruction in handwriting be postponed until the child can draw a vertical line, a horizontal line, a circle, a cross, a right oblique line, a square, a left oblique line, an oblique cross and a triangle. Amundson (2005) argues that 'letter formation requires the integration of the visual, motor, sensory and perceptual systems.' Teodorescu and Addy (2001) identify six main components of handwriting: legibility; spacing; letter size; slant; page alignment and formation.

Fundamental to the development of these components, regardless of whether a print or cursive style is adopted in schools, is the question of fine motor skills. These skills involve the ability to control the small muscles of the body and are usually defined as the ability to co-ordinate the action of the eyes and hands together in performing specific manipulations (hand – eye – co-ordination). Children need motor control in order to form various patterns and letter shapes, and they also need perceptual skills for letter size, spacing and orientation of letters.

Children require these hand-eye skills to develop good handwriting. It is poor handwriting that usually brings these children to teacher's attention, but it is important to remember that poorly formed letters may only be part of the problem. These children may be poor writers because of an underlying motor difficulty or they may be experiencing difficulties with posture, positioning / steadying the paper, or with pencil pressure. Developing good posture for writing is as important as a correct pencil grip. As children spend a considerable amount of their school day engaged in writing activities, poor posture may result in tiredness or shoulder/arm pain. Good posture provides trunk stability, which is essential for good mobility of the arms, wrists, hands and fingers. It may seem old fashioned, but ideally, children should be seated with both feet on the floor at a table that is neither too high nor too low as this could affect pencil pressure. The non-writing arm/hand should be steadying the paper and also bearing some body weight.

It has been the tradition in the Irish educational system that fine motor activities are introduced in an informal manner during the early morning classroom play/activity time. Throughout this activity/play period, children are usually grouped and given different activities. These activities are usually rotated on a daily basis so that each child may experience a variety of activities in the course of the school week. However, while the children are actively engaged in these activities, the teacher may also be occupied with other tasks (for example, correcting work or listening to a child's reading). This may result in very little direct observation of children's fine motor manipulation/development. Such an approach may be satisfactory if the child has the ability to automatically develop and perform fine motor tasks. However, the reality in classrooms is that for many children this informal approach is not sufficient for the development of these skills. The importance of the teacher's role in the early identification of children with fine motor, pencil grip, spacing, or possible reversal difficulties cannot be overstated. Until such time that a child has developed satisfactory fine motor skills, I believe s/he should not be introduced to formal handwriting worksheets/books.

The Revised Curriculum (1999) overlooks the whole area of fine motor skills. Perhaps this was an oversight or an assumption that by adhering to traditional practices, these skills will be automatically acquired. The closest it gets to fine motor skills is when it states (page 78) that

> 'the teaching of letter formations will be done as one of a number of activities that a child must practice (sic) in order to begin writing.'

Unfortunately, it neither defines nor proposes what these activities should be. Without guidance as to how children may perfect these areas of development, it is most likely that the traditional random approach to fine motor activities will continue, denying the opportunity for proper evaluation of progressive development. Landy and Burridge (1999) stress that young children 'need to practise visual-motor skills and develop kinaesthetic and tactile awareness.' Just as is the case with gross motor skills (involving large muscle movements such as crawling, walking, running, jumping, swinging, throwing, kicking, skipping, etc.), fine motor skills do not develop at the same pace for each child. Sometimes these skills develop rapidly and at other times very slowly. It is common for many children to experience difficulty with certain fine motor skills, but if these skills are considerably underdeveloped on school entry, then specialist assistance may be required. It is crucial that teachers need to model these skills/movements and provide daily opportunities for children to experiment and practise them.

One of the most significant fine motor milestones is the pincer grip – the ability to lift and hold objects between the thumb and index finger. This indicates that the child has moved away from the palmar grip - holding an object (for example, a baby's rattle) in the palm and wrapping fingers around it. In the literature, some experts state that children are able to form a pincer grip from as early as nine months. Others will argue that it is between the ages of twelve and fifteen months that such a grip develops. When the child reaches the toddler stage, manoeuvring objects becomes more advanced to include twisting, pulling, pushing, turning and using writing implements to produce scribbles.

To improve a child's fine motor skills is certainly more complicated than developing gross motor skills and does necessitate preparation, time and a variety of activities. It is possible to find children with a weakness in one or both gross/fine motor areas. A child who may be skilled at sporting activities may not possess the fine motor skills to write neatly. A child who possesses good artistic expression may not have the skills (or interest) to be involved in games in the schoolyard or sports field. It may also be argued that fine motor skills can be broken down further into skills needed to draw a picture and skills needed to write letters/numbers. Many children who state that they 'don't like drawing' or 'don't like writing' may be the very ones who find carrying out certain fine motor tasks quite difficult or frustrating.

By the age of four, most children will have developed a clear hand preference or dominance. The dominant hand develops expertise in performing tasks while the non dominant hand assists, e.g. cutting paper with a scissors. However, just as there are some children who may not have reached this stage there are others who may be quite proficient using both hands (ambidextrous). For the classroom teacher a greater cause of concern than hand dominance is the difficulty children experience with the development of their pencil grip. The Revised Curriculum (1999) states that

> 'from their earliest school experience, children should be encouraged to learn to grip the pencil appropriately.'

Although the word 'appropriately' is undefined, I assume that it refers to the tripod grip, which involves holding a pencil with the index finger, thumb and middle finger. According to Levine (1987)

> 'in order to hold a pencil effectively and produce legible handwriting at an acceptable rate, the fingers must hold the writing tool in such a way that some fingers are responsible for stabilising the tool and others for mobilising it. In a normal tripod grip, the index finger is responsible for stabilising the tool and the thumb and middle finger are responsible for mobilising the tool during writing.'

Many children enter our educational system without such a pencil (tripod) grip. These children may come to school with faulty habits perhaps picked up in the home, in the crèche or playschool. Research clearly indicates the importance of a correct pencil grip to allow the fine movements necessary for writing. The longer children use a faulty pencil grip, the more it becomes habitual and more difficult to correct. For older children, poor pencil grip impacts when the volume of writing increases. It usually leads to fatigue as well as slow/poor letter formation. If the child has not acquired a tripod grip, then activities/opportunities will have to be provided for its development. If these activities/opportunities have been afforded to the child and s/he still experiences difficulty with the correct grip, then as mentioned above, specialist assistance may be required from an occupational therapist.

A common and traditional occurrence in schools sees children with underdeveloped fine motor skills using 'chubby' crayons, pencils or paintbrushes. In such instances, the immature/underdeveloped tripod grip may have to be 'reinforced' with the ring finger and perhaps the small finger also. Having children with underdeveloped fine motor skills use heavier writing/painting implements they cannot manipulate, could exacerbate the problem. Lamme (2000) suggests that there is no real advantage in giving children such 'chubby' writing implements. It is fundamental that children be presented with writing instruments that they *are* able to manage. Once a teacher is satisfied that the child's fine motor skills are developing, the child should be given a 'normal' slim pencil to use. A short (golf size) slim triangular pencil is most suitable as it fits 'snugly' into the tripod grip. Another advantage of using a slim pencil is that the child will not have to change to different size writing implements, as s/he gets older. If there is to be a methodical development of fine motor skills children must be given opportunities to experiment, practise and improve new movements. Landy and Burridge (1999) outline a sequential order of pencil activities, namely; *scribbling, colouring, channelling, tracing* and *copying*. They define channelling as drawing a line between two guiding lines and assert that it is a prerequisite to tracing activities.

It is fundamental that children be presented with writing instruments that they are able to manage.

Activities to promote the development of fine motor skills

Activities to promote the development of fine motor skills are meant to be enjoyed and to relax the child. The Revised Curriculum states that 'in the junior infant class they should have plenty of experience in pre-writing, scribbling and pattern work. (p.14).' As it does not elaborate on these activities, the following list may be of use when developing a school policy on fine motor skills. Very young children have the tendency to knock objects down before building up, remove objects before inserting and pull objects apart before joining them together. The list of activities (see Appendix One), both bi-manual and uni-manual, are intended to assist the child to grasp, place, insert, build up, join, reach out, release, twist and write. They are not presented in developmental stages of difficulty, nor are they broken into the categories of grasping, manipulating or hand-eye co-ordination. In association with school policy, teachers will take the child's stage of development into consideration and select or adapt activities that will encourage rather than frustrate the child. For ease of access, the list is presented in alphabetical order and is illustrative rather than exhaustive.

Appendix 1 – Fine Motor Skills

Fine Motor Skills without Manipulatives

Bend and straighten fingers one at a time

Brush imaginary dust off clothes with dominant hand

Clap hands/fingertips together

Clap finger tips individually

Clap out syllables/beat

Clean imaginary window with circular movements (clockwise / anticlockwise)

Clench and open fist tightly / lightly

Clench and open fist quickly / slowly

Copy tapping/clapping movements

Cup hands together

'Cut' imaginary string using a scissors movement with index and middle finger of dominant hand

Dangle both arms limply and shake them

Dangle both arms limply but just move wrists backwards and forwards / in circles

Drum fingers individually on desktop

Fan out and then close fingers

Finger knitting

Finger tapping on table/desk each finger in turn

Finger tapping on table/desk with alternate fingers

Finger walk on flat surface

Flick each finger away from thumb

Interlock fingers to make both hands 'water – tight'

Lean on/press finger tips on table top / against wall / door

Make 'circle' (pincer) shape by joining thumb and index finger. Do the same with other hand. Now interlock both 'circles' and pull

Make stirring movement with closed fist (quickly / slowly)

Make stirring movement with open hand (quickly / slowly)

Make stirring movement with thumb, index and middle finger (quickly / slowly)

Mime the playing of various musical instruments

Open fingers of left hand and press fingers of right hand against each finger of left hand in turn.

Place dominant hand on table (palm facing downwards) and raise each finger in turn from the table

Place dominant hand on table (palm facing upwards) and raise each finger in turn to touch thumb

Place elbows on table and move hands in circular motion (clockwise/anticlockwise)

Play imaginary piano in the air /on the table top/desk

Play imaginary violin

Play with miniature toys (tea cups, saucers, etc.)

Pretend to tear paper, cardboard

Pretend to wring out clothes

Push fingers and thumb against table (two hands – then dominant hand)

Put both arms straight over head and make scissors movement

Put on / remove imaginary gloves

Rotate thumb around each finger tip (clockwise / anticlockwise)

Rub hands together

Shake hands

Snap thumb and middle finger

Spread and close fingers (quickly / slowly)

Thumb touching the tip of each finger in turn

Thumb touching the tip of alternate fingers

Touch nose with fingers (eyes open / shut)

Turn imaginary key using thumb, index and middle fingers

Twiddle thumbs (forward and reverse motion)

Twist imaginary door knob

Use dominant hand to squeeze fingers of other hand

Use pincer grip using thumb and index finger

Use pincer grip using thumb and other fingers

'Walk' index and middle finger up and down a pencil/ruler/desktop/wall

Wiggle fingers

Fine Motor Skills with Manipulatives

Break matchsticks / spaghetti

Build tower /tall structure with blocks (timed/un-timed)

Build a 'bridge' with three blocks

Build blocks (gradually increasing the number)

Build 'unifix train'

Build 'unifix train' (sequence colours)

Button coat

Carry case with thick handles

Clean vertical surfaces with cloth (circular, vertical and horizontal movements)

Clean table tops with cloth (circular, vertical and horizontal movements)

Click computer mouse to drag and drop file items

Coin rubbing

Complete simple puzzle (with or without insets)

Complete interlocking puzzles/jigsaws (increasing number of pieces)

Complete three/five piece inset puzzle (circles, triangles and squares)

Connect popper beads/Lego pieces

Crease paper with index finger and thumb

Crumple piece of paper into ball with dominant hand

Cup hand with palm facing upwards and hold as many buttons/dice/marbles as possible

Cup hands together to shake a die

Dial a telephone number with index finger

Draw line with ruler (see ***drawing and pre-writing*** exercises)

Dress dolls (big / small)

Fasten / unfasten safety pins

Fasten / unfasten zips

Fill moulds with various liquids

Fit shapes into correct frames

Flick marbles using thumb either index or middle finger of dominant hand

Flick paper ball using either thumb or index/middle finger of dominant hand

Flick table tennis ball either thumb or index/middle finger of dominant hand

Flip a coin (catch with two hands / one hand)

Fold /crease paper in half/quarters

Fold paper diagonally and crease it

Glue pieces of paper onto a paper plate

Glue various objects together

Hammer plastic/wooden pegs

Hold a marble between ring finger and small finger

Join / pull apart popper beads

Join / pull apart unifix cubes

Join lines with ruler

Knit

Knot latex tubing

Lace cardboard shoes

Lace real shoes

Make neckbands with wool

Make paper chains

Manipulate finger puppets

Move two marbles around in the palm of dominant hand

Needlework activities

Nest objects within each other (nest of rings/cubes, Russian dolls)

Open/close a variety of containers

Open/close large buttons/zip/fastenings

Open/close large safety pins

Open/close lock with key

Open knots using pincer grip

Paint fingernails

Pare a pencil (manually)

Peel orange

Peel sellotape off objects with thumb and index finger

Peel sticking plaster / blu-tack off objects with thumb and index finger

Peg small clothes on line

Pick coins/sweets/small objects from a plate/jar using thumb and index finger only

Pick out small objects from a sand tray using pincer grip

Pick up a die with thumb and index finger

Pick up block with thumb, index and middle finger

Pick up small objects using tweezers

Pick up small objects using two rulers (or other implements)

Pinch a zip-lock plastic bag shut using thumb and index finger
Place elastic bands around different sized containers
Place index/middle/ring/small finger on various objects
Place one piece in a single inset puzzle
Place small objects on table with voluntary release
Place string/wool on various outlines
Plait wool
Plant seeds in flowerpot
Play dominoes
Play drums / bongos
Play tiddlywinks
Play 'twiddle thumbs'
Play with miniature cups and saucers
Play with 'people figures' (small and large)
Play with 'transformers'
Poke /examine large/medium/small objects with index finger
Polish with cloth/small brush
Pop beads
Pour water / sand / rice grains from one container to another
Press rubber stamps onto paper
Pull apart Lego pieces / Duplo / Velcro
Pull zips up and down
Put assorted shapes (common/complex) into a shape box (untimed/timed)
Put large/medium/small objects in container
Put objects in box through a small/large hole (matching shape to hole)
Put paper clips on paper
Put pegs on clothes line/or edge of box
Put rings on a stick
Put shapes into correct shape containers
Reassemble blocks from a picture stimulus
Release block on to flat surface
Remove a pen/marker lid with one hand
Roll a large/small ball while sitting on floor (with two hands/with dominant hand)
Roll a marble/pen/pencil between thumb and index finger
Roll paper and twist it into shapes
Rotate pencil, biro, pen, coin or crayon using thumb, index and middle finger
Rotate pencil, biro, pen, coin or crayon using thumb and all fingers
Screw/unscrew lids
Scrunch a newspaper page into a ball using dominant hand
Sew around the outline of fabric (Hessian)
Shake containers filled with rice
Shake musical instruments (maracas, etc.)
Shuffle and deal playing cards
Sort buttons (by size, colour, holes) using thumb and index finger only

Sort dissimilar objects using thumb and index finger only

Sort similar size nuts and bolts (screwing and unscrewing these)

Spoon teaspoons of sand/sugar from one bowl to another

Spread wallpaper paste/ glue with 'paper' brush

Squeeze and burst bubble wrap

Squeeze putty (see ***clay, pastry, play-dough*** exercises)

Squeeze small sponge ball with dominant hand

Squeeze tennis ball with dominant hand

Squeeze squeaking toy with dominant hand

Squeeze water from eyedropper using thumb, index and middle finger

Squeeze water from plastic bottle with dominant hand

Squeeze water from sponge with dominant hand

Stack plastic coins / counters

Stretch elastic bands over a nail board (with two hands/with dominant hand)

Stretch elastic bands with thumb and all fingers

Stretch elastic bands with thumb, index and middle fingers only

String beads/macaroni/pasta rings

Sweep up rice grains / pasta with brush and pan

Tear paper/cloth using thumbs and index fingers

Tear paper/cloth using thumbs, index and middle fingers

Thread buttons onto string (by shape, size, and colour or to follow sequence)

Thread lace through sewing card

Thread large needle

Thread onion/orange bags with paper, string or ribbon

Throw beanbags into a bin

Throw/catch beanbag with dominant hand

Throw/catch bigger ball with two hands (high catch/low catch)

Throw/catch small ball with dominant hand

Tie bow, ribbon, or tie

Tie knots with thick/thin rope

Tile and mosaic work – copy patterns

Toss coins

Touch screen activities

Trace around coins and make a rubbing

Trace around stencils

Trace around tactile letters

Transfer water from one bowl to another using a sponge

Turn a key

Turn book pages (cardboard, fabric, plastic)

Turn knobs (large/medium/small)

Turn on/off 'play taps'

Turn over discs/buttons/counters/coins/playing cards (without slipping them to the edge of the table)

Twist caps on/off bottles

Twist dials / door knobs
Unwrap various objects (large/medium/small)
Use comb/plastic card to play 'push penny'
Use commercial circuit boards
Use complex shape holders (with stars / polygons)
Use computer game console / mouse
Use eraser (vertical / horizontal, left right movements)
Use eyedroppers to pick up and transfer liquid
Use geo boards
Use glue gun
Use hole-puncher (to make designs)
Use index finger to create a text message
Use keyboards
Use non-standard measurement materials (lollipop sticks / finger span)
Use origami books for paper folding exercises
Use interlocking blocks / cubes
Use interlocking rubber/foam puzzles
Use magnet to pick up / move pins
Use paper and pencil to curl a piece of ribbon
Use peg puzzles that require using thumb and index finger only
Use pencil sharpener
Use pipe cleaners to form shapes
Use plant sprayer to water plants
Use plastic garlic crusher with play dough
Use plastic tongs to lift and place objects
Use plastic whisk
Use remote control
Use ring stackers
Use rubber stamps
Use salad tongs
Use small brush to sweep up Rice Krispies / popcorn
Use snap beads
Use spray gun to spray plants
Use stamps and stamp pads
Use staple remover
Use stapler (increase the number of pages)
Use stencils to trace objects
Use toy screwdriver and screws
Use tweezers to pick up and place small items in containers
Use various size magnets to pick up paper clips, etc.
Use wool/thread to make letters
'Work' pencil through fingers
'Work' small items from fingers to palm and back again
Water play – fill different size containers

Wave ribbons/small flag on a stick
Weave paper / ribbons
Wind cord evenly on a spool
Wind thin/thick plastic thread onto bobbin/spool
Wind up toys (clocks/trains/robots)
Wrap potatoes/fruit in aluminium foil
Wrap present
Zipping / unzipping (bags, jackets, pants)

Using Child Safety Scissors / Paints / Clay / Pastry / Play Dough / Putty
a) Scissors
Cut 'fringe' on edge of paper
Cut along curved lines
Cut along dotted lines
Cut along thick straight lines
Cut along thin straight lines
Cut around items (animals/toys)
Cut around simple shapes
Cut cardboard/cloth
Cut corners off a page
Cut out complex shapes
Cut out items from template
Cut straws
Cut basic geometric shapes
Fold paper and cut out shapes
Hold paper for cutting
Make snips on paper
Move paper while cutting shapes
Open/close scissors
Snip fringes on a page
Speed up cutting of shapes
Use index finger to make cutting movement
Use plastic scissors to make small cuts

b) Paint
(i) Finger painting
Dabbing (one finger dab – five finger dabs)
Dabbing with different shaped sponges
Making letter like patterns
Pulling on continuous lines
Pulling on horizontal / vertical lines
Using toothbrush to spray paint

(ii) Brush painting (on flat horizontal and vertical surfaces)
Take paintbrush 'for a walk'
Use continuous strokes
Use cotton bud as paintbrush
Use different size brushes
Use toothbrush to spray paint
Use whole arm brush strokes
Use wrist action brush strokes
Vary the direction of these strokes (see ***drawing and pre-writing*** exercises)

c) Clay / Pastry / Play Dough / Putty
Begin to make letter shapes
Begin to make simple geometric shapes
Create objects with clay (pinch, prod, pull, push, and squeeze)
Create objects/shapes with two /three parts
Cut clay with plastic knife / pizza cutter
Hide coins in clay/pastry/dough and have child pull them out
Knead clay/pastry/dough
Make balls of clay
Make big / small balls of clay on table with one hand
Make crude objects
Make flat shapes
Make flat round cakes
Make rolled ropes
Pinch clay between thumb and index finger (e.g. to make a nest)
Plait clay 'strings'
Poke holes in clay/dough with index finger / pencil / toothpick
Pound clay
Pull clay apart
Pull off pieces of clay with just thumb and index finger
Roll balls of clay between two palms
Roll clay into tiny balls using fingertips
Roll clay on tabletop with one hand
Spread clay / dough / pastry with knife
Squeeze clay/dough using tripod grip
Use pegs / toothpicks to make designs on clay
Use plastic garlic crusher with play dough
Use plastic tea strainer with play dough
Use rollers to make shapes
Use shape / biscuit cutters
Weave clay 'strings/ropes'
Write on clay slabs with toothpicks

Drawing /pre-handwriting

* **Note:** *Be aware of the different movements for the right and left-hander.* *

'Channel' letters
'Channel' mazes
'Channel' patterns
Close shapes/patterns
Colour letters
Colour shapes within lines
Complete unfinished pictures
Copy a simple diagram
Copy a simple pattern on to a grid
Copy a simple shape
Copy cross / square shapes
Copy/follow patterns
Copy basic pencil strokes
Copy tile/mosaic work
Draw (channel) lines between two lines (channel narrows with development)
Draw a diagonal cross
Draw an upright cross
Draw a person
Draw a rectangle
Draw a square
Draw a triangle
Draw anticlockwise/clockwise circles (when shown how)
Draw anticlockwise/clockwise circle around a shape
Draw anticlockwise/clockwise circle within a shape
Draw anticlockwise/clockwise spirals
Draw continuous 'pigs' tails'
Draw horizontal lines from left to right
Draw flower petals
Draw simple shapes between two lines
Draw slanting lines from bottom left to top right
Draw slanting lines from top left to bottom right
Draw vertical upstrokes / down strokes
Draw upstrokes / down strokes (slanted)
Fold paper to make hat/ship
Imitate scribbles
Imitate shapes
Join dots to copy an existing pattern
Join numbered dots to make a picture
Join two dots (increase the number of dots to be joined)
Pasting activities
Play 'squares' game
Scribble chevrons, curves, and spirals

Scribble lines (left to right) that do not touch each other
Scribble lines (left to right) that do not touch edge of page
Scribble on vertical surfaces (chalkboard, whiteboard or easel)
Scribble with chalk / broad tipped markers / thin tipped markers / crayons
Sprinkle sand / glitter on to 'glue pictures'
Take crayon / pencil /paint brush for a walk
Trace around hand (fingers closed / fingers open)
Trace basic movements in air using a 'magic wand'
Trace over dots of simple shapes
Trace over felt/sandpaper letters
Trace over slanted lines from bottom left to top right
Trace over vertical, horizontal line
Use stencils / templates
Work out simple mazes
Write on easel / chalkboard / whiteboard
Write on sand trays

At home

Beat/whisk eggs
Butter bread
Clean tabletops
Clean vertical surfaces with cloth
Crack eggs into bowl
Crack nuts with nutcracker
Cutting (see exercises for using a ***scissors***)
Dip into jam, yoghurt, and other kinds of dips.
Fill salt/pepper shakers
Fill ice-lollipop moulds
Fold dish cloth / table cloth
Grate orange peel/cheese
Grind pepper corns/coffee beans
Make sandwiches
Mash banana with fork
Measure flour
Mix flour with hands
Mix flour with wooden spoon
Open bags (crisps/raisins/currants, etc.)
Peel orange/hard boiled egg with fingers
Peel apples/potatoes with peeler
Pick up raisins / Rice Krispies using pincer grip
Pick up raisins, grapes, olives, sausages or cheese cubes using toothpick
Pour liquid from one container to another
Pull weeds

Roll pastry / play dough / meatballs

Rub margarine into flour with thumb and fingertips

Scoop flour/ice cream/detergent/jelly/cooked rice into cup

Scrub tabletop / worktop

Scrunch tinfoil with dominant hand

Shake containers filled with rice

Snap matches/spaghetti/toothpicks

Spoon sugar/flour from one bowl to another

Spread butter/soft cheese using knife/spatula

Sprinkle chocolate from a shaker

Squeeze a squirt bottle (wash-up liquid / shower gel)

Squeeze orange for juice

Squeeze wet sponge

Stick cocktail sticks in sausages

Tear, break, snap (lettuce/carrots/banana, etc)

Use chopsticks to pick up sliced vegetables/meat

Use different types of spoons for stirring movements

Use egg beater

Use egg slicer

Use flour sieve

Use fork to pick up sliced vegetables/meat

Use plastic garlic crusher with play dough

Use salad tongs

Use vegetable peeler

Use whisk

Whip cream

Wipe plastic dishes/table

Wrap apples or potatoes in foil for baking

Commercial Games: Darts (Velcro tipped), Game of 'rings', Jenga / Lego / Operation / Mastermind / Dominoes / Connect Four / Battleship / Paint by Numbers / Marbles / Twister / Marble maze / Octons

Appendix 2 – Writing Evaluation Checklist

Posture	Very good	Good	Fair	Poor
Trunk stability	Very good	Good	Fair	Poor
Fine motor skills	Developed	Average	Low	Poor
Pencil grip	Very good	Good	Fair	Poor
Pencil pressure		Normal	Too much	Too little
Steadying of paper	Always	Often	Sometimes	Never
Ability to 'channel'	Very good	Good	Average	Poor
Ability to trace	Very good	Good	Average	Poor
Ability to copy	Very good	Good	Average	Poor
Letter formation	Very good	Good	Average	Poor
Correct starting point	Always	Often	Sometimes	Never
Letters closed	Always	Often	Sometimes	Never
Leading in/out	Always	Often	Sometimes	Never
Letters properly rounded	Always	Often	Sometimes	Never
Spacing of letters/words	Excellent	Good	Fair	Poor
Maintains spacing	Always	Often	Sometimes	Never
Slant of letters	Excellent	Good	Fair	Poor
Maintains uniform letter size	Always	Often	Sometimes	Never
Ability to keep letters on line	Excellent	Good	Fair	Poor
Using whole arm to write	Always	Often	Sometimes	Never
Near point copying	Excellent	Good	Fair	Poor
Copying from board	Excellent	Good	Fair	Poor
Left / Right Directionality and return sweep to next line	Always	Often	Sometimes	Never
Mirror writing	Always	Often	Sometimes	Never
Interspersing upper / lower case letters	Always	Often	Sometimes	Never
Letter/word reversals	Always	Often	Sometimes	Never
Uses eraser	Excessively	Frequently	Sometimes	Seldom
Speed of writing	High	Average	Low	Poor

Writes in different genres	Always	Often	Sometimes	Never
Willingness to write	High	Average	Low	None
Confidence in writing	High	Average	Low	None
Attitude to writing	Positive	Average	Poor	Negative
Amount of writing	High	Average	Low	None
Legibility	Very good	Good	Average	Poor
Interest / pleasure in writing	High	Average	Low	None
Readability of work	High	Average	Low	Illegible
Vocabulary range	Excellent	Good	Fair	Poor
Syntax	Excellent	Good	Fair	Poor
Grammar / punctuation	Excellent	Good	Fair	Poor
Sequence of thoughts	Excellent	Good	Fair	Poor
Descriptive vocabulary	Excellent	Good	Fair	Poor
Spelling	Very Good	Good	Plausible	Bizarre

+y **busy**	w+ **what**
+r **tear**	gr+ **great**
sl+ +y **slowly**	h+ +d **heard**
+e **care**	kitc+ **kitchen**

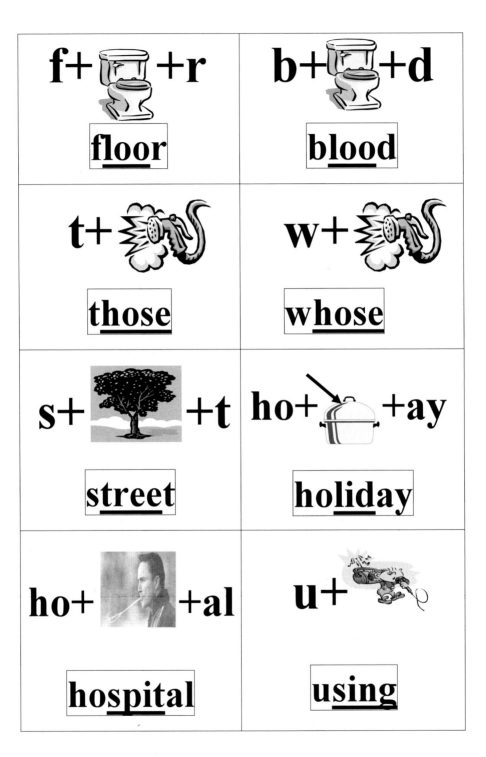

f+ 🚽 +r

f<u>loo</u>r

b+ 🚽 +d

b<u>loo</u>d

t+ 🐉

t<u>hose</u>

w+ 🐉

w<u>hose</u>

s+ 🌳 +t

s<u>tree</u>t

ho+ 🍲 +ay

ho<u>lida</u>y

ho+ 🚬 +al

hos<u>pita</u>l

u+ 📻

u<u>sing</u>

+an

began

t+

told

f+

farm

w+

warm

mi+ +e

minute

d+1

done

g+1

gone

c+1

cone

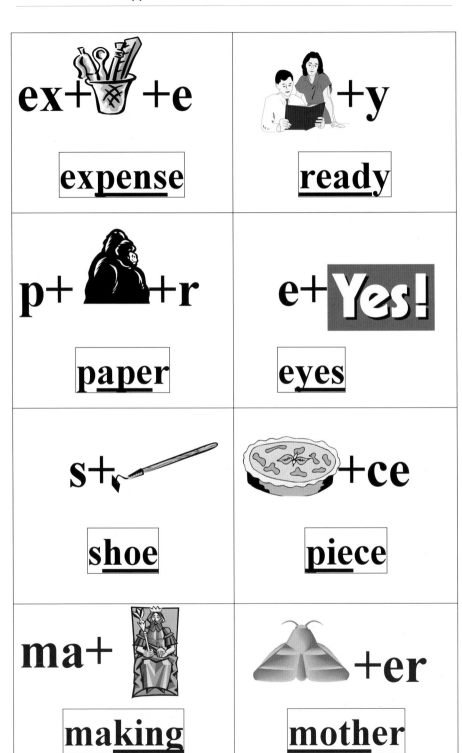

ex+🗑+e

expense

+y

ready

p+ +r

paper

e+ Yes!

eyes

s+ ✒

shoe

+ce

piece

ma+ 👑

making

+er

mother

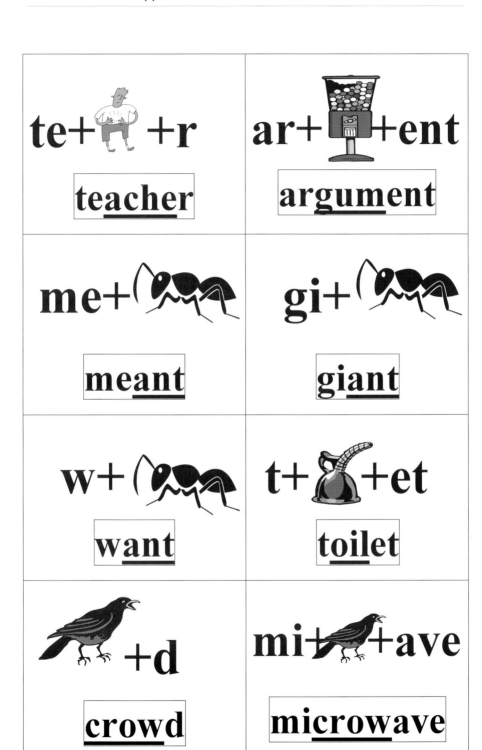

te+ +r
teacher

ar+ +ent
argument

me+
meant

gi+
giant

w+
want

t+ +et
toilet

+d
crowd

mi+ +ave
microwave

Appendix 4 –
Names / Letter Strings – Associations

Name	Words / Letter string(s)	Associations
Aaron	aar, aron, aro, ron	**aar**dvark, b**aron**, **aro**ma, ma**ro**on, ap**ron**, f**ron**t
Abigail	abi, big, iga, ail,	b**abi**es, c**iga**r, s**ail**
Adam	ad, ada, da, dam, am	m**ad**e, he**ada**che, m**adam**, **da**y, **dam**age, f**am**ily
Adrian	ad, dri, adri, rian, ian, an	m**ad**e, **dri**p, **adri**ft, histo**rian**, magic**ian**, brilli**an**t, pl**an**t
Aidan	ai, aid, idan, ida, da, an	**ai**r, p**aid**, s**aid**, afr**aid**, gu**idan**ce, hol**ida**y, **da**rk, w**an**t
Aideen	ai, aid, aide, ide, dee, een	ag**ai**n, p**aid**, s**aid**, r**aide**d, **ide**a, **dee**p, s**een**
Aifric	aif, if, fri, fric, ric	w**aif**, w**if**e, **Fri**day, **fric**tion, **ric**e, t**ric**k
Ailbhe	ail, il, ailb, lb, bhe, he	s**ail**, **il**l, m**ailb**ox, e**lb**ow, su**bhe**ading, **he**r
Aileen	ail, aile, ilee, ile, lee, een	sn**ail**, f**aile**d, jub**ilee**, tr**aile**r, sm**ile**, s**lee**t, b**een**
Aisling	ais, isl, sling, slin, ling, ing	pr**ais**e, w**ais**t, d**isl**ike, **isl**and, clothe**sline**, go**sling**, foo**ling**, crawl**ing**, w**ings**
Aislinn	aisl, ais, isli, slin, linn, inn	**aisl**e, w**ais**t, d**isli**ke, **slin**g, **linn**et, w**inn**er
Alan	al, ala, la, lan	p**al**e, s**ala**d, **lan**e, p**lan**et, **al**ready, **al**ways
Alex	ale, lex, ex	t**ale**nt, dys**lex**ia, f**lex**, **ex**it
Alice	alice, alic, ali, lice, ice	ch**alice**, it**alic**, he**ali**ng, po**lice**, r**ice**
Alison	al, alis, ali, lis, ison, iso, so, son	s**al**t, equ**alis**e, ste**ali**ng, **lis**t, pol**is**h, pr**ison**, po**iso**n, al**so**, per**son**
Alma	alma, alm, al, ma	sign**alma**n, p**alm**, p**al**e, **ma**y
Amanda	aman, am, mand, man, and, da	camer**aman**, l**am**e, de**mand**, wo**man**, s**and**, **da**y
Amy	amy, am, my	dre**amy**, g**am**e, **my**stery, ar**my**
Andrea	andr, and, an, dre, drea	d**andr**uff, w**and**, le**an**, hun**dre**d, **drea**m
Andrew	an, andr, and, dre, drew	p**an**, h**andr**ail, w**and**, h**and**, **dre**ss, with**drew**
Ann(e)	anne, an, ann, ne	ch**anne**l, l**an**e, sc**ann**ing, **ne**w
Anna	ann, na	t**ann**ing, **na**il

Annie	annie, anni, ann, nie, ni, ie	grannies, **anni**versary, b**ann**er, de**nies**, **ni**ce, **lie**
Anthony	an, ant, anth, antho, thon, tho, hony, hon, on, ony	me**an**t, w**an**t, p**anth**er, **antho**logy, py**thon**, **tho**ught, sym**phony**, p**hon**e, p**on**d, p**ony**
Aodán	ao, od, oda, dan	cha**o**s, extra**o**rdinary, **od**d, t**oda**y, **dan**ger
Aoibhinn	oi, ib, hinn, hin, inn	b**oil**, f**ib**, t**hinn**er, s**hin**e, s**inn**er
Aoife	ao, oi, ife	a**o**rta, b**oil**, kn**ife**
Arthur	ar, art, rth, thu, ur	**ar**e, p**art**, hea**rth**, ea**rth**, **thu**mb, t**ur**n
Audrey	au, aud, dre, drey, rey, ey	m**au**l, appl**aud**, **dre**am, **drey**, g**rey**hound, k**ey**
Austin	au, aus, aust, st, usti, sti, tin	**au**nt, c**aus**e, exh**aust**, **st**op, ju**sti**ce, **sti**nk, **tin**y
Ava	av, ava, va	h**av**e, car**ava**n, **va**se
Avril	av, ril	h**av**e, f**ril**l
Barbara	barb, bar, arba, arb, ara, ar	**barb**er, **bar**e, g**arb**age, m**ar**bles, ch**ara**cter, **ar**ea
Barry	ba, bar, barr, arr, arry, rry, ry	**ba**re, **bar**ber, **barr**ow, **arr**ive, c**arry**, so**rry**, dia**ry**
Bart	ba, bar, ar, art, bart	**ba**y, **bar**n, **ar**e, he**art**, **bart**er
Beatrice	beat, rice, eat, eatr, atri,	th**eatr**e, p**atri**ot, ave**rice**
Beckie	beck, eck, ckie, cki, kie	**beck**on, wr**eck**, lu**ckie**st, cra**cki**ng, s**kie**s
Ben	be, en, ben	**be**d, p**en**, b**en**d, **ben**efit
Bernadette	berna, ber, erna, ern, nade, nad, ade, det, ette	hi**berna**te, mem**ber**, fing**erna**il, conc**ern**, lemo**nade**, tor**nad**o, m**ade**, **det**ail, l**ette**r
Bernard	be, er, ern, berna, erna, nar, ard	tu**be**, b**e**ar, gov**er**nment, int**ern**et, hi**berna**te, int**erna**l, **nar**row, y**ard**
Breffni	bre, ref, eff, ni	**bre**ad, fib**re**, ca**ref**ul, **eff**ect, **ni**b
Brendan	bre, end, ren, rend, enda, ndan, dan	fib**re**, **bre**ad, f**ri**end, pa**ren**ts, sur**rend**er, cal**enda**r, atte**ndan**t, **dan**ger
Brian	br, bri, ian, rian	**br**ing, **bri**ght, p**ian**o, libra**rian**
Bridget	brid, rid, ridge, dge, get	**brid**e, **bri**ng, **rid**dles, f**ridge**, e**dge**, for**get**
Caitríona	ca, aitr, ait, trio, tri, ion, ona	**ca**t, w**aitr**ess, f**ait**h, pa**trio**t, **tri**p, act**ion**, pers**ona**l
Caitlín	ait, itl, tlin, lin	f**ait**h, t**itl**e, ou**tlin**e, s**lin**g
Caoimhe	aoi, oi, im, mh, he	Ta**oi**seach, c**oi**n, t**im**e, far**mh**ouse, **he**
Carl	carl, car, arl	s**car**let, **car**e, de**arl**y, b**arl**ey
Carmel	car, arme, arm, rme, mel	**car**e, w**arme**r, al**arm**ed, f**arm**, **arm**ed, **mel**t, ca**mel**
Carol	car, aro, rol	s**car**e, **aro**und, pet**rol**, **rol**e

Caroline	car, aro, rol, lin, ine	**car**e, **aro**ma, pet**rol**, b**lin**d, m**ine**
Catherine	cat, ather, athe, ath, ther, heri, her, erin, rin, ine	we**ather**, bro**ther**, bre**athe**, b**ath**, **ther**e, in**heri**t, **her**e, deliv**erin**g, **rin**g, p**ine**
Céire	cei, ce, eire, eir, ei, ire	re**cei**ve, a**ce**, h**eire**ss, w**eir**d, for**ei**gn, v**ei**l, f**ire**
Celine	cel, eline, elin, eli, line, ne	can**cel**, sid**eline**, fe**elin**g, r**eli**es, o**ne**
Charles	char, cha, har, arl, rles, les	**char**ge, **cha**in, **har**d, cle**arl**y, fea**rles**s, b**les**s
Charlotte	char, har, arlo, arl, lot, tte	**char**ge, **char**t, c**arlo**ad, sn**arl**, s**lot**, le**tte**r
Christina	Christ, rist, isti, stin, tin, ina	**Christ**mas, w**rist**, d**isti**nct, po**stin**g, **tin**y, f**ina**l
Christopher	christ, hris, hri, ris, rist, risto, stop, ophe, phe, her	**christ**en, c**hris**m, s**hri**nk, a**ris**e, w**rist**, B**risto**l, pro**phe**t, she**phe**rd, up**her**d, **ther**e
Cian	ci, cia, ia, ian, cian	**ci**ty, offi**cia**l, med**ia**, g**ian**t, magi**cian**
Ciara	cia, ci, iar, ara, iara	spe**cia**l, **ci**ty, l**iar**, g**ara**ge, har**ara**ss, sep**ara**te, t**iara**
Cillian	ci, cil, cill, ill, illi, illia, lian, ian	ra**ci**ng, coun**cil**, pen**cill**ed, p**ill**, gr**illi**ng, br**illia**nt, Ita**lian**, musi**cian**
Claire	clai, cla, cl, ire, re	**clai**m, **cla**n, un**cl**e, I**re**land, t**ire**d, **re**ad
Clare	clare, cla, lar, are	de**clare**, **cla**p, burg**lar**, sc**are**
Claudia	clau, cla, audi, aud, udi, dia	**clau**se, **cla**p, **audi**ence, **aud**io, st**udi**es, **dia**l
Clíona	ci, liona, lion, iona, ion, ona, na	**cli**p, mil**liona**ire, mil**lion**, dict**iona**ry, act**ion**, pers**ona**l, **na**p
Clodagh	clo, lod, oda, dag, agh	**clo**th, p**lod**, s**oda**, **dag**ger, band**age**, **agh**ast
Colin	col, coli, oli, olin, lin, in	**col**our, broc**coli**, p**oli**ce, co**olin**g, **lin**e, p**in**t, m**in**t
Colleen	colle, coll, col, olle, oll, lee, een	**colle**ct, **coll**age, **col**our, r**olle**r, tr**oll**ey, as**lee**p, b**een**
Colm	col, ol, olm, lm	**col**lect, petr**ol**, scho**olm**aster, pa**lm**, fi**lm**
Conor	con, cono, ono, on, nor, or	**con**e, e**cono**my, pr**ono**un, d**on**or, d**on**e, g**on**e
Cora	cora, cor, ora, ra	de**cora**te, **cor**ner, an**ora**k, t**ra**in
Cormac	cor, orm, orma, rm, mac, ac	**cor**k, w**orm**, n**orma**l, ha**rm**, **mac**hine, **ac**e
Damian	dam, ami, ian	**dam**age, f**ami**ly, brill**ian**t
Daniel	da, dan, ani, aniel, iel	**da**y, **dan**ger, cle**ani**ng, sp**aniel**, f**iel**d

Danielle	da, dan, anie, an, nie, iel, ie, ell, elle	**da**re, **dan**ce, comp**anie**s, **any**, **nie**ce, **y**i**eld**, p**ie**, cop**ie**s, s**ell**, exc**elle**nt
Darragh	dar, arra, agh	**dar**e, **arra**nge, sp**agh**etti
David	da, avi, avid, vid	**Da**d, s**avi**ng, h**avi**ng, **vid**eo, di**vid**e
Debbie	deb, de, ebbi, ebb, bie, ie	**deb**ate, **de**n, w**ebbi**ng, p**ebb**les, ba**bie**s, d**ie**t
Declan	de, dec, decla, ecla, cla, clan	i**de**a, **dec**ide, **decla**re, **ecla**ir, **cla**y
Deirdre	eird, eir, irdr, ird, dre	w**eird**, th**eir**, hair**dr**esser, b**ird**, **dre**am
Denise	deni, den, nise, nis, ise	**deni**m, gar**den**, orga**nise**, ten**nis**, r**ise**
Dermot	derm, der, ermo, rmo, erm, mot	un**derm**ine, won**der**, ev**ermo**re, a**rmo**ur, g**erm**, **mot**or
Desmond	de, des, smo, mon, on, ond, mond	**de**ad, si**des**, **smo**ke, **mon**ey, **on**e, p**ond**, dia**mond**
Dorothy	dor, oro, roth, oth, thy	a**dor**e, hum**oro**us, b**oth**, br**oth**er, fil**thy**
Dylan	dy, dyl, yla, lan	la**dy**, i**dyl**lic, sk**yla**rk, p**lan**e
Éadaoin	eada, ead, ada, oin	h**eada**che, r**ead**, r**ada**r, d**oin**g
Eddie	ed, edd, die, ie	push**ed**, w**edd**ing, **die**d, sol**die**r, l**ie**, tr**ie**d
Edel	edel, ede, ed, del,	r**edel**iver, ne**ede**d, push**ed**, mo**del**
Edward	ed, dwa, war, ward	lock**ed**, **dwa**rf, mi**dwa**y, **war**n, to**ward**s
Eileen	ei, eil, ile, lee, een	**ei**ght, v**eil**, p**ile**, s**lee**p, b**een**
Éilís	eili, eil, ilis, ili, lis	c**eili**ng, v**eil**, ut**ilis**e, ra**ili**ngs, foo**lis**h
Eimear	ei, ime, me, mear, ear	w**ei**rd, sl**ime**, co**me**, s**mear**, w**ear**
Elaine	ela, el, laine, lain, ain, ine	d**ela**y, cam**el**, exp**laine**d, chap**lain**, r**ain**, l**ine**s
Eleanor	elea, ele, lean, lea, ano, nor	r**elea**rn, **ele**phant, c**lean**, **lea**p, pi**ano**, s**nor**t
Elizabeth	eli, ab, abe, bet, th	fe**eli**ng, believe, st**ab**, l**abe**l, **bet**ter, **th**ey
Ella	ella, ell, lla	umbr**ella**, c**ell**ar, f**ell**, do**lla**r
Ellen	elle, ell, el, llen, lle, len	sp**elle**r, b**ell**, hot**el**, fa**llen**, bu**lle**t, **len**t
Emily	em, emi, mil, mily, ily	th**em**, se**emi**, re**mil**d, s**mil**e, fa**mily**, da**ily**
Emma	emma, em, mma, ma	dil**emma**, h**em**, co**mma**nd, wo**ma**n
Emmet	em, mme, met	m**em**ber, su**mme**r, co**mme**nt, **met**re
Enda	en, end, da, enda	s**end**, fri**end**, **da**b, ag**enda**, att**enda**nce
Eoghan	eo, eog, ogh, gh, han, an	p**eo**ple, g**eog**raphy, d**ogh**ouse, **gh**ost, c**han**ce, **an**y
Eoin	eo, oi, oin, in	n**eo**n, b**oi**l, c**oin**, d**oin**g, w**in**d

Erica	erica, eric, eri, ica	United States of Am**eric**a, cl**eric**, s**eri**ous, alphabe**tica**l, mus**ica**l
Eve	eve, ev, ve	**ev**er, s**ev**en, beli**eve**, d**ev**il, l**ive**
Fachna	fac, ach, chn, na	**fac**e, **each**, te**chn**ology, **na**il
Fergal	fer, erg, ga, gal	**fer**ry, em**erg**e, ov**erg**row, **ga**in, **gal**lon
Fergus	fer, erg, rgu, gus	dif**fer**, cl**erg**y, a**rgu**e, Au**gus**t
Fiachra	fia, fi, ach, chr, ra	ruf**fia**n, **fi**rst, **fi**ght, e**ach**, **ach**e, y**ach**t, co**ach**, **chr**isten, w**ra**p
Fidelma	fidel, fide, fid, idel, del, elm, lma	**fidel**ity, con**fide**nt, **fid**dle, s**idel**ine, **del**ay, **elm**, mai**lma**n
Finn	fin, inn	**fin**ger, **fin**al, gr**inn**ing, d**inn**er
Fíona	fi, iona, ion, ona	**fi**x, addit**iona**l, tens**ion**, d**ona**te
Fionn	fio, ion, ionn, onn	**fio**rd, act**ion**, quest**ionn**aire, c**onn**ect
Frances	fra, France, ranc, ran, ance,	a**fra**id, b**ranc**h, c**ran**e, c**ance**l
Frank	fran, fra, rank, ank	**fran**tic, **fra**me, d**rank**, **ank**le
Francis	fra, anc, anci, cis, is	a**fra**id, c**anc**el, ch**anc**e, d**anci**ng, de**cis**ion, exer**cis**e, s**cis**sors, th**is**
Gabriel	gab, ab, abri, bri, brie, rie, ie, iel	**gab**le, **ab**ove, f**abri**c, **bri**ng, **brie**f, d**rie**d, l**ie**, f**iel**d,
Gary	gar, ar, ary, gary	**gar**age, **gar**den, f**ar**, w**ar**, sc**ary**, su**gary**
Gemma	emma, gem, mma,	dil**emma**, enga**gem**ent, co**mma**nd,
Gene	gene, ge, gen, ene,	**gene**ral, strange**ne**ss ur**ge**, **gen**tle, ur**gen**t, b**ene**fit,
George	geo, orge, eor, rgè	**geo**graphy, f**orge**, th**eor**y, la**rge**
Geraldine	gera, ger, erald, eral era, ral, ald, dine, din, ine	exag**gera**te, an**ger**, h**erald**, min**eral**, op**era**, cent**ral**, b**ald**, sar**dine**, **din**e, m**ine**
Gerard	gera, ger, era, ar, ard	exag**gera**te, big**ger**, op**era**te, av**era**ge, h**ard**, e**ar**, he**ard**
Grace	gra, race, rac, ace, ce	**gra**b, b**race**let, cha**rac**ter, pe**ace**, **ce**nt
Gráinne	grain, gra, rain, inn, inne, nne, ne	**grain**, **gra**pe, b**rain**, sk**inn**y, p**inne**d, cha**nne**ls, fi**ne**
Grant	gran, gra, rant, ran, ant	**gran**d, emi**gra**nt, cur**rant**, war**rant**, **gra**pes, w**ant**, me**ant**
Hannah	hann, han, ann,	c**hann**els, t**han**, pl**ann**ing
Harry	harr, har, ar, arry	**harr**ow, **har**m, **ar**e, c**arry**
Helen	hel, he, ele, le, len	**hel**p, **she**, t**ele**phone, ab**le**, p**len**ty
Henry	hen, enr, nry, ry	t**hen**, **enr**ol, maso**nry**, sca**ry**

Hillary	hill, illar, illa, lary, ary	**chill**y, **pillar**, vi**lla**ge, sa**lary**, di**ary**
Hollie	holl, olli, lli, lie	**holl**ow, c**olli**de, mi**lli**on, be**lie**ve
Homer	ho, hom, ome, mer	**ho**ur, **ho**t, **home**, w**hom**, r**hom**bus, s**ome**, w**ome**n, kil**ome**tre, **mer**ry
Hugh	hu, hug, ugh	**hu**mp, **hug**e, t**hug**s, la**ugh**, eno**ugh**, co**ugh**
Ian	ian, ia, an	g**ia**nt, d**ia**l, soc**ia**l, p**an**e
Imelda	ime, imel, mel, eld, Ida, eld	a**ime**d, t**imel**ine, ho**mel**and, ho**ld**all, fi**eld**
Irene	iren, ire, rene, ren, ene, ne	s**iren**, t**ire**, **rene**w, child**ren**, sc**ene**, **ne**xt
Isabelle	isab, isa, sab, abelle, elle, ell	d**isab**le, v**isa**, u**sab**le, l**abelle**d, exc**elle**nt, b**ell**
Ita	ita, it, ta	cap**ita**l, gu**ita**r, b**it**e, **ta**pe
Jacinta	jac, acin, aci, cin, inta, int, ta	**jac**k, r**acin**g, cap**aci**ty, **cin**ema, **inta**ct, p**int**, s**ta**b
Jack	ja, ac, ack, jack	**ja**m, **ac**e, p**ack**et, t**ack**le, hi**jack**, **jack**et
Jacqueline	acqu, quel, eline, eli, lin, ine	**acqu**ire, se**quel**, guid**eline**, beli**eve**, **lin**k, **ine**pt
James	jam, am, ame, me, mes	g**ame**s, dre**am**er, c**ame**l, di**ame**ter, ho**me**s, **mes**s, ti**mes**
Jamie	jam, ami, mie, ie	py**jam**as, f**ami**ly, pre**mie**r, l**ie**
Jana	ja, jan, ana	**ja**b, **Jan**uary, c**ana**l
Jane	ja, an, ane	**ja**w, lo**an**, pl**ane**t
Jason	as, so, ason, son, on	**as**k, h**as**, cha**s**e, w**as**, re**ason**, **on**ly, **son**g, ma**son**
Jennifer	enni, enn, nifer, nife, fer	t**enni**s, k**enn**el, co**nifer**, k**nife**, of**fer**
Jenny	enn, enny, nny	op**enn**ess, p**enny**, fu**nny**
Jessica	jes, essi, ess, sica, ica	**jes**t, conf**essi**on, car**ess**, mu**sica**l, electr**ica**l
Joan	jo, oa, oan	**jo**b, l**oa**d, b**oa**t, l**oan**
Joanne	jo, oan, anne, ann, ne	**jo**y, m**oan**, m**anne**rs, **ann**oy, **ne**t
Joelle	jo, oe, ell, elle	**jo**in, t**oe**, b**ell**, s**elle**r
John	jo, oh, hn	**jo**b, ban**jo**, **jo**in, **jo**urney, alc**oh**ol, ric**hn**ess
Joseph	jo, ose, sep, eph	**jo**y, h**ose**, wh**ose**, **sep**arate, el**eph**ant, tel**eph**one
Josephine	jos, ose, sep, eph, phi, hine, hin, ine	ban**jos**, r**ose**, **sep**arate, n**eph**ew, grap**hi**c, s**hine**, bat**hin**g, l**ine**

Joy	joy, jo, oy	en**joy**, **jo**b, b**oy**
Jude	jud, ju, ude	**jud**ge, **ju**st, attit**ude**, st**ud**ent
Julie	jul, uli, lie	**Jul**y, fo**uli**ng, be**lie**ve
Karl	kar, arl, rl	tan**kar**d, ne**arl**y, gi**rl**
Kate	kate, ka, at, ate	s**kate**, **ka**le, e**at**, w**ate**r
Katherine	atheri, ather, kat, ther, heri, erin, rine	g**atheri**ng, f**ather**, s**kat**e, **ther**e, s**heri**ff, ball**erin**a, cla**rine**t
Kathrina	ka, athr, ath, thr, rina, rin, ina	**ka**le, b**athr**oom, **ath**letics, **thr**ough, ma**rina**, g**rin**, f**ina**l
Katie	kati, ati, at, tie, ie	tal**kati**ve, e**ati**ng, **at**e, **tie**s, p**ie**
Keith	ke, ei, eith, it, ith, th	**ke**y, rec**ei**ve, **it**em, **eith**er, w**ith**, fa**ith**, **th**ey
Kenneth	kenn, ken, ke, en, net, th, eth	**kenn**el, to**ken**, week**en**d, **ke**g, ten**ni**s, **net**tle, **th**en, t**eeth**, m**eth**od, tog**eth**er
Kerri	ker, erri, err, ri	con**ker**, t**erri**ble, **err**or, c**ri**es
Kevin	ke, evi, evin, vin	**ke**ep, beli**evi**ng, achi**evi**ng, **evi**l, d**evi**l, **evi**dence, **vin**egar
Kian	ki, ia, ian, an	**ki**ll, d**ia**ry, g**ia**nt, m**an**y
Kieran	ie, ier, era, eran, ran	n**ie**ce, dr**ier**, funn**ier**, op**era**, vet**eran**, g**ran**d
Killian	illian, killi, illi, lian, ian	br**illian**t, **killi**ng, m**illi**on, civi**lian**, p**ian**o
Kim	kim, ki, im	s**kim**, **ki**te, t**im**e
Kyle	kyl, yle, le	s**kyl**ine, st**yle**, unc**le**
Laura	laur, lau, aura, aur, ura	**laur**el, app**lau**d, rest**aura**nt, thes**aur**us, nat**ura**l
Lauren	lau, aur, ure, ren	**lau**ndry, dinos**aur**, s**ure**, w**ren**
Leah	lea, eah, ah	c**lea**n, **lea**rn, t**eah**ouse, hurr**ah**
Lee	lee, le, ee	as**lee**p, b**lee**d, ab**le**, f**ee**t, s**lee**t
Leo	leo, le, eo	**leo**pard, **leo**tard, tab**le**, vid**eo**
Lewis	lew, ewis, ewi, wis	f**lew**, like**wis**e, ch**ewi**ng, **wis**e
Leyla	ley, le, ey, yla, la	hur**ley**, ab**le**, **ey**es, sk**yla**rk, **la**nd
Liam	liam, lia, li, ia, iam, am	par**liam**ent, **lia**r, bril**li**ant, **li**p, a**ia**rial, d**iam**ond, j**am**,
Lily	lil, il, ily	**lil**ac, penc**il**, fam**ily**
Linda	lind, lin, ind, da	b**lind**, s**lin**g, k**ind**, **da**y
Lisa	lis, is, isa	rea**lis**e, m**is**ter, d**isa**ppear
Lorcan	lo, lor, orc, can	**lo**w, **lor**ry, g**lor**y, f**orc**e, t**orc**h, **can**e

Lorna	lor, orna, orn, rna, na	ex**plo**re, **orna**ment, b**orn**, jou**rna**l, s**na**p
Lorraine	lorr, lor, orr, raine, rain, rai, ine	**lorr**y, **lor**d, b**orr**ow, **rain**ed, t**rai**n, af**rai**d, p**ine**
Louis	lo, lou, ou, ui, uis, is	**lo**t, **lou**d, jealo**us**, o**ur**, wo**u**ld, b**ui**ld, br**uis**e, disg**uis**e, w**is**e
Louise	lou, uise, uis, ui, ise	c**lou**d, br**uis**e, n**uis**ance, b**ui**ld, surpr**ise**
Lucy	luc, ucy, uc, cy	**luc**k, sa**ucy**, kn**uc**kle, bi**cy**cle
Luke	lu, luk, uke, ke	**lu**ck, f**luk**e, d**uke**, **ke**ep
Madeline	made, line, deline, deli, elin	gui**deline**, **deli**ght, fe**elin**g
Maeve	ma, eve, ve	cine**ma**, **eve**r, **ve**ry
Maggie	mag, aggie, aggi, agg, gie, ie	i**mag**e, b**aggie**s, dr**aggi**ng, **agg**ressive, hy**gie**ne, p**ie**
Máiréad	mai, ma, aire, air, irea, ire, rea, read	**mai**n, **ma**y, rep**aire**d, ch**air**, f**ire**arm, f**ire**, a**rea**, b**read**
Máirín	mai, airin, airi, irin, iri, rin	**mai**d, rep**airin**g, d**airi**es, t**irin**g, sp**iri**t, p**rin**t
Malcolm	mal, alco, col, olm, lm,	nor**mal**, b**alco**ny, cho**col**ate, d**olm**en, fi**lm**, a**lm**ost
Margaret	marg, mar, arga, arg, garet, gare, gar, are, ret	**marg**in, **mar**ry, b**arga**in, **arg**ue, ci**garet**te, dun**gare**es, **gar**den, c**are**, p**ret**ty
Maria	mar, aria, ria	s**mar**t, veget**aria**n, f**ria**r
Marianne	mari, mar, ari, aria, ian, ann, ne	sa**mari**tan, re**mar**k, **ari**se, libr**aria**n, magic**ian**, **ann**ounce, n**ea**t
Marie	mar, ari, rie	gram**mar**, sh**ari**ng, t**rie**d
Marion	mar, ario, ari, rio, ion	**mar**ket, v**ario**us, **ari**thmetic, **rio**t, mans**ion**
Mark	ma, mar, ar, ark	**mar**ry, gram**mar**, **mar**ket, **ar**e, d**ark**, sp**ark**le
Martha	mart, mar, arth, rth, tha	s**mart**, gram**mar**, e**arth**, bi**rth**, **tha**n
Martin	ma, mar, art, arti, tin	night**mar**e, **mar**ket, p**arti**es, **art**ist, s**tin**g, **tin**y
Martina	mart, mar, arti, art, tin, ina	s**mart**, night**mar**e, **art**ist, he**art**, **tin**y, **ina**ctive
Matthew	ma, mat, att, the, he, hew, ew	**ma**y, **mat**e **att**ack, b**att**le, nep**hew**, c**hew**, st**ew**, s**ew**
Maurice	mau, ma, au, aur, rice, uri,	**mau**l, **ma**t, **au**nt, h**au**l, rest**au**rant, b**uri**es, d**uri**ng
Max	max, ma, ax	cli**max**, cine**ma**, rel**ax**,

Megan	mega, egan, meg	o**mega**, b**egan**, home-g**rown**
Melanie	mela, mel, elan, lan, nie	ho**mela**nd, ca**mel**, I**re**l**and**, **lan**e, **nie**ce
Meriel	meri, mer, erie, eri, iel	**mer**it, sum**mer**, s**erie**s, int**eri**or, f**iel**d
Michael	mic, ich, icha, cha, ae, el	**mic**e, co**mic**, r**ich**, multi**cha**nnel, **cha**nge, **ae**rial, h**el**p
Michelle	mic, iche, chel, che, elle, ell, le	**mic**e, r**iche**st, ba**chel**or, **che**at, trave**lle**r, te**ll**, unc**le**
Miriam	miri, mir, iri, ria, am	ad**miri**ng, **mir**ror, I**ri**sh, spi**ri**t, mate**ria**l, **am**ber
Monica	moni, mon, oni, onic, nica, ica	**moni**tor, **mon**ey, p**oni**es, ph**onic**s, tech**nica**l, pel**ica**n
Morgan	organ, orga, morg, gan	**organ**ise, forg**ave**, **morg**ue, cardi**gan**
Naomi	na, omi, mi	tu**na**, co**mi**c, **mi**ght
Natasha	natas, nat, tash, asha	so**natas**, domi**nat**e, s**tash**, w**asha**ble
Niall	nial, ni, ia, iall, ial, al, all	de**nial**, **ni**ce, l**ia**r, d**iall**ed, tr**ial**, soci**al**, **all**ow, **al**so
Niamh	nia, ia, am, mh	Nar**nia**, man**ia**c, di**al**, n**am**e, **armh**ole
Nicholas	nich, icho, ich, holas, ola	**nich**e, art**icho**ke, wh**ich**, sc**holas**tic, c**ola**
Nicola	nico, nic, icol, ico, cola, col, ola	u**nico**rn, **nic**e, mult**icol**our, **ico**n, cho**cola**te, **col**our, vi**ola**
Niki	ni, iki, ki	**ni**ne, l**iki**ng, **ki**nd
Noel	noe, oe, oel, el	ca**noe**, volca**noe**s, h**oe**, sh**oel**ace, **el**bow
Norma	norma, norm, nor, orma, orm, rma, ma	**norma**l, e**norm**ous, s**nor**e, f**orma**l, w**orm**, supe**rma**rket, **ma**y
Odile	odile, odil odi, od, dile, dil, ile	cro**codile**, daff**odil**, b**odi**es, c**od**, **dile**mma, **dil**ute, sm**ile**, fail**ed**
Oisín	oi, ois, oisi, isi, sin	**oi**l, m**ois**t, p**oisi**on, n**oisi**er, r**isi**ng, **sin**ger
Olive	oli, live, liv,	p**oli**ce, brocc**oli**, ho**liv**day, **live**ly, a**live**
Oliver	olive, oli, live, ive, ver	p**oli**ce, de**live**r, **live**ly, g**ive**, dri**ver**, ri**ver**, **ver**y, e**ver**, se**ver**al
Olivia	livi, ivia, via, ia	**livi**ng, tr**ivia**l, de**via**te, d**ia**l
Orla	orl, or, rla, rl, la	w**orl**d, f**or**, ove**rla**p, gi**rl**, cu**rl**, **la**st
Órlaith	or, rl, lait, lai, ith	b**or**n, swi**rl**, twi**rl**, p**lait**, c**lai**m, w**ith**
Owen	ow, owe, wen, en	c**ow**, t**owe**l, flower, burr**owe**d, **wen**t, tw**en**ty, **en**ter
Patricia	patr, pat, atri, tric, tri, rici, icia, ici, cia, ia	**patr**ol, **pat**ch, the**atri**cal, me**tric**, **tri**p, p**rici**ng, mag**icia**n, sl**ici**ng, offi**cia**l, tr**ia**l

Patrick	pa, pat, atri, tri, ric, tric, trick, ick	**pa**th, **pat**ient, **pa**triot, **tri**p, **ri**ce, elec**tric**, s**trict**, s**ick**
Paul	pau, au, aul, ul	**pau**se, **au**nt, m**aul**, ass**ault**, f**ault**, r**ule**
Paula	pau, aula, aul, au, ul	**pau**se, h**aul**age, c**aul**iflower, h**aul**, p**ull**
Pauline	paul, au, ulin, uli, ul, line	tar**paul**in, s**au**ce, r**ulin**g, t**uli**p, fo**ul**, **line**n
Peter	pe, pet, ete, ter	**pe**a, **pet**al, comp**ete**, athl**ete**, let**ter**
Philip	phil, ph, hil, ili, lip	**phil**osopher, **ph**one, **hil**l, fi**li**ng, tu**lip**
Philomena	philo, phil, ph, hil, ilom, ilo, lom, omen, ena	**philo**sopher, up**hil**l, gra**ph**, ch**ilo**d, k**ilom**etre, p**ilo**t, dip**lom**a, w**omen**, p**ena**lty
Rachel	rach, rac, ra, ach, ache, chel, hel	pa**rach**ute, t**rac**k, ext**ra**, **race**, y**ach**t, te**ache**r, sat**chel**, **hel**p
Rebecca	reb, ebe, bec, cca	**reb**uild, r**ebe**l, bar**bec**ue, o**cca**sion
Richard	ric, ich, rich, cha, char, har, hard,	p**ric**e, wh**ich**, **cha**t, **char**ge, **char**acter, **har**m
Rita	rita, rit, ri, it, ita	B**rita**in, ir**rit**ate, spi**ri**t, **ri**ce, b**it**e, cap**ita**l
Robert	ro, rob, robe, ober, be, ber, bert, ert	**ro**om, s**ob**er, exp**ert**, mem**ber**, li**bert**y, **cert**ain, over**take**
Róisín	rois, roi, ro, ois, isin, isi, sin	he**rois**m, emb**roi**der, **ro**ll, m**ois**t, adv**isin**g, r**isi**ng, **sin**gle
Ronan	ron, ro, on, ona, onan, nan	w**ron**g, f**ro**nt, **ro**w, **on**e, d**ona**te, cons**onan**t, ba**nan**a
Rosaleen	rosa, ros, osal, osa, sale, lee, een	**rosa**ry, **ros**e, prop**osal**, disp**osa**ble, b**een**
Ruth	ruth, rut, ru, uth	t**ruth**, c**rut**ch, b**ru**te, p**ru**ne, mo**uth**
Ryan	ry, yan	ve**ry**, **ry**e, anno**yan**ce
Samuel	sam, amu, mue, uel	**sam**ple, **amu**se, **mue**sli, f**uel**, cr**uel**
Samantha	sama, amant, ant, ama, anth, tha	**Sama**ritan, ad**amant**, w**ant**, **ama**ze, **anth**em, **tha**nk
Sarah	sar, ara, rah	di**sar**m, p**ara**de, ch**ara**cter, hur**rah**
Seamus	sea, eam, amu, mus	di**sea**se, **seam**, **am**, t**eam**, **amu**se, **mus**ic
Sean	sea, ea, ean	**sea**t, h**ea**d, cl**ean**, oc**ean**
Selina	selin, sel, elin, ina	ba**selin**e, my**sel**f, kne**elin**g, f**ina**l
Shane	sha, han, an, ane	**sha**pe, **han**d, p**an**, m**ane**, mo**ane**d
Sharon	shar, har, aron, aro, ron, on	**shar**e, **shar**p, **har**d, mac**aron**i, **aro**und, he**ron**, d**on**e
Sinéad	sine, sin, inea, ine, nead, nea, ead	bus**ine**ss, cou**sin**, p**inea**pple, f**ine**, k**nead**, **nea**t, r**ead**

Siobhán	sio, obh, ob, han	pension, jobholder, robe, thank
Sophie	sophie, sophi, so, oph, phi, ph, hie, ie	philosophies, sophisticate, soon, videophone, dolphin, graph, shield, copies
Stephanie	step, ep, phan, hani, han, ie	wastepaper, steep, elephant, mechanic, handle, tie
Stephen	ste, step, ephe, eph, he, hen	sister, shepherd, nephew, telephone, shed, then
Steven	ste, teve, eve, even, ven	mister, instead, whatever, seven, eleven, evening
Stewart	stew, stewar, tewa, ewar, art	steward, whitewash, beware, apart
Susan	sus, usan, usa, san	misuse, thousand, usage, sane
Suzanne	su, za, ann, ne	sum, zap, planned, annoy, net
Tamara	tamara, tam, mar, ara	catamaran, stamp, grammar, earache
Tara	tara, tar, ara, ra	tarantula, stare, harass, train
Terence	tere, ter, renc, ere, ence	entered, watered, interest, wrench, conference, there, presence
Theresa	there, ther, here, ere, resa, res, esa	gathered, mother, hemisphere, cereal, resale, cares, lifesaver
Therese	ther, there, here, eres, rese, res, ese	further, interest, present, rest, these
Thomas	tho, ho, oma, mas	thought, who, woman, mass, master
Timothy	ti, im, moth, oth, th, thy	tie, time, mother, other, the
Tom	to, tom, om	into, tomorrow, custom, automatic, come
Ursula	ursu, urs, rsu, sula, sul, ula	pursue, burst, persuade, insulate, sulk, ambulance
Vincent	vince, vin, in, ince, cent, ent	convince, vinegar, saving, mince, centre, enter
Walter	alter, walt, alte, lted, ted	waltz, salted, bolted, tedious
William	willi, illi, ill, ia, liam	willing, brilliant, spilling, caterpillar, diary, parliament
Yvonne	vo, onne, onn, nne, ne	vote, bonnet, connect, tunnel, lane
Zachary	ach, char, ary	each, character, weary
Zara	zar, ara	hazard, caravan
Zoe	zo, oe	zoom, toe, canoe

Appendix 5 – Name/Word Webs

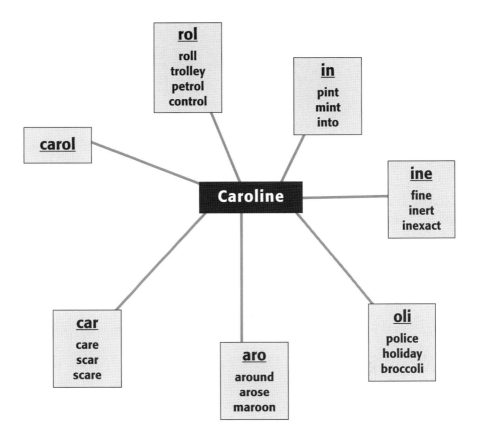

Finding small words in bigger words

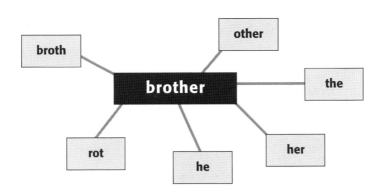

Name/Word Webs

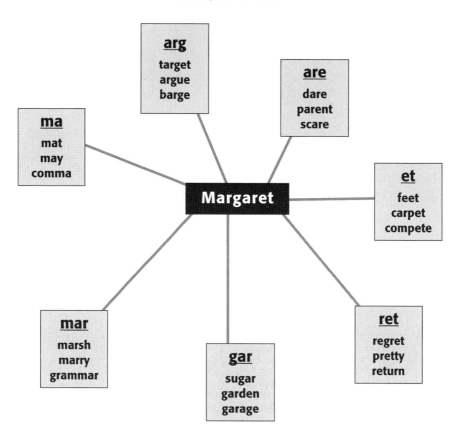

Finding small words in bigger words

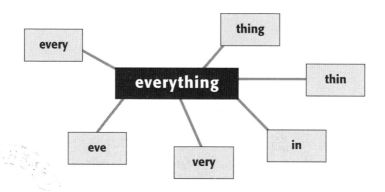

Name/Word Webs

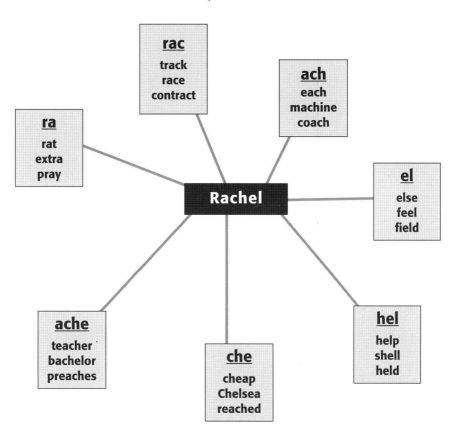

Finding small words in bigger words

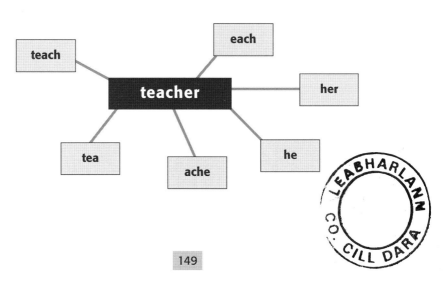

Name/Word Webs

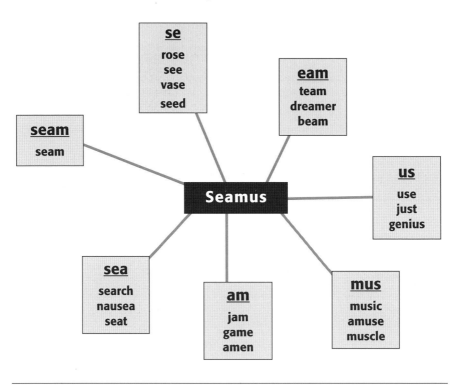

Name/Word Webs

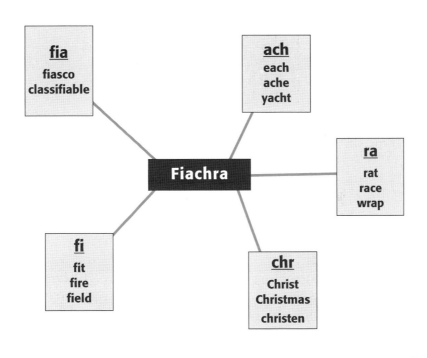

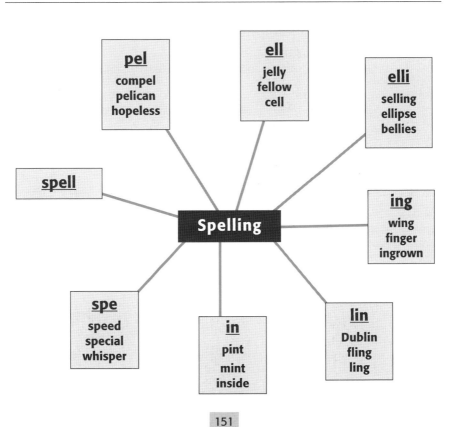

(a)

against
all right
already
alone
although
animal
arrived
arriving
awful

(b)

bake
baking
banana
basket
bath
beach
beginning
behave
believe
biggest
board
bodies
bottom
breakfast
bridge
business
busy

(c)

captain
carried
centre
chicken
choose
climb
club
comic
cool
corner
countries
crash
cried

(d)

dance
dead
desert
digging
doctor
drank
drive

(e)

earth
easy
electric
elephant
eleven
else
enjoy
except
excuse
expect

(f)

families
favourite
felt
fifteen
fifth
fifty
flew
forest
free
frighten
fruit

(g)

ghost
giant
goal
grand-mother
grew
grey
group
grown

(h)

hardly
heavy
held
high
hitting
hoping
hospital
hundred
hungry
hurried

(i)

ice-cream
insect
instead
invite
island

(j)

jelly
juicy

(k)

kitchen
kite
knife
knives

(l)

laugh
lawn
leaving
library
listen
living
lovely

(m)

mail
mean
middle
mind
missed
month
mountain
mouth
move
museum

(n)

neck
ninety
noise
number
nurse

(o)

office
often
oil
orange
order

(p)

paid
parcel
passed
pick
picnic
plenty
police
ponies
potatoes
power
prefer
princess
promise

(q)

quarter
queen

(r)

racing
radio
really

(s)

scared
sentence
shoot
short
showed
sitting
sixth
skipping
slowly
snow
soap
soccer
sore
spent
steep
stories
strong
sudden
sugar
surprise
sweet

(t)

taught
team
teeth
telephone
television
themselves
thousand
threw
throw
travel
trouble
truck
twelve
twenty

(u)

usually

(v)

vegetables

(w)

we'll
we're
whole
wide
wife
wild
woke
wonderful
wore
worried
written

Corewords 3 – Dictation Exercises
(Set One)

1. After eating some chicken, my grandmother and grandfather were very sick, but now they are all right again.

2. I went to the library yesterday to find a book about animals.

3. Does everybody else enjoy ice cream as much as I do?

4. The number of people killed in the crash is thought to be between ninety and one hundred.

5. The teacher tried to bake a banana cake but he made an awful mess of it.

6. When the farmer put the potatoes on the truck, the bottom fell out of the bags.

7. The doctor is so busy she hardly ever leaves the hospital.

8. We have a strong soccer team this year and we don't expect to be beaten very often.

9. I will choose twelve children to invite to my party.

10. We had such a wonderful holiday on the desert island that we hated coming back home.

11. When we arrived at the museum it had already closed for the day.

12. I wonder what it is like being in fifth or sixth class.

13. They got a great surprise seeing themselves on television.

14. I am having awful trouble with my new telephone.

15. Somebody will have to go to town to order new chairs for our sitting room.

16. We showed the ghost where the teacher's house was.

17. They hurried home because they didn't want to miss their favourite television show.

18. They had to drive their lorries slowly over the high mountains.

19. One quarter of the school children missed the huge snow fight.

20. The captain of the winning team carried the cup across the bridge into the county.

21. Those oranges we bought yesterday were really lovely.

22. During the party fourteen children played pass the parcel.

23. We listened to the horse racing on the radio.

24. If we had some knives we could have cut the fruit.

25. We got in free because our aunt worked in the ticket office.

26. I couldn't believe what the elephant could eat for breakfast.

27. He warned us to behave or else we would be sent to the office.

28. We promised the princess that we would pick the largest vegetables in the garden and then bring them to the kitchen.

29. Instead of buying ice cream every day he saved his money to buy an electric train.

30. The baby cried and cried when his father was giving him a bath.
31. Too much sugar is bad for our teeth.
32. They were serious at the start but all of a sudden the children started to laugh.
33. Who taught you to shoot like that?
34. He was asked to leave the club because he couldn't behave himself.
35. There are plenty of comics in the corner of the classroom.
36. I don't think that giant would frighten anyone.
37. Although his mouth was quite sore, he could just manage to eat some jelly.
38. We wanted to free the ponies but our aunt and uncle said that it was none of our business.
39. My cousin says that she has been to visit fifteen different countries.
40. We were going to have a picnic on the lawn but there were too many insects around.
41. His knife slipped and cut through the centre of the kite.
42. After the crash he found it difficult to move his neck.
43. We couldn't keep the cats in the basket any longer because they grew too big.
44. He started digging early in the morning and he never took a break.
45. After hurting her leg, she was afraid to start skipping again.
46. The postman threw the whole lot of the mail into a large bag.
47. My stolen car cost eleven thousand euro.
48. The queen will be arriving at twelve o'clock.
49. We heard many awful stories about wild animals.
50. His wife always wore a hat with apples and bananas sticking out of it.
51. Our teacher was angry when she saw what was written on the blackboard.
52. I paid three hundred euro/pounds to learn how to drive and I still failed my test.
53. When he woke up he couldn't move his neck because it was sore.
54. I was quite scared when I heard a loud noise coming from the room next to mine.
55. The nurse taught him to how to walk again.
56. I always thought I was a very strong player but I had no excuse when I was beaten.
57. We spent all their money buying all kinds of sweets.
58. The army tried to steal quietly up the steep hill.
59. Eleven thousand fans are expected to travel to the soccer match.
60. We put soap on our aunt's toothbrush because she wouldn't tell us any bedtime stories.
61. When we climbed to the top of the mountain we had a rest to cool off.
62. He was only sleeping for a short while when the noise suddenly woke him.

63. I didn't really mind standing but I was hoping to get a chair.
64. Nobody knows how many dead bodies will be found under the bridge.
65. The weather really turned cold last month.
66. Ever since the crash he has no power in his right hand.
67. Do you ever get fed up listening to the teacher all day long?
68. He promised us that it would only take a few minutes to throw twenty boxes onto the truck
69. The spaceship is arriving back to Earth tomorrow evening.
70. She felt much better when she drank some cold water.
71. She was skipping on our front lawn with twelve other girls.
72. We're going to have to dress up if we want to get into the dance.
73. I wasn't laughing when I was left alone in the big old house.
74. We were not allowed to bring comics into the clubhouse.
75. There was so much oil on the beach that some of the birds had to be cleaned in a bath.
76. I think we'll put salt into the teacher's tea instead of sugar.
77. Would you prefer to meet a giant or a ghost?
78. I cried and cried when I was told that my pet rabbit was dead.
79. Fifty people helped the farmer to pick all the potatoes in two of the fields.
80. My grandmother and grandfather brought us up the mountain for a beautiful picnic.
81. He banged his mouth against the corner of the wall and he had to go to hospital.
82. Our families are always trying to surprise one another.
83. We began to get worried when our captain was carried off.
84. Fifty children wanted to go camping in the forest but their parents were too scared.
85. Going to school sometimes can be a real pain in the neck!
86. The farmer got really angry when we chased the chickens into the centre of the field.
87. She wore a different dress each time she was invited to a party.
88. The queen is supposed to arrive at a quarter to twelve.
89. It is really lovely living in the country.
90. The sky looked very grey when we left the library.
91. We will be arriving for breakfast at half past eight.
92. After baking the bread, I put it into a basket to cool it down.
93. The fighter jet flew at great speed high above the clouds.

94. Everybody except me seemed to have grown much bigger.

95. I am not trying to drive across that broken bridge.

96. We spent all our money on sweets and ice cream.

97. He stayed sitting on the wall for a short while and then he walked slowly home.

98. When we came out of his office we all started laughing.

99. He drove a large truck right across the beautiful lawn.

100. I never want to play in goal again because everyone was laughing at me.

101. We always believed that teachers came from a different planet!

102. She got the biggest surprise of her life when her favourite singer arrived for breakfast.

103. It's really none of our business, but we think you are making too much noise.

104. I wonder if the queen and princess ever listen to the radio.

105. There is no excuse for giving the children so much homework.

106. He promised to invite me to the party but I don't expect to enjoy it.

107. The shopkeeper was sure that we never paid for the tank of oil.

108. Those men and women keep themselves fit by eating lots of fruit and vegetables.

109. The trouble with grandmother is that she has no teeth left!

110. I called into the travel office, but they were much too busy to answer my question.

111. In the beginning, the trees grew very slowly.

112. When I woke early in the morning, the place was covered in snow.

113. Although the beach was dirty, many people still went swimming.

114. I got quite hungry in the middle of the night.

115. Sometimes I find it difficult to choose a good book in the library.

116. There were fifteen lovely ponies in the field at the bottom of the street.

117. After the break-in there was a large number of things missing from the museum.

118. We couldn't find a knife in the kitchen to cut the fruit.

119. Do you think there is enough oil in the truck?

120. We had awful trouble writing some of these sentences.

121. It is very difficult to travel across a desert.

122. We hurried to the hospital hoping that he was still alive.

123. Every year plenty of parcels seem to be lost in the post-office.

124. She held the heavy electric train in one hand.

125. Do those awful stories about insects ever frighten you?

126. We had to drive a group of nurses back to the hospital.

127. They were hoping that they didn't have to write on the blackboard.

128. I couldn't believe it when they started hitting the ponies.

129. We decided to free the elephant from behind the electric fence.

130. The princess wore a beautiful grey dress.

131. They thought they would be allowed to climb up the steep side of the mountain.

132. I tried to telephone their friends but I couldn't get through to them.

133. We passed the centre of the island at twelve o'clock.

134. They flew over the forest to see how much damage was done during the storm.

135. Teams from fifty different countries will arrive next month to play against each other.

136. They cried and cried when someone threw oranges at them.

137. Instead of baking some bread, we decided to go on a picnic.

138. We're all very happy because we have written wonderful stories.

139. Mother showed us how she wanted the vegetables cut.

140. The police did not remove the bodies until the doctor arrived.

141. We had to choose a strong knife to cut the fruit.

142. I had to go to the hospital because I had an orange stuck in my mouth.

143. We were very worried when we saw smoke rising from the centre of the forest.

144. I am used to the doctors and nurses ordering me around.

145. After racing for twenty minutes their legs felt very tired.

146. I often have to clean the kitchen, but I don't really mind.

147. We have to tell the teacher not to throw soap around the toilet, but he never listens to us.

148. Although he worked alone, he found it easy to clean all the knives.

149. The farmer sold ponies to each of the eleven families.

150. He woke his wife when he thought he heard a noise downstairs.

151. The garden has grown wild because there is no one to look after it.

152. Everyone told him to shoot, but when he did the ball went wide.

153. Thousands of children go hungry every day.

154. In the beginning the captain of the boat promised that the boat had enough power and get us safely back to land.

155. They felt sure that their business would last.

156. All of a sudden the giant didn't seem that strong.

157. The water around the island is full of jellyfish.

158. We put a drawing of a ghost on the kite to scare the birds.

159. The captain taught us how to play better.

160. During the bad weather the farmer carried the sheep to higher ground.

161. We could hardly see the bottom of the river.
162. When I passed by fifth class there was a very heavy smell!
163. I had a wonderful time when they showed me how to stay out of trouble.
164. We'll be having our favourite dinner tomorrow night.
165. Our families have already arrived home from their holiday in the country.
166. In springtime the farmers are always busy with young animals.
167. If you were alone, would you watch television or listen to the radio?
168. The game was held up for twenty minutes because the goal post was broken.
169. My grandmother threw her telephone over the bridge because it wouldn't work.
170. The birds flew from the forest because some animals frightened them.
171. My wife has spent almost all of my money.
172. I must learn how to fix the basket on my new bicycle.
173. When we arrived at the beach we warned the teacher to behave!
174. We spent the whole day digging the earth at the bottom of the garden.
175. It's lovely to drink milk when it is really cold.
176. I didn't get any mail because the postman said he didn't know where I was living!
177. He must have missed the turn because he never arrived at the library.
178. Those stories about wild animals were very interesting.
179. We had to bake a large number of cakes but we didn't have enough fruit.
180. We didn't really mean to cause so much trouble.
181. That must have been the biggest surprise he ever got.
182. It was very difficult not to laugh when we saw the teacher skipping.
183. He slipped on a banana skin and crashed into the grandfather clock in the corner of the room.
184. We spent yesterday afternoon sitting in sixth class because our teacher left early.
185. I didn't really mean to throw the basket into the bath.
186. I felt wonderful when I drank some cold water.
187. We decided to leave the old comics in the corner of the clubhouse.
188. You wouldn't believe who we caught trying to break into the soccer shop.
189. Do your legs ever get tired from skipping?
190. The truck didn't have enough power to climb the steep hill.
191. How are we expected to have enough potatoes cut for dinner, when we don't have a knife?

Corewords 3 – Dictation Exercises
(Set Two)

1. It's all right for my grandmother and grandfather to eat the chicken, but it would make me sick.
2. I'm not interested in going to the library to find out about wild animals.
3. Nobody enjoys ice cream as much as I do!
4. Many people thought that ninety or a hundred were killed in the crash.
5. The teacher is sure that he didn't make an awful mess of the banana cake.
6. The farmer placed the bags of potatoes near the back of the truck.
7. The hospital is so busy that the doctors have very little free time.
8. We never expected to be beaten by their soccer team.
9. If I could choose I would only invite twelve children to the party.
10. That desert island isn't such a wonderful place to go on holiday.
11. The new pictures arrived at the museum just before it closed.
12. The children in fifth and sixth class wonder why they don't have fun anymore.
13. I got a great surprise when I saw colour television for the first time.
14. My new telephone is causing me awful trouble.
15. Who ordered these new chairs for the sitting room?
16. The ghost wasn't interested in the teacher's house.
17. If they hadn't hurried home they would have missed their favourite television show.
18. We couldn't manage to drive the lorries over the steep mountains.
19. There was a huge snow fight in school, but a quarter of the children missed it.
20. When we won the cup, the county captain brought it across the bridge.
21. Who bought those lovely juicy oranges?
22. Fourteen children wouldn't play pass the parcel during the party.
23. We don't like listening to horse racing on the radio; we prefer to watch it on the television.
24. These knives are even useless for cutting fruit!
25. Maybe I can get you in free because my aunt works in the ticket office.
26. You wouldn't believe what the elephant ate for breakfast.
27. We promised the man in the office that we would always behave ourselves.
28. When we picked the largest vegetables in the garden we brought them into the kitchen.
29. Instead of saving her money to buy an electric heater, the princess bought ice cream every day.
30. The baby cried when his father fell into the bath.
31. At the time we didn't think it was serious, but when we ate too much sugar our teeth started to ache.
32. At the beginning of the story the children were happy but all of a sudden they started crying.

33. Whoever taught you that should be shot!
34. He will be asked to leave the club because he is not behaving.
35. The corner of the classroom is not the place to put those comics.
36. Anyone who saw the giant would be very frightened.
37. He managed to eat some jelly although his mouth was quite sore.
38. Our aunt and uncle wanted to save the ponies but we said that it was none of their business.
39. When she was fifteen my cousin visited many different countries.
40. It is awful having a picnic when there are lots of insects around the place.
41. When he slipped, his knife cut through the centre of the cloth.
42. He stayed in bed after the crash because it was too difficult to move his neck.
43. Those baskets are useless now because those cats have grown too big for them.
44. If we start digging early in the morning we will need a break at eleven o'clock.
45. She was afraid her leg would start hurting again if she joined in the skipping.
46. The whole lot of the stolen mail was thrown into a large sack.
47. It will cost you eleven thousand euro/pounds to change your car.
48. Three queens will be arriving at twelve o'clock tomorrow.
49. The stories we heard about those animals were really awful.
50. Why does his wife always wear a hat with apples and bananas sticking out of it?
51. If our teacher knew what we wrote about her on the blackboard, she would be very angry.
52. I have spent hundreds of euro/pounds learning how to pass my driving test.
53. His neck was so sore when he woke up he decided not to go to school.
54. I heard a loud noise coming from next door and I began to feel quite scared.
55. After the crash he had to be taught how to walk again.
56. I hate making excuses when I am beaten.
57. The army was supposed to steal quietly up the hill.
58. We started buying all kinds of sweets with their money.
59. Thousands of fans are expected to travel to watch the teachers playing soccer.
60. If our aunt doesn't tell us stories tonight we will hide her toothbrush.
61. It was very cool at the top of the mountain.
62. I had just fallen asleep when a loud noise suddenly woke me.
63. She was really hoping to get a chair because she hated standing.
64. When the bridge fell nobody knew how many bodies would be found.
65. It was only early in the month that the weather turned cold.
66. He has no power left in his left hand ever since he crashed his car.
67. When teachers talk and talk we really get fed up listening to them.
68. I promise you that twenty minutes will not be enough to throw all those boxes onto the truck.

69. We expect the spaceship to arrive back to Earth late tomorrow.

70. I always feel much better after drinking some cold water.

71. I warned those twelve children not to be skipping on my front lawn.

72. We usually put on our best clothes when we go dancing.

73. He stopped laughing when he was told he had to stay on his own in the big old house.

74. Nobody will be allowed to bring comics into the clubhouse.

75. When oil was spilled on the beach, some birds were cleaned in a bath.

76. I would much prefer to meet a giant than a ghost.

77. We'll get in trouble if we put salt in the sugar bowl.

78. When I found out that my pet rabbit died, I couldn't stop crying.

79. The farmer needed fifty people to pick all the potatoes in the field.

80. We brought our grandparents up the mountain for a beautiful picnic.

81. He had to go to hospital because he banged his head against the corner of the table.

82. We are always thinking of different ways to surprise our families.

83. When our captain was carried off, the fans began to get worried.

84. Fifty children went camping in the forest but their parents were too scared to go.

85. Having to sit quietly in class is a real pain in the neck.

86. If we chase the chickens into the centre of the field we will make the farmer really angry.

87. Every time she was invited to a party she made sure she wore a different dress.

88. It is now a quarter to twelve and the queen hasn't arrived yet.

89. We always supposed that it would be lovely to live in the country.

90. As soon as we left the library we knew it would rain because the sky was very grey.

91. They are supposed to be arriving for breakfast at a quarter past eight.

92. Put the bread into that basket to cool it down.

93. We knew the fighter jet flew at a great speed but we couldn't see it because of the clouds.

94. Why has everyone grown much bigger except for me.

95. Nobody should be allowed to drive over that dangerous bridge.

96. I can't understand why they spent so much money on sweets and ice cream.

97. Some of the children walked slowly home while the others stayed sitting on the wall.

98. All the children started laughing as soon as they left the office.

99. The angry truck driver ruined his beautiful lawn.

100. I will never play in goal again because I don't like people laughing at me.

101. We were not surprised to discover that our teacher was from a different planet.

102. We wanted to surprise her so we invited her favourite singer to join her for breakfast.

103. We told them they were making too much noise but they told us to mind our own business.

104. It was wonderful listening to the queen and princess on the radio.

105. I am trying to find an excuse to give the children more homework.

106. After all the trouble last year, he promised not to invite me to their party again.

107. My parents were sure that they had paid for the oil but the shopkeeper kept saying that they hadn't.

108. By eating lots of fruit and vegetables, those men and women will keep themselves fit.

109. Grandmother has lost all her teeth and has great trouble eating anything.

110. The lady in the travel office never called me back because she was much too busy.

111. The trees are beginning to grow very slowly.

112. I got up early in the morning and I couldn't believe it when I saw the place covered in snow.

113. I can't understand why so many people still go swimming at that dirty beach.

114. Although I had a big dinner I was still hungry during the night.

115. There are so many interesting books in the library it is always difficult to choose one.

116. It was awful to hear that a truck killed fifteen ponies at the bottom of the street.

117. The guard at the museum was sure that a large number of things would be missing after the break in.

118. It's almost impossible to find a good kitchen knife that will cut fruit properly.

119. The truck wouldn't start because it didn't have enough oil.

120. Some of these sentences are so difficult I have awful trouble writing them.

121. We knew it wouldn't be easy to travel across the desert.

122. As they hurried to the hospital, everyone hoped that their friend would still be alive.

123. The post-office seems to lose plenty of parcels every year.

124. That electric train is too heavy to hold in one hand.

125. They are always trying to frighten me with awful stories about killer insects.

126. The nurses couldn't get back to the hospital on time because there was no one to drive them.

127. I was hoping the teacher wouldn't ask me to write on the blackboard.

128. I heard that all those who started hitting the ponies are in big trouble.

129. It was going to be difficult, but we decided that we must free the elephant from behind the electric fence.

130. Everywhere she goes, the princess always wears a beautiful dress.

131. They were angry because they thought that they should have been allowed to climb the steep mountain.

132. Although I tried very often, I couldn't telephone their friends because the line was busy.

133. It was exactly twelve o'clock when we passed by the centre of the island.

134. When they flew over the forest they knew how much damage had been done by the great storm.

135. Next month we will have to plan how the teams from fifty different countries will play against each other.

136. I cried when someone threw oranges at me and hurt my eye.

137. We decided to do some baking when we returned from the picnic.

138. We have written some wonderful stories and we are very pleased with ourselves.

139. They wanted to show their mother that they could cut vegetables too.

140. The doctor told the police not to remove the bodies until he arrived.

141. When you choose your favourite fruit you can cut it with this sharp knife.

142. We stuck a banana in the teacher's ear and he had to go to the hospital.

143. When we camped in the centre of the forest we were worried that someone would see the smoke rising from our fire.

144. I found it difficult to get used to the doctors and nurses ordering me about.

145. Their legs felt really tired because they had been racing quickly for twenty minutes.

146. It doesn't really bother me when I have to clean the kitchen.

147. I wonder if he was listening at all when he was told not to throw soap down the toilet.

148. Although he had to clean all the knives, he wanted to work alone.

149. Our families told the farmer that they wished to buy eleven ponies.

150. He thought he heard a loud noise downstairs so he decided to wake his wife.

151. It is no wonder that the garden has grown wild because nobody lives there anymore.

152. Everyone wanted him to shoot but he was afraid the ball would go wide.

153. It is difficult to believe that thousands of children still go hungry every day.

154. The boat just had enough power to get us back safely, but in the beginning we didn't think it would.

155. I felt sure that their business would not last very long because there was always lots of trouble with the workers.

156. When I stood on the giant's small toe, he didn't seem that strong all of a sudden.

157. There were so many jellyfish in the water around the island that everyone stopped swimming.

158. The birds were scared when they saw the drawing of a ghost on the kite.

159. If the captain wanted us to play better he should have taught us what to do.

160. All the sheep had to be carried to high ground during the flooding.
161. The water was so dirty it was difficult to see the bottom of the river.
162. As I passed by, there seemed to be a very heavy smell in fifth class.
163. They told us that if we stayed out of trouble that we would have a wonderful time.
164. Tomorrow night I will be cooking our favourite dinner.
165. When we arrived back from our holiday in the country, our families were home before us.
166. All the young animals keep the farmers busy in springtime.
167. When I am alone I prefer to listen to the radio than watching television.
168. When I broke the goalpost, the game was held up for twenty minutes.
169. When my grandmother's telephone wouldn't work, she just threw it over the bridge.
170. The birds were frightened because the wild animals rushed through the forest.
171. I don't have enough money to buy a paper because my wife has spent all of my money.
172. I had to learn how to fix a new basket on to my bicycle.
173. As soon as we arrived at the beach the teacher started to misbehave.
174. There was so much earth at the bottom of the garden that we spent the whole day digging it.
175. It's a lovely feeling drinking cold water on a really warm day.
176. Our postman hates delivering our mail because we are living on the side of a mountain.
177. I suppose that he never arrived because he missed the turn at the library.
178. I was always interested in stories about wild animals.
179. If we don't have enough fruit we won't be able to bake very many cakes.
180. He causes so much trouble and then he tells us that he really didn't mean it.
181. What was the biggest surprise you ever got?
182. The teacher found it difficult to skip so we started laughing at him.
183. He slipped on a banana skin and knocked his grandfather onto the floor.
184. We spent most of yesterday just sitting around doing nothing.
185. It was really mean of her to blame me for throwing the basket into the bath.
186. It was wonderful to discover the pool of water in the desert.
187. The captain decided that the corner of the clubhouse was not a safe place to leave the comics.
188. When we were caught breaking into the soccer shop the police wouldn't believe us when we told them that we lived there!
189. My legs got so tired from skipping that I thought they would fall off.
190. I don't think that truck will have enough power to climb up the steep street.
191. We were expected to have the potatoes cut for dinner but we didn't have enough knives.

Appendix 7 – Corewords Four

(a)
accident
acting
ahead
allow
amount
angry
April
area
arithmetic
attack
August
available
avoid
awoke

(b)
balance
base
battle
bead
beaten
below
beside
blew
blow
boring
bottle
bowl
branch
brave
Britain
brush
bunch
burn
bush

(c)
calves
capital
careful
case
castle
cause
certain
change
cheese
chimney
circus
citizen
clear
climate
clock
clothing
coast
common
continue
control
correct
court
crept

(d)
damage
dangerous
daughter
deaf
December
dentist
dirty
disease
distance
downstairs
dream
drew
dropped
drum

(e)
either
empty
engine
escape
especially
Europe

(f)
fail
famous
feast
February
film
finally
finger
finish
flat
flies
flood
fold
follow
Form
fought
fresh

(g)
glove
goat
golden
greedy

(h)
headache
heart
heat
hole
honey
horn
hotel
huge
hung

(i)
idea
illness
imagine
important
injured
Ireland

(j)
January
July
June

(k)
knocked

(m)
main
market
meal
melt
mess
mouse

(n)
nail
newspaper
none
northern
November

(o)
October
outdoors

(p)
page
panic
parade
personal
piano
plain
pleasant
pocket
poem
point
policeman
port
possible
prize
probably
problem
programme
proud
puncture
pushed

(q)
question
quiz

(r)
reach
reason
receive
repair
replied
reply
ripe
roar
robber
rocket
roof

(s)
sail
science
seal
season
serious
settle
sew
shine
shining
shirt
sign
silly
silver
size
sliding
slipped
soil
soldier
sound
speak
square
squeeze
stamp
stepped
stomach
storm
strange
stream
stuck
subject
suppose
swing

(t)
terrible
thankful
theatre
thick
thirsty
throne
tied
tiny
tore
track
tractor
triangle
trousers
true
twice
tyre

(u)
upstairs
useful

(v)
valley
view
village
voice

(w)
warn
weekly
weigh
wheel
whether
whose
window
wipe
wishes
wonder
wooden
worse
wrong

(y)
you'll
you're

Corewords 4 – Dictation Exercises

(Set One)

1. The baker got very angry when his helper dropped a drum of flour on his finger.

2. I have no reason to believe that the punctured tyre caused the accident.

3. I can't remember but I think that it was either in January or February last year that we had terrible flooding.

4. When I grow up I will probably go acting in a famous theatre in the city.

5. She was so thirsty at the finish of the race that she drank five bottles of water.

6. We had to be careful putting on the final bead because if our hands slipped the whole thing may not balance properly.

7. The robber escaped by running downstairs and avoiding all the policemen.

8. There was no fresh fruit at the market because the ship had failed to arrive from Britain.

9. At the beginning of the programme, I hadn't an idea what was happening.

10. All the citizens of Europe made it quite clear that they don't like the change in climate and they want something done about it.

11. They had a great view of the northern lights shining in the distance.

12. The circus master was injured when he lost control of the lions.

13. The hotel in which we were staying wasn't very pleasant.

14. It is important for the doctors to find a cure for that illness.

15. The general ordered his soldiers to attack the castle but they couldn't break through the huge wooden gate.

16. I wonder if I will be given another chance to catch the mouse.

17. The king tried to reach for the knives that he kept beside his throne.

18. I found it almost impossible to learn that poem off by heart.

19. Her daughter wishes to become a dentist when she grows up.

20. We stepped carefully when we tried to cross the dirty stream.

21. The farmer doesn't know whether the tractor's engine can be repaired or not.

22. Will you weigh that bunch of bananas and then follow me to the checkout?

23. I have to wear white gloves if I want to be the leader of the parade.

24. I arrived for my piano lessons on the wrong day.

25. Are you sure you are taping the correct programme?

26. He receives personal voice mail every morning.

27. It is not possible to push a wheel chair through the village because of the amount of potholes.

28. It's rather silly asking us to write ten sentences in our science copies.

29. I only prefer certain cheeses after my meal.

30. I wrote a letter about all the trucks using the roads in the valley, but so far I haven't had a reply.

31. Not every citizen knows all the capital cities in Europe.

32. After catching the disease, all the calves were killed and burned.

33. During the battle they had to blow up an important bridge.

34. My biggest problem in arithmetic is finding the highest common factor.

35. In my dream I was swimming with seals off the west coast of Ireland.

35. Our team dropped too many points this year but we hope to do better next season.

37. When I was cleaning the chimney, the brush got stuck.

38. When I become a famous film star I will invite all my friends to a huge feast.

39. All those terrible things she said about me are not true.

40. Everyone thought it would be better if I settled out of court.

41. He lifted the newspaper very slowly and knocked the flies off the ripe bananas.

42. When I was getting the area of the triangle I forgot to halve the base.

43. When he went to the clothesline there was no sign of his shirt.

44. She kept running upstairs and downstairs trying to lose weight.

45. If I took a huge bite of the apple I knew they would say I was greedy, so I took a tiny one instead.

46. I wasn't allowed to shine the silver teapot.

47. I really don't have any favourite subject in school…I hate them all.

48. He crept up quietly behind the baby and pushed him off the swing.

49. I was lying flat on my stomach so that I wouldn't be seen.

50. It wasn't a very good idea to hang the large picture at the bottom of the stairs.

51. 'Don't speak to me, don't even make a sound.'

52. 'You're too proud and I hope that you're knocked out of the quiz.'

53. We decided not to go on holidays during June or July because it would be too warm.

54. He fought a brave fight but finally he was beaten.

55. We managed to squeeze all the clothing into a square shaped case.

56. It was strange that none of the goats was killed in the terrible storm.

57. The roar from the rocket engines was so loud we thought we would go deaf.

58. He pulled off a tiny branch and the whole tree crashed down on his head.

59. He threw out the clock and it landed on a bush just below the window.

60. Last December when the roof was blown off our house, I stayed with my favourite aunt.

61. When I was sliding on a branch I tore my new trousers and my mother had to sew them.

62. The rabbits stamped on the loose soil to warn the others of great danger.

63. I could no longer lift the huge weight, but at least I tried.

64. When we finally tracked down the lost tribe we brought a tiny golden calf as a sign of friendship.

65. In April it wasn't pleasant when the northern winds blew so cold.

66. You're the last person to finish his bowl of soup.

67. You'll be in trouble if you don't fold the clothes and put them in the hotpress.

68. When the snow began to melt the whole place was in a terrible mess.

69. The body of the dead lamb was covered with flies.

70. There is always dirt under your nails so wash them carefully.

71. It was much too cold to sleep outdoors during October and November.

72. When the ice-cream van comes to our village the driver always blows the horn.

73. I didn't know whose turn it was to lift the main sail.

74. She awoke twice during the night with an awful headache.

75. The teacher went bananas when I dropped honey on his clothes.

76. From now on, my favourite comic will be available weekly.

77. The thick branch was useful when I was trying to beat my way through the forest.

78. It was plain to see that his drawing would win first prize.

79. There was great heat coming from the wall of the chimney.

80. When we got back to port we had to wipe our shoes on a special mat.

81. Mother was really thankful that I had hung out the clothes.

82. When I saw the teacher coming I pushed the page quickly into my trouser pocket.

83. Instead of signing his name on the form, he just drew a picture.

84. I especially love July and August because I am free from school.

85. There was terrible panic when the lion escaped from the circus.

86. The policemen said that there was no way the accident could have been avoided.

87. Although he knocked the bottle off the wall he was surprised that it didn't break.

88. It will not be possible to make certain changes to their programme.

89. The size of the tractor tyre is at least twice that of the truck.

90. It was very frightening when the engine below deck blew up.

91. I know he has received my letter and I can't understand why he hasn't replied.

92. My aunt believes that the castle is haunted ever since the soldier was killed.

93. You'll go deaf if you don't turn down the sound of the radio.

94. Do you remember that during the wet season lots of water came in through the roof?

95. Until the storm stopped, none of us could settle down to sleep in the tent.

96. It was clear to everyone that the dog would continue to bark until someone gave him a bone.

97. He had to dive into the flowerbed to avoid being attacked by the girls!

98. The king tried to escape but we managed to tie him to his throne.

99. My mother expected me to clean my room and she was very angry when she saw the amount of dust under the chair.

100. The storm was caused by strong northern winds blowing across the sea.

101. I was supposed to go to the doctor because I had a pain in my stomach.

102. When the policeman asked me to empty out my pockets he found my knife.

103. He thought it was a wonderful idea, but in my heart I knew it was impossible.

104. If he continues like that the lion will go out of control.

105. I can't imagine why he crept so close to the tractor.

106. It is important to look after your teeth properly.

107. What he said was probably true, but we weren't so sure.

108. The farmer has to be careful when he goes to feed the calves and goats.

109. He didn't want to burn his mouth so he blew on his soup.

110. The police had to make sure that the parade passed through the village without any trouble.

111. The robber left the upstairs rooms in a terrible mess.

112. When I tried writing my sentences, my pen started sliding all over my copy.

113. The soldiers tore their trousers when they dived through the hotel windows.

114. I tried to balance ten bottles on the teacher's head, but he wouldn't stand still.

115. I was in a terrible panic because I couldn't find the poem I was supposed to have ready.

116. Can you imagine how awful it must be to have a headache everyday?

117. He left his watch beside the door and when he returned someone had taken it.

118. There was only a slight chance that the soldiers would escape.

119. His feet were always sore, especially after a soccer match.

120. We were warned not to stand near the windows during the storm.

121. After the flood the people were not allowed back to their houses for two months.

122. Throughout February, he either goes to the pictures or to the theatre.

123. When he got to the hotel door the lorry driver blew his horn.

124. The baker had to battle his way through the crowd to get his prize.

125. When my cousin got a puncture, he had to push the car because he didn't have a spare wheel.

126. My daughter wants to have the chimney cleaned early in December.

127. I have a loose tooth and I need to go to the dentist as soon as possible.

128. It was a huge problem moving the piano upstairs.

129. I know I am not supposed to do it, but I cut squares and triangles on the bark of the tree.

130. There were lovely beads right around the side of the bowl.

131. When the coast was clear, we decided to cross the river.

132. If you continue to point at those citizens, they might get very angry.

133. We were very thankful when our country cousins arrived safely.

134. When we reached the stream we knew we had taken the wrong road.

135. I didn't understand the question, so there was no way I could answer it.

136. The strange illness was reported in every newspaper during January and February.

137. Which soccer teams do you follow in Ireland and Britain?

138. My aunt got very angry with me when I couldn't control the horse.

139. Those golden shoes are no longer available.

140. He couldn't be brought before the court because he was away on business.

141. You can't imagine how proud my family was when we won first prize in the quiz.

142. There was no real reason to believe either of their stories.

143. She didn't know whether to choose the golden or the silver ear-rings.

144. When I left the circus early, I got my hand stamped so that I could return later if I wanted to.

145. All the people were very thirsty after running through the forest.

146. I suppose that you believe everything he says is true?

147. When we followed him we tied our bicycles together near the track through the wood.

148. He wouldn't fill out the hotel form because he said he was so famous that everyone ought to know who he was.

149. Our doctor told us that honey was good for the heart.

150. There is no point in having the heating on, if you leave all the windows open.

151. I don't know which subject is worse, arithmetic or English.

152. The manager was wrong when he thought none of his players was injured.

153. Whose wheel is this, I wonder?

154. We tried really hard not to laugh when the teacher slipped on a banana and fell flat on his face.

155. They fought over the sweets because they were very greedy.

156. As they crept nearer the house they had an idea that they might be in great danger.

157. I had an awful dream about digging holes in the desert.

158. They couldn't control the disease and it spread very quickly from village to village.

159. They fog was so thick that they couldn't finish their game.

160. If I get the chance, I will probably change to a different team.

161. My mother warned that she would throw the television out the window, but I don't really think she is serious.

162. Although my pet mouse is usually good, he made an awful mess with the newspaper.

163. The main part of the sail came loose and was left lying across the deck.

164. The loud bang of the drum frightened me so much that I dropped the bowl of fruit on the floor.

165. He squeezed my stomach so hard that I was beginning to panic.

166. When we arrived at the science room the place was empty.

167. His glove got caught in the wheel of the bicycle and caused an accident.

168. In every capital city in Europe there seems to be a problem with hospital waiting lists.

169. They thought they would never escape from the flooded area.

170. Hundreds of people had to squeeze into the small theatre to receive their prizes.

171. Their daughter wants to be a long distance runner.

172. We were thankful that the weather was so pleasant during our holidays.

173. We have a wonderful library in our school where we can all settle down and read quietly.

174. Have you any idea whose piano this is?

175. I really have no favourite subject in school.. they are all boring!

176. Famous people don't usually have any worries about money.

177. The shop had no bread because the baker was not available for work.

178. He tore his trousers when he fell off the bicycle.

179. I don't see the point of having to learn all these poems.

180. The huge flood caused great damage throughout the country.

181. Every week we brought fresh flowers to the people in the hospital.

182. If you lose balance on a swing, you could be seriously injured.

183. The robber slipped his hand so quickly into my pocket that I did not notice.

184. If you continue to listen to very loud music, you might go deaf.

185. Although she has become very famous, she is still a close personal friend.

186. We wrote twelve letters to him but he never once replied.

187. They had to sign three forms at the airport before their clothing was returned to them.

188. At the end of October children usually have a great feast of fruit and nuts.

189. I had a very sick stomach after eating an unripe banana.

190. The damage done to the bicycle was much worse than we thought.

Corewords 4 – Dictation Exercises

(Set Two)

1. Wouldn't you get angry too, if the baker dropped a flour drum on your fingers?

2. We first thought that the punctured tyre caused the accident, but now there is no reason to believe that.

3. Can you remember the terrible floods that happened last January and February?

4. He is probably the most famous actor to ever work in that theatre.

5. We had lots of bottles of water because we knew the runners would be very thirsty when the race finished.

6. Before putting your weight on the chair, make sure that it is balanced properly.

7. The robber thought he could escape by running downstairs and avoiding the police.

8. We didn't receive any fresh fruit from Britain this morning because the ship never arrived in port.

9. The beginning of the programme was so strange that most of the viewers had no idea what to expect.

10. The change of climate hasn't suited all the citizens of Europe.

11. When the sunspots blew out we got a great view of the northern lights.

12. When the circus master saw a light shining in the distance, he lost control of the animals.

13. The hotel where we stayed was so pleasant that we will certainly return there again.

14. The doctors know that it is very important that a cure for the illness is found before people begin to panic.

15. In general, the soldiers don't find it too difficult to break through the large wooden gates of the castle.

16. I wonder how many more chances they need to catch the troublesome mouse.

17. The king always kept some knives beside his throne just in case that someone wanted to kill him.

18. I have decided that it is almost impossible to learn that poem off by heart.

19. I really don't know why his daughter wishes to be a dentist when she grows up.

20. When we reached the dirty stream, we stepped carefully from stone to stone.

21. I'm so busy at the moment that I don't know if I will be able to repair the farmer's tractor.

22. I want you to follow me to the checkout when you have weighed those bananas.

23. Why does the leader of the parade have to wear a pair of white gloves?

24. My mother forgot to tell me that my piano lessons had been changed and I arrive at the wrong time.

25. I am always afraid that when I am taping their favourite programme I won't do it properly.

26. It is correct to say that I receive personal voice mail each morning.

27. It is important that those potholes are repaired because it is very difficult for people with wheelchairs to move around the village.

28. Teacher warned us to keep our sentences neat and tidy in our science copies.

29. Certain truck drivers always choose the same cheeses with their meal.

30. I would much prefer not using those awful roads through the valley.

31. The quiz questions were all about the capital cities of Europe and I was unable to answer any of them.

32. The farmers had to kill and burn all the calves that caught foot and mouth disease.

33. Many soldiers were killed or injured during the battle for the important bridge.

34. It's a pain in the neck trying to work our arithmetic based on the highest common factor.

35. I had a wonderful dream that I was swimming with seals off the West Coast of Ireland.

36. Our team must play better next season, because we dropped far too many points last year.

37. Dad went bananas when the cleaning brush got stuck in the chimney.

38. The famous film star invited most of his friends to a huge feast by the swimming pool.

39. Not one of those terrible things they said about me is true.

40. He wouldn't settle the case out of court as he thought there was a chance that he could get more money.

41. He lifted the newspaper carelessly and knocked over the bowl of bananas.

42. I could never remember to halve the base when I was getting the area of a triangle.

43. He didn't hang his shirts on the line, as there was no sign of the rain stopping.

44. A good way to lose weight is to keep moving up and down the stairs.

45. Instead of taking a tiny bite of the apple, I knew the greedy child would take a huge one.

46. Although the silver teapot was always in use, nobody was ever allowed to shine it.

47. I hate when my aunt and uncle ask me about my favourite school subject.

48. The baby crept quietly behind her mother and pushed her into the pram!

49. Although he was trying to hide by lying flat on his stomach, everyone knew he was there.

50. Whose bright idea was it to hang that picture at the bottom of the stairs?

51. The people next door don't speak to me anymore because my car makes too much noise when I return in the middle of the night.

52. I wasn't careful enough with the answers and I got knocked out of the quiz very early.

53. The weather was so awful during June and July that we decided that we wouldn't go anywhere on holidays.

54. They fought bravely but were finally beaten by a much stronger team.

55. When he flies away to Europe he always manages to squeeze his clothing into a square shaped case that's years old.

56. A stranger came into our village during the storm and stole some of our goats.

57. If we are not careful, the noise from those engines could deafen us.

58. When the tiny car crashed, it knocked down the whole tree.

59. He was hiding in a bush just below the window when someone inside threw a clock at him.

60. During the storm last December, my favourite aunt was blown off the apple tree!

61. If my mother caught me sliding down the branch again, she said she wouldn't repair my trousers.

62. Although it was dangerous, some rabbits stamped on the loose soil to warn the others.

63. He was upset when he couldn't lift the huge weight, but at least he tried.

64. They brought a tiny golden calf to the lost tribe as a sign of friendship and to show they weren't going to cause any trouble.

65. April wasn't a very pleasant month because the cold northern winds kept blowing.

66. The last person to finish his bowl of soup must wash all the dishes.

67. If you don't fold your clothes and tidy your room, you could be in mighty trouble.

68. The whole street is always in a terrible mess when the snow begins to melt.

69. We better put something over the body of the dead lamb before it is covered with flies.

70. Wash under your nails carefully and get rid of all that dirt.

71. You're not allowed to sleep out in the garden during October or November, as it's much too cold.

72. Why does the ice-cream driver always blow his horn when he comes through the village?

73. 'I don't care whose turn it is, I want the main sail lifted now,' roared the captain.

74. Twice this month, I awoke from my dream with a terrible headache.

75. Just because I dropped his new silver watch into the water, the teacher went bananas.

76. Is your favourite comic available weekly or monthly?

77. A good saw is useful when you are trying to cut through a very thick branch.

78. His drawing of the animals in the forest is sure to win first prize.

79. All the people stood around because there was great heat coming from the wall of the chimney.

80. Because of the disease we had to wipe our shoes on a special mat when we arrived at the port.

81. When my mother arrived home and saw that I had washed and hung out the clothes, she was very thankful.

82. I quickly pushed all the money into my trouser pocket because I thought it might be stolen.

83. He was unable to sign the form so he drew on it instead!

84. Children love school especially during July and August!

85. When the elephants escaped from the circus, it caused terrible panic in the city.

86. I don't think there was any way that I could have avoided the accident.

87. She was certainly surprised that the bottle didn't break when I knocked it off the table.

88. They don't believe that it is possible to make any more changes to their radio programme.

89. The front tyre of the tractor is at least twice the size of the back one.

90. It was very frightening below deck when the first engine blew up.

91. He said he hadn't received any letter I had written and that was the reason he never replied.

92. Everyone believes the castle is haunted since the day the soldier killed my aunt.

93. If the sound of the radio is too loud, it may cause deafness.

94. Do you remember last season when the water flooded in through the hole in the roof?

95. It was almost impossible to settle down to sleep in the tent until the storm stopped.

96. It was clear that if someone had given the dog a bone sooner, he wouldn't have continued to bark through the night.

97. The pop star hid behind the wall to avoid being attacked by the girls.

98. We tried to stop the king from escaping by tying him to the throne.

99. If your mother expects you to clean your room, don't make her angry by brushing the dirt under the chair.

100. When the strong northern winds blew across the sea, they caused terrible flooding all along the East Coast.

101. I was supposed to revisit the doctor if my stomach pains returned.

102. The policeman found my penknife when he asked me to empty my pockets.

103. I thought it was impossible but my friends believed it was a wonderful idea.

104. If he continues to train the lion like that, he will lose control.

105. Can you imagine why he crept so close to the tractor wheel?

106. Dentists keep telling us that cleaning our teeth is very important.

107. It could probably happen but we weren't really so sure.

108. It is true that you must be careful when feeding the calves and goats.

109. He blew on his tea because he didn't want to chance burning his mouth.

110. The parade passed through the village without any trouble because of all the police that were present.

111. The rooms downstairs were left in an awful mess after the robbery.

112. The teacher couldn't write any sentences on the board because his hand kept slipping all over the place.

113. The children were careful not to tear their trousers when they climbed in through the broken window.

114. I tried to balance three bottles on top of each other but I couldn't manage it.

115. We began to panic when we couldn't find the homework we were supposed to have ready.

116. We can't imagine how awful it must be to always have a headache.

117. When he returned to his room to watch his favourite programme, he discovered that his television had been stolen.

118. We had only a slight chance of escape before the soldiers came back.

119. My lips get very sore especially if the weather is cold.

120. We were warned to close all the windows and doors before the storm began.

121. They weren't allowed back to their houses for months because there was still a danger of flooding.

122. January is a great time of year to go to the theatre.

123. The hotel manager warned the lorry driver not to blow his horn.

124. He wasn't too happy when he found out that he had to battle his way through the crowd to get his prize money.

125. My cousin hasn't got a spare wheel and I don't travel with him in case he gets a puncture.

126. Why does your daughter always want to get the chimney cleaned in early December?

127. If your tooth is loose, go to the dentist as soon as possible.

128. It must have been a huge problem getting the piano downstairs.

129. You are not supposed to cut squares or triangles in the bark of any tree.

130. The coloured beads around the side of the bowl looked lovely.

131. When you decide to cross the river, make sure the coast is clear.

132. Those citizens might get angry if you continue to point at them.

133. When my cousins arrived in this country they thanked me for the money I sent.

134. If you finish up at the stream, it means you must have followed the wrong track.

135. How am I expected to answer these questions if I don't understand them?

136. Do you remember the news reports about that strange illness last January and February?

137. Why do so many people in Ireland follow soccer teams in Britain?

138. I knew my uncle would get mad with me when I couldn't control the horse.

139. What do you mean that those golden shoes are no longer available in the shops?

140. The court case was stopped until he returned from a business trip in Europe.

141. I can imagine that your family was delighted to win the table quiz.

142. Their stories were so different that it was impossible to believe either of them.

143. The women couldn't decide whether to choose the gold or silver watch.

144. If you leave the circus early you can get your hand stamped in case you wish to return later.

145. Running through the large forest would make me very tired and thirsty.

146. I suppose your friends believe everything you say is true!

147. When we reached the track through the woods, we got off our bicycles and followed on foot.

148. Famous people always get someone else to fill in the forms when they arrive at hotels.

149. The school doctor tried to tell us that homework was good for the heart, but we didn't believe him.

150. It's so warm outdoors; there is no point in turning on the heating.

151.   Which is worse, arithmetic or English?

152.   The manager thought that three of his best players were injured, but he was wrong.

153.   We began to wonder whose horse was in the field.

154.   If your teacher slipped on a banana, would you try hard not to laugh?

155.   The four greedy children fought over the sweets.

156.   I had an idea that if we crept near the haunted house it might be dangerous.

157.   We spent months digging holes in the desert looking for gold and silver.

158.   If the doctors can't control the disease, it will spread from village to village.

159.   The game was stopped because of the thick fog.

160.   I would love to change to a different team, but I probably won't get a chance.

161.   Do you believe my mother is serious when she promised to throw the television out the window?

162.   My pet mouse always makes a terrible mess with newspapers.

163.   The main sail came loose during the storm and we had awful trouble getting it off the deck.

164.   We got such a fright that we dropped our bowl of fruit.

165.   I got in a panic when he squeezed my stomach too tightly.

166.   When we arrived early in school, everywhere was empty except for the science room.

167.   Be careful, because if your glove gets caught in the wheel of the bicycle it could cause an accident.

168.   No matter what capital city you visit in Europe, people are angry about hospital waiting lists.

169.   It wasn't possible for everyone to escape from the flooded area.

170.   Why do children have to squeeze into small theatres every year to accept their prizes?

171.   If your daughter wants to be a long distance runner, she will need to do lots of training.

172.   Our holidays were very pleasant because the weather was really beautiful.

173.   It's wonderful to settle down quietly in the school library and have a good read.

174.   They had no idea whose piano fell off the lorry.

175.   School subjects are so boring; I don't understand how anyone could have a favourite one.

176.   When you become famous you won't have any worries about money!

177.   If the baker is unavailable for work the shops may run out of bread.

178.   I fell off the bicycle but my trousers weren't torn!

179.   Can anyone tell me the point of learning these hundred poems off by heart?

180.   There was terrible damage throughout the country because of the floods.

181.   We make sure that everyone in hospital receives a bunch of fresh flowers each week.

182.   He was seriously injured when he lost his balance on the swing.

183.   I didn't notice a thing when the robber slipped his hand into my pocket and stole my money.

184.   The sound coming from the rocket was deafening.

185.   A close friend of mine has become a very famous theatre actor.

186.   He never replied to any letters he received.

187.   If they didn't sign the forms at the airport, their clothing in the cases would not be returned to them.

188.   Children usually enjoy their feast of fruit and nuts at the end of October.

189.   If that banana isn't ripe you might have an upset stomach in the morning.

190.   We thought the damage to the building couldn't be worse, but we were wrong.

Appendix 8
Corewords 3 / 4 – Revision Exercises

1. My grandmother and grandfather went to the library yesterday. Before they went on holidays they wanted to find out as much as they could about wild animals. On the way home they stopped off to have some chicken and chips. Grandfather wanted to buy some ice cream as well but he wasn't allowed, as he was getting too heavy. When they had finished their meal they saw an awful crash between a lorry and a car. Between ninety and a hundred sheep escaped from the lorry and ran along the street. The police had a difficult time when they tried to catch them. (103)

2. When the farmer lifted the potatoes off the back of the truck he didn't expect the bottom to fall out of the bag. They rolled everywhere. When the children saw what had happened they started laughing. This made him very angry and he threw a potato at them. The children ducked when they saw the potato coming but it went right through the school window. To make things worse, the teacher was sitting at his table and he was hit on the head. He had to be brought to hospital. The doctor told him to stop crying because he would be all right. The children were happy because they had a free day.(113)

3. In the beginning it seemed like a great idea to go on holiday to a desert island. The pictures in the catalogue looked very inviting. However, they had awful trouble getting there. Then, when they arrived they were very surprised because it was not what they had expected. Instead of beautiful golden sand and clear water the place was a mess. There was no telephone so they couldn't make their feelings known to their travel agent. They decided they would have to make the best of it and started to look for a clean place to stay. Although the weather was lovely they couldn't help feeling cheated, but they were going to make sure that their money was going to be returned to them. (124)

4. It is usual for teachers to bring their class on a tour. Sometimes they might visit the museum or travel to some place in the country. After our last tour, the teacher promised that he would never ever take us anywhere again. We don't really know why he got so upset. After all, it really was an accident when we pushed him into the pool. How were we supposed to know that he didn't have a change of clothes and that he would have to sit on the bus all day? To tell the truth it wouldn't have made any difference if we had known. We are hoping he will change his mind. Even if he doesn't, we will never forget the look on his face as he climbed out of that pool. (134)

5. The four lorries hurried across the bridge high up in the mountains. So far it had been a difficult journey. They had not expected so many things to go wrong. Apart from all the trouble and delays, something else was also on their mind. They had a feeling that they were being watched ever since they had arrived in the country. At first they thought nothing about the white truck that always seemed to be around. The drivers decided that the two lorries at the back would pretend to have broken down and allow the white truck to pass. Then they would start up again and trap the truck in the middle. (113)

6. Dad went bananas when he arrived home. He had completely forgotten that he allowed his son to have a sleepover. All he wanted was a nice quiet evening and instead all he got was non-stop noise. He couldn't listen to his favourite radio programme. He wanted to watch the car racing on television but that too was out of the question because someone had hooked up his play-station to it. His son had promised that he was only having two friends staying, but he finished up with twelve. Dad knew that it was going to be a very long night and he just prayed that nothing would happen and that everyone would behave. (114)

7. Our aunt was always warning us to be careful with the sharp knives in the kitchen. She hated to see us using them. She was a nurse in a big hospital and had seen many people arriving there with badly cut hands. One day we were bored and we decided to play a trick on her. We found a half-empty bottle of tomato sauce and put it on our hands and clothes. Then we started screaming. She rushed in the kitchen and almost fainted at the sight. She became very angry with us. She had visited to surprise us with concert tickets for our favourite group, but when she discovered what was going on she said she would give them to our country cousins instead. (126)

8. I never want to read stories about princes and princesses again. I am really fed up with them. Did you ever notice that it is some brave prince who usually killed those poor dragons? For his troubles he then probably married the beautiful princess. They always seem to live happily ever after and that really makes me sick. I feel sorry for those dragons because they were wonderful creatures and never did anything much except guard some treasure or maybe eat a few people. I would just love to read a story where the dragon is the winner instead of being the loser. Maybe I will have to write it myself and have an ending that no one will be expecting. (122)

9. It happened all of a sudden. I had just picked up the sugar from the shelf and was heading to get some vegetables when a bright light hit me right between the eyes. I couldn't move. I tried to call for my parents but nothing happened. People passed me as if I wasn't there. I even overheard my father saying that I couldn't be very long and would return soon with the sugar and potatoes. I reached out to touch him but my hand went right through his arm. Something awful was happening. I decided to go back to where I got the sugar to find out what caused this. I put the sugar back on the exact spot where I found it, but nothing happened. It was then that I saw it …. a tiny creature calling me into a wonderful golden light. (144)

10. Our aunt and uncle keep lots of ponies on their farm. Each one of my three cousins has to spend a certain amount of time helping every week. They were all given different jobs but they usually change twice a month. The most difficult one is to clean out the stables. They all hate when it is their turn. I think it is the smell that gets to them. Not only do they have to clean out the manure but also they have to spread it on the lawn and roses. I went to help them once but I slipped and fell straight into a big pile. My uncle had to hose me down before my aunt would allow me into the house. Although I realise that some insects live in it, I cannot understand how it helps to give us beautiful roses. (144)

11. The robbers threw all the mailbags into the centre of the sorting room. They ordered the workers to open them. Some of the postmen had been working throughout the night and were quite tired. The robbers didn't care. If anyone refused to do what they were told they were tied up and tape was put over their mouth. The robbers knew they had to be quick. The next group of workers would be arriving shortly. When one of the robbers had counted out fifteen thousand pounds they seemed to be happy with that. As they were leaving they fired some shots into the air and warned that nobody was to follow them. They escaped in a blue van and to this day they have not been caught. (128)

12. 'I am sure that must be eleven times this year that we have found dead fish', said Tom to his friend, as he rushed home to tell his parents. Time after time his father had reported it to the manager of the local factory, but all he heard was one excuse after the other. This time would be different as he could now prove that it was the factory's fault that the fish were dying. Although he didn't tell anyone, he had lately spent a great deal of time watching where the factory pipes emptied into the river. He had brought his video camera with him and now all he has the evidence he needs. He decided he wouldn't visit the manager again and instead he passed on the video evidence to the guards. (134)

13. Although they had a beautiful view from the top of the mountain, they knew they couldn't stay much longer. The clouds were closing in and the weather was changing. Over the past number of years many people had been trapped until the weather cleared. Some had not been so lucky and other climbers later discovered their bodies. They decided to start down. They knew it was going to be tough in the beginning but they hadn't expected it to be so dangerous. They couldn't believe how strong the wind was and the driving rain had them all worried. As they move slowly and carefully they were glad that they had tied themselves together with a rope. It was a long slow journey but they were all delighted to reach the bottom safely. (133)

14. They had always wanted to see their favourite television programme being made but they never realised that they were going to be part of it. It all began when the families went on their usual Saturday picnic. When they arrived they found it difficult to find a parking space. Then they noticed a huge man running towards them. He was very angry and saying awful words. He had expected five other actors to arrive but they never showed up. He explained that they were trying to take some shots. When their mother heard this she fainted because she thought he had a gun! When she recovered he suggested that they could stand in for these actors. They thought about it for a while and then agreed. They got fifty pounds each and forgot all about having a picnic. (139)

15. I was beginning to believe that our family was unusual. First of all we had no telephone or television. We only had a very old radio to help us keep up with the outside world. Our relations rarely came to visit us. When they were invited to dinner they always had some excuse not to turn up. The last time my grandparents arrived we all missed lunch because granny got lost. We found her twenty minutes later in the middle of a field. She was angry with us because she said she knew exactly where she was! She said that she was just talking to the lovely ponies. She finally allowed us to bring her home when we promised to cook her favourite meal. I do get worried about her sometimes and I often wonder if other families have a granny like ours. (144)

16. It was a huge surprise to hear that my friend's business was in trouble. It wasn't really his fault as he had tried everything possible to keep it going. He now had to break the story to his fifty workers and he certainly wasn't looking forward to that. Right now he would probably prefer to be somewhere else. Although the workers realised that things were tough, they would not be expecting to be out of a job. He decided the only way to break the news was to gather everyone in one large group and tell them exactly what had happened. He was hoping that they would understand and that the meeting would not be too difficult. (118)

17. The loud sound woke him. Robert could tell that his brother, who was sleeping in the bottom bunk, had heard nothing and was still fast asleep. Reaching out to turn on the light beside his bed, he stopped suddenly as he heard the sound again. He decided to stay in the dark and slipped quietly out of bed. Although he crept carefully towards the window, he tripped over his science book and lost his balance. Things wouldn't have been so terrible if he hadn't grabbed at the curtains to stop himself from falling. As he hit the floor, the curtain pole went crashing through the window. He picked himself up slowly and looked out. He certainly didn't expect to see the pole sticking through the window of the policeman's van and the curtains thrown over the policeman's head. (137)

18. I always dream about being a famous video game inventor. I spend hours playing with my play station. I know many experts say that this is bad for my health but what else can I do? My brothers and sisters are much older than I am and all my school friends live too far away. My parents are always giving out to me but I think they are over-reacting. I have a wonderful idea for my new game and it is almost finished. With a few certain changes it will be perfect. It is not like those other boring games with nothing but beaten soldiers falling all over the place. When I sort out these little problems it will certainly be on the best sellers list within a few months. When all that money starts to roll in, I wonder will everyone still say that I have been wasting my time. (152)

References

Adams, M.J., (1990), _Beginning to Read_. (Cambridge, Massachusetts: MIT Press).

Alston, J., (1994) _Spelling Helpline – A Guide for Parents, Teachers, Adults and Children with Spelling Difficulties_. (Manchester: Dextral).

Amundson, S.J. (2005) Prewriting and handwriting skills. In Case-Smith (Ed.) _Occupational Therapy for Children_ (London: Mosby).

Anderson, P.S., and Lapp, D., (1988), _Language Skills in Elementary Education_. 4th Edition. (New York: MacMillan).

Apel, K. (2002) Toward an Understanding of Literacy Issues in Multicultural School. (The American Speech-Language-Hearing Association).

Ardvidson, G.L., (1977), _Learning to Spell_. (Oxford: Pergamon Press).

Barone, D., (1992), Whatever happened to spelling? In _Reading Psychology_. Vol. 13, No. 1. pp. 1-17.

Barr, J., (1985), Understanding _Children's Spelling_. (Edinburgh: Scottish Council for Research in Education).

Beard, R., (1993) Teaching Literacy: Balancing Perspectives (Sevenoaks, Kent: Hodder & Stoughton).

Bell, G.H., (1994), _Action Research, Special Needs and School Development_. (London: David Fulton Publishers).

Bentley, D., (1990), _Teaching Spelling: Some Questions Answered_. (Earley: University of Reading).

Beery, K, (1992) Wide Range Asst., Visual Motor Abilities (Cleveland: Modern Curriculum Press).

Bissex, G.L., (1980), _GNYS AT WRK, A Child Learns to Write and Read._ (Cambridge, Mass: Harvard University Press).

Blumenfeld, S, L. (1994). How Should We Teach Our Children to Write? The Blumenfeld Education Letter, Vol. 9, No. 9.

Bradley, L., (1981a), The organisation of motor patterns for spelling: an effective remedial strategy for backward readers. In _Developmental Medicine and Child Neurology_. Vol. 23, pp 83-97.

Bradley, L. & Bryant, P., (1985), _Children's Reading Problems_. (Oxford: Blackwell Press).

Bragg, M., (2003) _The Adventure of English – the Biography of Language_. (London: Hodder & Stoughton).

Brown, G., and Ellis, N., (1994), Issues in spelling research – an overview. In Brown, G. and Ellis, N., _Handbook of Spelling – Theory, Process and Intervention_. (Chicester: Wiley & Sons).

Brown, E. N., (1990) Children with spelling and writing difficulties: an alternative approach. In Pumfrey, P. & Elliott, C.D.(Eds.) _Children's Difficulties in Reading, Spelling and Writing_. (Basingstoke, Hants.: Falmer Press).

Bruner, J., (1996) _Towards a Theory of Instruction_ (Harvard).

Bullock Report, (1975), _A Language for Life_. Report of the Committee of Inquiry into Reading and the Use of English. (London: H.M. Stationery Office).

Byers, R. & Rose, R (1995) Planning the Curriculum for Pupils with Special Educational Needs: A Practical Guide (London: David Fulton Publishers).

Carless, S., (1989), Spelling in the primary school curriculum. In P. Pinsent (Ed.) _Spotlight On Spelling – Current Approaches for Teachers_. (Oxon: A.B. Academic Press).

Cataldo, S. & Ellis, N. (1990), The role of spelling in learning to read. In _Language and Education_. Vol. 4, No. 1. pp. 1-28.

Chandler, K., (2000) Squaring up to Spelling: A teacher research group surveys parents.
In *Language Arts*. Vol. 77, No. 3 (January).

Chomsky, C., (1970), Reading, writing and phonology. In *Harvard Educational Review*. Vol. 40.

Clark, L., (1994), *Help Your Child with Reading and Writing*. A parents' handbook.
(London: Headway: Hodder & Stoughton).

Cook, W.A. & O'Shea, M.V. (1914), *The Child and his Spelling*. (Bobbs-Merrell: Indianapolis).

Corley, BMG (2001) In *Dyslexia Review*. The spelling strategies of children with specific
learning difficulties. (Vol. 12, No. 3 Summer).

Cotton, P., (1992), Let's all join up. In *Child Education*. April edition,
(Leamington Spa: Scholastic Publications).

Cox, C.B., (1988), *English for Ages 5 to 11*. (HMSO).

Cripps, C., (1985), *Stile Spelling Programme*. (Wisbech: Learning Development Aids).

Cripps, C. & Cox, R., (1989) *Joining the ABC* (Cambs: LDA... Learning Development Aids).

Cripps, C., (1978), *Catchwords, Ideas for Teaching Spelling*.
(London: Harcourt, Brace & Jovanovich).

Cripps, C. & Peters, M., (1990), *Catchwords*. (London: Harcourt, Brace & Jovanovich).

Cripps, C. & Bushell, R., (1994), *Spelling : A Visual Approach*
(Sheffield: Home and School Council).

Cripps, C., (1995), *A Hand for Spelling* (New Edition) (Cambs: Learning Development Aids).

Culligan, B., (1993), The Teaching of Spelling, Anybody for 'Fonix'. In *Learn Journal,*
(Dublin: Association of Remedial Teachers of Ireland).

Culligan, B., (1996), Investigation of spelling achievement in the Greater Dublin Area.
In *Learn Journal*, (Dublin: Association of Remedial Teachers of Ireland:
also in *Education Today*, Dublin: I.N.T.O. Autumn/Winter Edition).

Culligan, B., (1997), *Improving Children's Spelling*. (Dublin: Culligan).

Culligan, B. (2000), Putting spelling in context. In Bates, Galvin, Swan & Williams (Eds.)
Words Alone. (Dublin: University College Dublin Press).

Czerniewska, P., (1992), *Learning About Writing* (Oxford: Blackwell).

Daw, P., Smith, J., & Wilkinson, S., (1997), Factors associated with high standards of spelling in
years R-4. In *English in Education*, Vol. 31, No.1, Spring. pp. 36-47.

Department of Education, (1971), *Curaclam na Bunscoile, Cuid 1*
(Dublin: The Stationery Office).

Department of Education and Science & National Council for Curriculum and Assessment
(1999), *Primary School Curriculum* (Dublin: The Stationery Office).

Dodds, J. (1994), Spelling skills and causal attributions in children.
In *Educational Psychology in Practice*. Vol. 10, No. 2.

Educational Company, (1993), *Spelling Workshop*. (Dublin: Educational Company).

Ehri, L.C. & Wilce, L.S. (1980), The influence of orthography on readers' conceptualisation of
the phonemic structure of words. *In Applied Psycholinguistics*, 1, pp. 371-385.

Ellis, N. & Cataldo, S., (1990), The role of spelling in learning to read.
In *Language and Education*. Vol. 4, No. 1. pp. 1-27.

Feiler, A., & Gibson, H., (1997), Spelling mnemonics: a critical commentary on the use of
mnemonics as a spelling strategy with primary – aged children. In *Education 3-13*.
Vol 25, No. 2.

Fernald, G.M., (1943), *Remedial Techniques in the Basic School Subjects*.
(New York: McGraw – Hill).

Fitzgerald, J.A., (1953), The Teaching of Spelling. In *Elementary English*. Vol. 30, pp. 79-85.

Folens, (1986), *Spellings and Tables*. (Dublin: Folens Publishing Company).

France, L., Topping, K. & Revell, K. (1993), Parent tutored Cued Spelling. *Support for Learning*. Vol. 8, No. 1. pp. 11-15.

Fresch, M.J., (2000) What we learned from Josh: sorting out word sorting. In *Language Arts*. Vol. 77, No. 3 (January).

Frith, U., (1980), Unexpected spelling problems.
In Frith, U., (Ed.) *Cognitive Processes in Spelling*, (London: Academic Press).

Geedy, P.S., (1975), What research tells us about spelling. In *Elementary English*. February. pp 233-236.

Gentry, J.R. (1981), Learning to spell developmentally. In *The Reading Teacher* Vol. 34, January. pp. 378-381.

Gentry, J.R., (1987), *Spel.. Is a Four Letter Word*. (Leamington Spa: Scholastic).

Gentry, J.R. & Gillet, J.W. (1993) Teaching Kids to Spell. (Portsmouth NH: Heinemann).

Gildea, M.T., (1991) *Self-concept in Children with Specific Learning Difficulties*. (Unpublished M. Ed. Thesis).

Gill, C.H. & Scharer, P.L. (1996). 'Why do they get it on Friday and misspell it on Monday'? Teachers inquiring about their students as spellers. *Language Arts* 73.

Gladstone, K (2000) Illegibility: can America write? Some facts on our handwriting crisishttp://www.global2000.net/handwritingrepair/KateHwR.html).

Goldstein, N. (1994), *Toys, Play and Child Development*. (New York: Cambridge University Press).

Goswami, U., (1988), Children's use of analogy in learning to spell. In *British Journal of Developmental Psychology*. Vol. 6, Part 1. pp. 21-33.

Goswami, U., & Bryant, P., (1990), *Phonological Skills and Learning to Read*. Essays in Developmental Psychology. (East Sussex: LEA).

Goswami, U., (1995) The role of analogies in reading development. In Shiel, Ní Dhálaigh & O'Reilly, (Eds.) *Reading Development to Age 15 – Overcoming Difficulties,* (Dublin: Reading Association of Ireland).

Goswami, U., (1992). Phonological factors in spelling development. In *Journal of Child Psychology and Psychiatry*. Vol. 33, No. 6.

Goulandris, N. K., (1996) Assessing reading and spelling skills. In Snowling, M. & Stackhouse, J. Eds. (1996), *Dyslexia, Speech and Language,*(London: Whur).

Graham, S., Harris, K.R., Mac Arthur, C. & Schwartz, S., (1998), Writing instruction. In B.Y.L. Wong (Ed.) *Learning About Learning Disabilities*, 2nd Edition. (Toronto: Academic Press). pp 391-423.

Graves, D.H., (1983), *Writing: Teachers and Children at Work*. (Exeter: Heinemann).

Gulliford, R., (1985), *Teaching Children with Learning Difficulties*. (Windsor: NFER – Nelson).

Hanna, P, Hanna, J., Hodges, R., and Rudorf, E. (1966) *Phoneme grapheme Correspondences as Cues to Spelling* (Washington; Government printing office).

Hannon, P., (1995), *Literacy, Home and School: Research and Practice in Teaching Literacy with Parents*. (London: Faber Press).

Henderson, A., (1994), Mathematical Concepts, Difficult or Easy? In *Learn Journal*. (Dublin: Association of Remedial Teachers of Ireland).

Henderson, E.H., & Templeton, S. (1986), A developmental perspective of formal spelling instruction through alphabet, pattern, and meaning. In *Elementary School Journal* (University of Chicago). Vol. 60, No. 3.

Horn, E. (1926) *A Basic Vocabulary of 10,000 words most Commonly Used in Writing* (Iowa: University of Iowa).

Humphreys, T., (1993), *A Different Kind of Teacher*. (Cork: Humphreys).

Jarman, C., (1979), *The Development of Handwriting Skills*. (Oxford: Blackwell).

Joss, J. (2001) "BJU Pre-Cursive and Cursive Handwriting." *Teacher to Teacher,* Vol. 5, No. 1, April.

Jowett, S., Baginsky, M., & MacNeil, M.M. (1991), *Building Bridges: Parental Involvement in Schools*. (Windsor: NFER-Nelson).

Kramer, C., (1996), Individualised spelling: a teacher's journal. In *Primary Voices K-6.* Vol. 4, No. 4 November. pp 28-32.

Lamme, L. L. (1979). Handwriting in an early childhood curriculum. *Young Children, 35*(1), 20-27.

Landy, J.M. & Burridge, K.R. (1999) *Fine Motor Skills and Handwriting Activities for Young Children* (New York: Centre for Applied Research in Education).

Lerner, J. W., (1985), *Learning Difficulties*, 5th Edition. (Boston: Houghton Mifflin).

Levine, M.D.,(1987) Developmental Variation and Learning Disorders. (Massachusetts: Educators Publishing Services Inc.).

Lurçat, L. (1980) *Etudes de L'Acte Graphique* (Paris, Mouton).

MacArthur, C. A., Graham, S., Haynes, J. B., & DeLaPaz, S. (1996). Spell checkers and students with learning disabilities: Performance comparisons and impact on spelling. In *Journal of Special Education*, 30, pp. 35-57.

McGuinness, D. (1998) *Why Children Can't Read, and what to do about it*. (London: Penguin).

McNally, J. & Murray, W. (1968) *Key Words to Literacy and the Teaching of Reading* (2nd Edition). (London: Schoolmaster Publishing).

Makay, F (2003) *Teaching Spelling* (Wiltshire: Hopscotch Educational Publishing).

Manning, M.L. (1988). Handwriting instruction. In *Childhood Education* (Vol. 65, pp. 112-114).

Marschark, M. (1993) *Psychological Development of Deaf Children* (Oxford: Oxford University Press).

Medwell, J & Wray D (2007) Primary English: Teaching Theory and Practice (Achieving QTS) (UK: Learning Matters Ltd).

Merttens, R., Newland, A., & Webb, S. (1996) *Learning in Tandem – Involving Parents in Their Children's Education*. (Warwickshire: Scholastic).

Moats, L.C. (1998), Reading, writing and spelling disabilities in the middle grades. In B.Y.L. Wong (Ed.) *Learning About Learning Disabilities*, 2nd Edition. (Toronto: Academic Press). pp 367-389.

Moatts, L.C. (2005). How Spelling Supports Reading (In *American Educator* – Winter Edition 2005/2006).

Montessori, M., (1972), *The Discovery of the Child*. (New York: Ballantine).

Montgomery, D., (1997), *Spelling, Remedial Strategies*. (London: Cassell Educational).

Moseley, D., (1990), Suggestions for helping children with spelling problems. In Pumpfey, P. & Elliott, C.D. (Eds.) *Children's Difficulties in Reading, Spelling and Writing*. (Basingstoke, Hants: Falmer Press).

Moseley, D., (1989), How lack of confidence in spelling affects children's written expression. In *Educational Psychology in Practice*. Vol. 5. No. 1.

Mountford, J., (1998), *An Insight Into English Spelling*. (London: Hodder & Stoughton).

Mudd, N., (1994), *Effective Spelling: A Practical Guide for Teachers*. (London: Hodder & Stoughton – In association with United Kingdom Reading Association).

Mudd, N., (1997), *The Power of Words: Guidelines for Improving Spelling and Vocabulary*. (Shepreth: United Kingdom Reading Association).

Nisbet, S.D., (1941), The Scientific Investigation of Spelling Instruction in Scottish Schools. In *British Journal of Educational Psychology*. xi, 150.

Olsen, J.Z. (1998) *Handwriting Without Tears*: Kindergarten Teacher's Guide (http://www.hwtears.com).

O'Sullivan, O. & Thomas, A. (2000) *Understanding Spelling* (London: CLPE).

Pain, H., (1980), *Analysis of Errors in Spelling*. (Edinburgh: Department of Artificial Intelligence, University of Edinburgh) Working paper No. 61.

Pape, B., (1999) Involving parents lets students and parents win. In *The Education Digest.* Vol. 64, No. 4, pp. 47-51.

Parkinson, C., McLaughlin – Cook, N., & Melling, R., (1994), Year 6 spelling: group tests vs. personal programmes. In *Educational Psychology In Practice*. Vol. 9, No. 4.

Peters, M. L. (1970), *Success in Spelling*, (Cambridge: Institute of Education).

Peters, M. L., (1975), *Diagnostic and Remedial Spelling Manual*. (London: MacMillan Education Ltd).

Peters, M. L., (1985), *Spelling, Caught or Taught*? *A New Look* (London: Routledge & Kegan Paul).

Peters, M. L. & Smith, B., (1993), *Spelling in Context*. (Berkshire: NFER Nelson).

Phenix, J., & Scott – Dunne, D., (1994), *Spelling for Parents*. (London: Picadilly Press).

Ramsden, M, (1993), *Rescuing Spelling*. (Southgate: Credition).

Read, G., (1991), Arriving at a spelling policy. In *Child Education*. May. (Leamington Spa: Scholastic Publications).

Reason, R. & Boote, R., (1994), *Helping Children with Reading and Spelling.* (London: Routledge).

Redfern, A., (1993), *Practical ways to Teach Spelling*. (University of Reading: Reading and Language Information Centre).

Redfern, A., (1995), *Spelling and Language Skills*. (Leamington Spa: Scholastic).

Roberts, G., (1989), *Teaching Children to Read and Write* (Oxford: Blackwell).

Sassoon, R., (1990), *Handwriting – The Way to Teach It*. (Cheltenham: Stanley Thornes).

Schickedanz, J.A & Casbergue, R.M. (2004) *Writing in Preschool*. (International Reading Association).

Schonell, F.J., (1965), *Backwardness in Basic Subjects*. 10th Ed. (Edinburgh: Oliver and Boyd).

Schlagal, R.C. (1989) Constancy and change in spelling development. In *Reading Psychology, 10*. pp 233-253.

Scragg, D. G. (1974) *A History of English Spelling*. (Manchester: Manchester University Press).

Sheahan, M., (1998), *A Study of the Teaching of Spelling in a Selected Number of Primary Schools in the Republic of Ireland*. (M. Ed. Thesis) Unpublished.

Sipe, R.B. (2003), *They Still Can't Spell*. (Portsmouth NH: Heinemann).

Smith, F., (1982), *Writing and the Writer,* (New York: Holt, Rinehart & Winston).

Stakes, R. & Hornby, G. (1996) Meeting Special Needs in Mainstream Schools: A Practical Guide for Teachers (London: David Fulton publishers).

Stewig, D., (1993), *Language Arts in the Early Childhood Classroom*. (London: Wadsworth).

Stubbs, M., (1980), *Language and Literacy – the Sociolinguistics of Reading and Writing*. (London: Routledge & Kegan Paul).

Sturges, J., & Sterling, C., (1994), Children's use of analogy in spelling. In *Education Section Review*. Vol. 18, No. 2.

Swap, S.M., (1993), *Developing Home-School Partnerships: From Concepts to Practice.* (New York: Teachers' College Press).

Tansley, A.E., (1967), *Reading and Remedial Reading,* (London: Routledge & Kegan Paul).

Templeton, S. & Morris, D. (1999), Questions teachers ask about spelling. In *Reading Research Quarterly* (Vol. 34, No. 1) International Reading Association.

Teodorescu, I. & Addy L.M. (2001) *Write from the Start, Book II: Developing fine-motor and perceptual skills for effective handwriting* (LDA).

Thomas, F. (1998) Une question de writing. In Support for Learning, Volume 13, No 1, February 1998, pp. 43-45(3).

Thompson, G.B., (1987), Three studies of predicted gender differences. In processes of word reading, *Journal of Educational Research*, 80.

Thompson, M., (1991), The teaching of spelling using techniques of simultaneous oral spelling and visual inspection. In Snowling, M., & Thompson, M. (Eds.) *Dyslexia: Integrating Theory and Practice*. (London: Whurr).

Thorndike, E.L. and Lorge, I. (1944). *The Teacher's Word Book of 30,000 Words.* (Teachers College, Columbia University, New York).

Todd, J., (1982), *Learning to Spell: A Book of Resources for Teachers*. (Oxford: Blackwell).

Topping, K., (1986), *Parents as Educators*. (London: Croom Helm).

Topping, K., (1995), *Paired Reading, Spelling and Writing*, (London:Cassell Education).

Torbe, M., (1977), *Teaching Spelling*. (London: Ward Lock Educational).

Vallins, G.H., (1954), *Spelling*. (London: Andre Deutsch Ltd.) (Revised by Scragg, D.G. 1965).

Vernon, P.E. (1977), *Graded Word Spelling Test*. (Hampshire: Hodder & Stoughton).

Vincent, D. & Claydon, J., (1982), *Diagnostic Spelling Test – Teacher's Guide*. (Berkshire: NFER – Nelson).

Webster, A., & McConnell, C., (1987), *Children with Speech and Language Difficulties*. (London: Cassell Educational).

Westwood, P. (2003), *Commonsense Methods for Children with Special Needs*, 4th Edition. (London: Routledge).

Wilde, S., (1996), What is our responsibility in helping children learn to spell? In *Primary Voices K – 6*. Vol. 4, No. 4, November. pp 2-6.

Wolfendale, S., (1985), *Parental Involvement in Children's Reading*. (London: Croom Helm).

Venezky, R.L. (1999). *American way of spelling: The structure and origins of American English orthography.* New York: Guilford.

Vygotsky, Lev (1986). *Thought and Language*. Cambridge, Massachusetts: The MIT Press.

Young, D. (1987), *Spar – Spelling and Reading Tests*. (London: Hodder & Stoughton).

List of Authors

Subject Index